D1823013

THE

GREAT PALACE

OF

CONSTANTINOPLE

BY

THE LATE DR. A. G. PASPATES

TRANSLATED FROM THE GREEK

BY

WILLIAM METCALFE, B.D.

WITH A MAP

ALEXANDER GARDNER

Publisher to Her Majesty the Queen

PAISLEY; AND 26 PATERNOSTER SQUARE, LONDON

1893

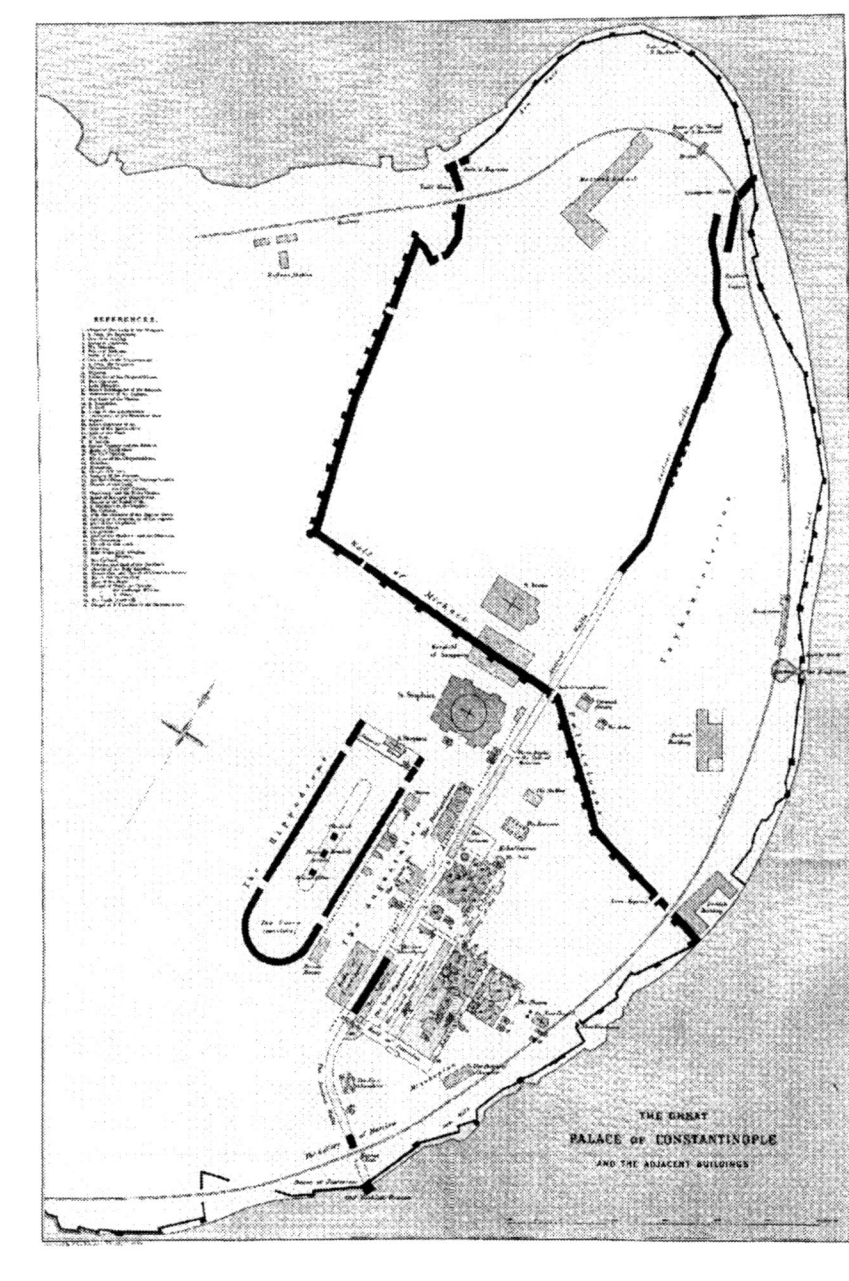

THE GREAT
PALACE OF CONSTANTINOPLE
AND THE ADJACENT BUILDINGS

NOTE BY TRANSLATOR.

In offering this translation of Dr. Paspates' work, Τὰ Βυζαντινὰ ᾿Ανάκτορα, to the English public, the Translator desires to state that he has carefully verified all the references to the works of the Byzantine writers, and such others as were accessible to him. The translation was undertaken with the consent of the Author, who, up to the time of his death, had read the proofs of the first eight chapters. Those of the remaining chapters were read by the k. D. Bikelas, to whom also the Translator is indebted for many valuable suggestions. The map, with the exception of the names, is an exact reproduction of that which appeared in the original work.

ERRATA.

Page 154, *for* follis, *read* folles.

,, 177, note 2, *for* προς, *read* πρòς.

,, 239, *for* Giúno, *read* Gioún.

CONTENTS.

INTRODUCTION.

In the following account of the Palace of Constantinople, the Hippodrome, and the neighbouring Augustaion, I often recall the difficulties of the task. Students of the Palace as it is presented in the latest works of Greek and Western writers, can form some idea of the confused nature of the subject, which, indeed, none admit more frequently than the writers themselves. Many are convinced that in this inhospitable country, inhabited only by the Turk, no remains can now be found. They have never inspected the place for themselves, but derive all their information from the extant Byzantine historians and from modern topographers. The majority of the Byzantine historians mention buildings and localities which were well-known to their original readers, and give no detailed accounts of the situation and size of the different parts of the Palace. Their pages are almost entirely occupied with theological controversies, bloody encounters between the ungovernable Factions, and popular risings. The topographers of Constantinople lived in the sunset of her power. The palaces were then mouldering away uncared for. The festivals, so frequently mentioned by Constantine VII., Porphyrogennetos, were forgotten, except a few which were performed in the palace at Blachernai. Many buildings, which had not been repaired, had fallen into ruin, and with them had perished the memory of the founders of the palaces on the Akropolis. A number of buildings were afterwards erected in imitation of them in the spacious precincts of Blachernai, and are vaguely described by the historians, who wrote after the Conquest. The identity of their names has occasioned great confusion in the accounts given of the Palace of the Akropolis, and the ignorance of these writers is beyond belief.

It is useless to search in the writings of our historians for the minute descriptions which characterise modern topographers. Had our forefathers taken thought for their descendants, and given more exact descriptions of the buildings then existing, our labours to-day would have been lighter, and our knowledge clearer. The study of ancient buildings in ruins, is indeed a difficult task. An impenetrable mist obscures almost all the monuments of our forefathers. Yet all that we so painfully strive to learn, could have been made perfectly clear by a methodical description of them.

This has often been brought home to me amid the difficulties of my work. The unintelligible patchwork of our own Byzantine and later historians, the works of Western authors, and the maps even of Labarte, the most eminent of them all, can hardly be said to invite the reader to their further study. Is it possible then that I can make any substantial contribution to the history of our country, on a subject which has already engaged the attention of so many men of ability?

I frankly acknowledge that I often began the study of the Palace of Constantinople, and as often abandoned it dispirited and hopeless. I spent much time in unprofitable researches. Things seemed sometimes plain, sometimes obscure. I could not reconcile the apparent vagaries of the historians. They would sometimes describe as close together a number of buildings, which were subsequently found far apart. At other times, they give descriptions of buildings of which the very foundations have perished and not one stone remains upon another, while other writers describe them as if in their original splendour. These discrepancies are, no doubt, partly due to the mistakes of ignorant copyists.

For a true account of the Palace buildings of Constantinople, we are—in my opinion—largely indebted to the Thracian Railway, which was begun in 1870, and ran through the whole length of the Akropolis and the ancient Byzantine Palace. Shortly before its commencement a great fire destroyed the seafront of the Sultan's palace, which lay beside the gate, formerly known as S. Barbara's and now as *Tóp Kapusú*. The Sultans erected new and more magnificent buildings on the Thracian side of the Bosphorus. The navvies pulled down some of the Sultan's buildings which had been abandoned, cut down the ancient trees, and tore away the climbing plants which had everywhere concealed the walls. Hither, without fear of savage eunuchs and armed sentinels, came a crowd of men of every rank and country, eager to inspect the scene of the hitherto fabled pleasures of the Sultans.

The excavations of the workmen, first uncovered the ruins of the often mentioned shrine of the Archmartyr Demetrios, which was richly adorned by the Palaiologoi. The next discovery was the great Cyclopean wall which extended to the sea, and on which the Byzantine Emperors subsequently built the landward or western wall of the Palace. Further on, beside the sea-wall and under a hillock, were revealed the wonderful and massive vaults of the Boukoleon. Within these lay in shapeless heaps, as if cast down by an earthquake, fragments of marble columns, bases, capitals, and lovely cornices with sculptured heads of oxen and lions. Upon these vaults, above the sea-wall, was built a beautiful palace, overlooking the sea and the opposite shores of Asia Minor.

I myself often inspected this place. To me it was a godsend, that might be the means of removing my despair, and throwing light on many historical events hitherto unexplained.

The land, or western wall, rising from the sea, and the buildings about the Boukoleon, at once convinced me that the place laid open by the excavations was part of the ancient Byzantine Palace. I followed the excavators with the closest attention as far as the Karean Gate, a vaulted structure supported on four marble pillars. This gate was one extremity of the site of the Palace. It stood in the middle of the projected line, and was demolished by the workmen.

To the right of this gate, within some Turkish gardens, the lofty walls of which had been pulled down, there stood some ancient remains. These belonged to the so called gallery of Marcian, which extended inland to a point behind the grounds attached to the mosque of Sultan Achmet. After many months' study, all things led me to the conclusion that we were mistaken in regarding the present walls of the Sultan's palace as the ancient walls of the Byzantine Palace mentioned by Porphyrogennetos and earlier historians. I had not been alone in making this mistake. All who describe the Palace have alike erred in taking these for the walls of the earlier Byzantine Emperors. They were erected by Michael Palaiologos, and have led all modern historians and topographers astray. All the descriptions and accounts by Byzantine historians are far from agreeing with the actual topography of the Palace and the celebrated Akropolis. This is the problem which I have endeavoured to solve in the following work, in which I often recall the difficulty of the task, and the vexation I experienced before finding the wished for solution of these historical puzzles.

This work cannot, unfortunately, profess to explain all the accounts left of the Byzantine buildings. We cannot determine with certainty the site of those only once or twice mentioned. Others more fortunate may perhaps complete these studies by further investigating the ruins which remain, and penetrating into the huts and cellars of the poorer Turkish population; for there, I think, such remains are still preserved, as will throw light on passages yet obscure.

I do not make these remarks in any spirit of boastfulness at having solved this difficult problem. In the proper part of this work, I mention the labours and opinions of writers on the history and topography of Constantinople, all of whom are entitled to every honour.

In consequence of the almost complete change of the names of places, and the total indifference of the inhabitants to the events which transpired in their city, Constantinople has been to this day but imperfectly described. Gyllius, who resided in Constantinople about the beginning of the sixteenth century, bitterly upbraids the Greek inhabitants for having so soon forgotten the names of churches and historic spots, and for their ready adoption of the Turkish nomenclature.[1]

Those who make comparisons between Constantinople and Rome, forget that in the latter there is no restraint placed on the excavation of ancient buildings, and that every relic of the past is preserved with the greatest care. In Constantinople however, ancient buildings are pulled down, master-

---

[1] Adde Græcorum inertem inscitiam, qui videntur totum oblivionis flumen ebibisse. Illorum enim nemo jam reperitur, qui ubinam essent vestigia antiquorum monumentorum sciat, aut scire curet, ut ne sacerdotes quidem ulli recognoscant loca, ubi paucis ante annis ædes sacræ deletæ sunt, et valde mirentur si quis talia inquirat. Gyllius, *De Constantinopoleos Topographia,* lib. ii., cap. 1.

pieces of art are broken in pieces, and inscribed slabs chiselled smooth. Excavations have never been made to discover works of art or historical remains. Even at the present moment, foreigners have difficulty in obtaining access to most of the surviving Byzantine buildings. Nowadays the Turks set more store on the historical relics treasured up in the Imperial Museum ; but the populace hate everything that is not Mussulman, and those in power unfortunately share their prejudice.[1]

This natural prejudice which characterises the warlike Ottoman, is inherited not only by their fellow-citizens, the descendants of the original Byzantines, but also by many of ourselves. Before the day of our national resurrection, our histories of Byzantion were few in number, and mere compilations from European works. The majority were the work of Catholics. The object they had in view, was not a faithful narrative of facts, but the dense ignorance of the Byzantines, and their stubborn resistance to the Pope and his claims. According to some writers the conquest in 1453 came fortunately to conceal entirely the enormities of the vile Byzantines, and to inflict on them the punishment they deserved.[2] To prove this, and to convince

---

[1] *Ibid.*

[2] Ils croyent que le Saint-Esprit ne procede que du Père, et non du Fils et ne veulent point admettre l'adjonction, *filioque.* . . . En punition de quoy il semble que Dieu ait permis la ruine de leur Empire, et la prise de Constantinople par les Infidèles. *Théâtre de la Turquie,* par Michel Fevre. Paris, 1686, p. 402. On p. 418 the writer says that he and his companions entered S. Sophia on horseback.

the ignorant, they described what they called the religious frenzy of the Byzantines, vigorous even at the moment of the death struggle with Mahomet. It is a matter of regret that these writings have corrupted not only the vulgar, but also our leading writers.

To this day the histories of the Byzantines have been regarded by most with little favour. Neither the just laws of the earlier Emperors nor the successful struggle against the Arab fanatics at the beginning of the eighth century, which if it had resulted otherwise, might have left the way open for all Europe becoming Mussulman, nor the numerous works of the Byzantine historians, to which we owe our knowledge of life in mediæval Europe and the neighbouring countries, nor their wonderful inventions of hydraulic machinery, nor the distinctively Hellenic form given to Christian ritual, not even the great Cathedral of S. Sophia, a surpassingly worthy house of God, has availed to bridle the tongues of those who speak evil of the Byzantines.

Many Western writers have warmly commended to us Greeks the study of the history of our own country and of the Byzantine Empire, in which not a few difficult problems invite our consideration. I am sure that we are better fitted than Europeans to elucidate them. This conviction has encouraged, and will continue to encourage me, in this difficult task. One of the first essentials for the student of Byzantine history is to proceed regardless of the unmerited accusations made by many Western writers, and by many also of our own wise men, who derive their stock of learning from other writers, in preference to investigating the sources of history for themselves. Examples of this are to be found in the works of Du Cange and Banduri, who described Constantinople without leaving their studies, and fell into numerous topographical errors. From their voluminous works the more recent historians of Byzantion have compiled their books. Others again, though living in Constantinople, shirked the trouble of perambulating a large city, and drew the bulk of their material from other writers. Witness Von Hammer's description of Constantinople, an unpardonable tissue of ignorance, on which many yet rely as a guide in their studies.[1]

Though I have never extolled the virtues of the Byzantines, I have never admitted the unjust accusations, so plentifully made by some writers. We literally shudder when we read in Byzantine history of malefactors being mutilated or having their eyes put out. What shall we say of men in Europe who were not malefactors, whose only fault lay in their opinions, being stretched on the rack, or burnt by the merciless followers of Christ—of the God of mercy and love ?

My opinion is that if we were first to study the history and politics of Byzantion in the original authorities and in our native tongue;[2] and then

---

[1] *Constantinopolis und der Bosporos, örtlich und geschichtlich beschrieben,* von Jos. von Hammer. 2 Bde. Pesth, 1822.

[2] Skarlatos D. Byzantios, Κωνσταντινούπολις, vol. III., p. 66.

proceed to Western historians and commentators, our countrymen would form a more correct estimate of the latter, and we should at least learn not to revile the life and polity of our forefathers.

This work, one, as I said above, full of difficulties, is the proof of all my statements. Taking the Byzantine historians as my authorities, I have tried to confirm the results of my investigations which have been made during many years of wandering in this place of palaces. In all cases I give references to such of our writers as describe the Palace, to convince every one of the accuracy of what I have written, and to assist those who are anxious to prosecute the study of the subject.

Such studies are wearisome to many. Students, however, should bear in mind that without a knowledge of the country whose history they are studying, the events recorded can be at best but imperfectly understood.

In conclusion, I hope that this description of the famous Palace of Constantinople may excite my countrymen to a fuller and more intimate study of Byzantine history.

A. G. PASPATES.

THE GREAT PALACE OF CONSTANTINOPLE.

CHAPTER I.

I HAVE never undertaken the discussion of any Byzantine problem more difficult than the present. My intention is to attempt to determine the site and boundaries of the Byzantine Palace in the Akropolis of Constantinople,[1] which is often called the Great Palace, to distinguish it from other palaces erected by our Emperors both in Constantinople and in the suburbs of Thrace and Anatole; namely, those of Eleutherios and of the Mangana, the Pegaia near to the Church of the Blessed Virgin styled the Life-receiving Spring (Ζωοδόχος πηγή), the Palace of the Virtues now *Daout Pasha*, that of Aphameia the present Makrochorion, the Heraion,[2] and various others, where they resided during the summer.[3]

According to the historians, the Akropolis, as it

---

[1] Χρὴ γινώσκειν ὅτι τοῦ Βύζαντος τὰ παλάτια ἐν τῇ 'Ακροπόλει ἦσαν. G. Kodinos, p. 24.

[2] τῶν παλατίων τῆς 'Ιερείας. Constantine Porphyrogennetos, Vol. I., pp. 373, 438, 497, 504; Nikephoros Patriarches, p. 28. Τὰ ἐν τῷ 'Ηραίῳ παλάτια. G. Kodinos, pp. 117, 276.

[3] Du Cange, *Constantinopolis Christiana*, lib. ii., p. 125. G. Kodinos, p. 117,

appeared in Byzantine times, was the work of Severus.[1] Xenophon calls it Akra.[2] It was sometimes called the Eastern Akropolis, to distinguish it from the Pentapyrgion and Heptapyrgion, to which the name Akropolis was also frequently applied.[3]

When I say I have undertaken a most difficult task, the reader must not suppose that I desire to unduly magnify the labour which such works involve. It would indeed be well if any one desirous of going through this work, would first read all that has been written both in Greece and in the West on the topography of the Palace in the Akropolis. For upwards of a thousand years this famous spot has been the scene of the most noteworthy events in our own history, and in that of the present Ottoman dynasty. Yet all accounts of the Palace are obscure or utterly unintelligible.[4] The student of the many years of Byzantine history, as he reads of the horrors perpetrated within the Palace—of men blinded or put to death, of the collisions between the populace and the rulers —is perplexed, because up to the present day we have no knowledge of the Palace, or of the walls that once surrounded its magnificent buildings,

---

[1] Εἰς μείζονα καὶ περιφανῆ κόσμον ἐπανήγαγε τὸ Βυζάντιον [i.e., Severus]. *Ibid.*, p. 12.

[2] *Anab.*, vii., 1, 5.

[3] *Opolis Christiana,* lib. i., p. 44; lib. iv., p. 171 ; Nikephoros Gregoras, Vol. II., p. 779.

[4] Les révolutions. du palais tiennent en effet beaucoup de place dans l'histoire de l'empire d'Orient. . . . . Dans l'ignorance absolue où l'on est de la disposition des lieux cités, le récit devient obscur pour le lecteur J. Labarte, *Le Palais Impérial,* p. 2.

and protected them against popular risings and pillage.[1]

As for the history of the Akropolis before the time of Severus, it does not lie within the scope of the present work. Very little is said of it in the histories of Byzantion.[2]

Our Byzantine historians enumerate all the Emperors, from Constantine the Great downwards, who built or adorned the Palace;[3] but it never occurred to them to describe its walls. Of the many halls, and splendid churches and chapels, raised within the Imperial precincts, nothing has been preserved to us, except some pillars, bases or capitals, some sarcophagi with inscriptions, and several foundations and vaults. These alone bear witness to the former greatness of the Akropolis, once filled with the wonders of Greek art and Byzantine architecture.

I have often had occasion to complain bitterly of the Byzantine historians. Most of the accounts of Constantinople preserved in their writings are by no means clear. Writing for contemporaries, they never thought of posterity. To this short-sighted neglect of the Mediæval writers, we all alike owe the depth of our ignorance and the barrenness of our labour on this subject.

The Akropolis and its Palace are, as I before said,

---

[1] S. Byzantios, Κωνσταντινούπολις, Vol. I., p. 206.

[2] Nam quae fuerint Byzantii antiqui, antequam oversum fuisset a Severo, monumenta, nemo scribit. Gyllius, *De Topographia Cpoleos.*, lib. iv., c. 11.

G. Kodinos, p. 18,

mentioned by all the Byzantine historians, especially by Constantine VII. (Porphyrogennetos), who gives us, in his invaluable Ἔκθεσις τῆς βασιλείου τάξεως, an account of the religious and civil ceremonial of the Emperors. This record is a work of great value to students of Byzantine history, and from it alone much information about the Palace may be derived. It belongs to the tenth century, when the Palace and all the buildings surrounding it, were still uninjured.[1]

From that time the Emperors erected no more buildings of any importance in the Akropolis. Many enemies were coveting the wealth of the Empire. The Byzantine traders were embarrassed by the opposition of the Italian merchants, and the Government was in financial straits.

I am convinced, however, that the extant Byzantine historical writers, whether civil or ecclesiastical, do not enable us to form a clear idea of the boundaries of the wide area in which so many palaces were built, and where stood the strong walls to which they so often allude.

None of our countrymen have described the fate of the Palace after the victory of the Crusaders in 1204. We do not know why the Emperors, during the last two centuries of their power, forsook the Great Palace on the Akropolis for the palace of Blachernai, which lay in marshy ground, exposed to bitter and pestilential winds.

From the capture of Constantinople by the Turks

---

[1] Labarte, p. 5.

in 1453 to our own day, many foreigners and some of our own countrymen have written on this Palace, and attempted, with praiseworthy zeal, to fix its true site and to reconstruct its former magnificence. The earliest of these is Peter Gyllius, who spent several years in Constantinople at the beginning of the sixteenth century,[1] and at great risk explored the whole of Byzantion that he might recount the ancient greatness of the city. This learned and accomplished traveller is compelled to admit, that not only did nothing of the old Palace survive in his day, but also that the very site was hard to find. His words are repeated by Labarte, the latest investigator, who says that absolutely nothing of the old Palace is now preserved.[2] Nevertheless, certain relics escaped the eyes of both these learned writers, and still exist to shed great light on the topography and history of the city. Gyllius, moreover, was not aware that two centuries before the capture by the Turks, parts of the Palace, which had long been neglected, were pulled down by the Emperors, while others had fallen into ruins through age. Yet even in his day some objects were preserved, both within and outside the Imperial precinct, such as pillars and statues, which are clearly described by him, and explain the history of the adjoining buildings as

---

[1] Non accusanda, sed damnanda fortuna, in quam me conjecit Francisci Regis mors, cujus nutu in Græciam accesseram, non diu ut desiderem Byzantii, sed ut conquirerem Codices Græcorum antiquos. *De Topographia Cpoleos*, lib. iv., *ad fin.* (Tr.)

[2] Labarte, p. 220; Gyllius, lib. i., cc. 1, 17.

well as of the Palace. His account, however, of
the ancient walls is confused, since he was unacquainted with the Byzantine historians, more
especially Constantine Porphyrogennetos, whose
works have since been published.

Another writer, who resided in Constantinople
at the same time as Gyllius, was Busbequius,[1] the
ambassador of the German Emperor ; but the particulars he gives are of no great importance.

After Gyllius I cannot name a single traveller or
writer before the publication of Du Cange's invaluable treatise *Constantinopolis Christiana.*[2] This indefatigable writer gives a description of Constantinople based on the works of Byzantine civil and
ecclesiastical historians, as well as on those of
Western travellers and Crusaders. His book is
not a little remarkable as the work of a man who
never saw Constantinople. Though he borrows
from Western writers, his principal authorities, at
least, are Byzantine, so far as they were then
available. At that time the Byzantine historians
had not all been published, and he was therefore confined to the few which were then accessible. Published two centuries ago, his work is still without
question the leading authority on the subject. He
has fallen into some errors, due chiefly to inferior
MSS., and the ignorance of travellers, and his statements on many points in connection with the

---

[1] *A. G. Busbequii omnia quæ extant.*   Lugdun. Batavorum, 1633.

[2] *Constantinopolis Christiana, seu Descriptio urbis Constantinopolitanæ
qualis extitit sub Imperatoribus Christianis.*   Lutetiæ Parisiorum,
MDCLXXX.

palaces both in the Akropolis and outside the city, are made simply on the authority of the then known Byzantine writers.

Next there was published at Paris, in two volumes, the work of Anselm Banduri, entitled *Imperium Orientale.*[1] Though a more pretentious performance than that of Du Cange, and conveying more information respecting the Byzantine Empire, Du Cange is, in my opinion, a safer guide. But no one who reads these invaluable works, now scarce and accessible to few, can fail to be struck by the wealth of learning and the patient industry of these two esteemed writers.

I pass over Gibbon and von Hammer, the historians of the Byzantine and Ottoman Empires, and our own Paparregopoulos, from whose writings we gain but few particulars concerning the Palace of Constantinople.

Two of our countrymen, the Patriarch Constantius (ever to be remembered) in 1824, and the celebrated Skarlatos Byzantios in the year 1852, described Constantinople and its ancient Palace. Both borrowed freely from the above mentioned works of Du Cange and Banduri; but the reader soon discovers that they had not personally inspected the numerous remains described by their authorities, on account of the dangers which beset the traveller in Constantinople. Byzantios' book contains a very minute account of the Palace buildings, and

---

[1] *Imperium Orientale, sive Antiquitates Constantinopolitanæ in quatuor partes distributæ.* Parisiis, MDCCXI.

the festivals there celebrated. We may pass over the many travellers who have described Constantinople, and portrayed Byzantine life, or sometimes made mention of the antiquities of the city.

In 1861 there was published at Paris the work of Jules Labarte, *Le Palais Impérial de Constantinople.*[1] Labarte's principal authority was Constantine Porphyrogennetos, and he follows his guidance in describing the site and dimensions of the buildings within the Imperial precinct. The account which this distinguished writer gives of these numerous ecclesiastical and civil buildings is in many places confused, since, as he himself confesses, he had not a clear conception of the walls encircling the Palace. Of the remains which still exist he makes no mention. I must, however, acknowledge that his account of the Palace is extremely accurate, and more clear and full than that of any previous writer. He also endeavours to determine the dimensions of the buildings, the domes, corridors, and varied adornments of the Imperial halls, where the governors and foreign ambassadors were wont to do obeisance to the Emperor. The reader of Labarte's work is struck by his quickness of perception and soundness of judgment. But it seems to me that any attempt to describe buildings of which no representations have been preserved, and no traces survived, must always be hazardous. Those, however, who

---

1 *Le Palais Impérial de Constantinople et de ses abords, Saint-Sophie, le Forum Augustéon, et l'Hippodrome, tels qu'ils existaient au dixième siècle.* Paris, 1861.

are interested in such studies as the present, may profit much from the work of the learned Labarte. I have myself learned much from it.

After the mention of so many writers and such elaborate books, I am not without justification in saying that I have undertaken a most difficult task. The reason for the great want of precision in the accounts of the Palace is that some of the writers never saw Constantinople, and that very few went through the streets of the city inspecting the existing walls, digging up heaps of rubbish, and studying the remains of ancient Byzantine buildings, which are still everywhere preserved.

To make the site of the ancient Byzantine Palace clear to all, it will be well to describe, first the walls built by Severus and Constantine the Great, and then the walls of the Sultan's Palace, which are those now visible.

The cuttings for the Thracian railway in the previously inaccessible Akropolis threw great light on many points of Byzantine history, by the discovery of the chapel of the Archmartyr Demetrios, the famous Palace of the Boukoleon, and the neighbouring harbour of the same name, where the Chelandia or Imperial barges were stationed.

At the spot where the railway coming from the east curves towards the south, a great wall was discovered, in the track of the line, some eight feet below the surface of the ground. It extended to the shore, and was dug up so far by the workmen for the sake of the large stones composing it, which were built into a retaining wall on the right, to support the cutting above. This wall bore no resemblance to the foundations of any known Byzantine walls. While these are built of various sized stones fastened together with mortar, this was what is commonly known as a Cyclopean wall, built of large stones, some as much as 10 feet long by 2½ broad and 1½ thick. On the right similar foundations appeared, on which subsequent generations had reared a wall of the ordinary Byzantine type. This Cyclopean wall is probably the work of Severus, or some one of the early rulers of Constantinople. On the right side of the railway, it runs inland to the top of the rising ground, and is of various degrees of thickness. Here and there strong stone walls, built up like buttresses, support it where it threatens to fall. The eastern part of the wall, as it runs up the hill, is built of smaller stones, and is in some parts very steep. This wall, now decayed with age, seems to have been renewed by various Emperors, and, doubtless, by the Sultans as well. On the foundations of the southern portion the stone treasuries of the Sultans were built, and the eight domes of the Sultan's kitchens, mentioned by Gyllius.[1] Farther on, slight walls were built on the same foundations as far as the old Ottoman Mint, which lay on the inner side of the Sublime Porte. Beyond this, again, it meets the great walls of the Sultans. I can find no mention of this wall in the works of the writers I referred to.

---

[1] Lib. i., cap. 7.

To the east of the great Ottoman mosque called *Sultan Achmet*,[1] or *Alty Minarely*, and along the eastern side of the Hippodrome, a Byzantine wall is preserved, almost entirely concealed by poor Turkish houses. This quarter is called *Ak bughiûk mahalesé*,[2] or the street of the white mustached, and the southern portion *Arista sokaghí*. This non-Turkish word ἀρίστα recalls the following passage from Anna Komnena :—"The Augusta was overjoyed, and received him outside the door of her chamber, in the apartment formerly called ἀριστήριον."[3] Constantine Porphyrogennetos calls this part of the Palace ἀριστητήριον.[4] To the great significance of this word I shall refer in my account of the Palace.

This wall is about 150 paces long. At the north end a low arched doorway, clearly of Byzantine construction, is preserved. The bricks are Byzantine, large and squared, such as appear in the oldest walls. The stones, which are laid in alternate courses with the bricks, are dark-coloured and skilfully wrought. In some places battlements appear. Through the backdoor of an Ottoman house, I caught a glimpse of a vaulted chamber. Owing to its situation in an obscure quarter of the town seldom visited by travellers, this wall is unno-

---

1 It was built by Sultan Achmet I. about 1610. Byzantios, Κπολις., Vol. I., p. 223.

2 *Ibid.*, p. 67.

3 Lib. xiv., p. 351, ed. Venice, 1751 [Vol. I., p. 287, ed. Bonn.]; *Cpolis. Christ.*, lib. ii., p. 121.

4 Εἰς τὸ βῆλον τὸ πρὸς τὸ ἀριστητήριον, ἤγουν ἔμπροσθεν τοῦ κοιτῶνος. Vol. I., p. 529.

ticed even at the present day. I searched the neighbouring streets and houses carefully, but found
nothing. There are probably other remains in the
Turkish gardens of this quarter.

We proceed now to another Byzantine wall, lying
to the right of the railway, in a Turkish garden
opposite a lofty tower overlooking the sea, on
which a beacon used to be kindled before the erection of the modern lighthouse, which is situated to
the north of the gate *Ahér Kapusú.* Beside this
tower are preserved some brick arches on the sea
wall, which I regard as the remains of the house
occupied by Justinian the Great before he became
Emperor. I say this by way of warning, that those
who wish to inspect the ruins may not be misled.

This wall, which is about 65 ft. long, is double,
and in some places, traces are found of arches con-
necting the inner and outer portions. Thus
citizens and soldiers could cross by a passage
everywhere under cover. From the arches or roof
to the rampart is about a man's height. Here the
soldiers could muster safely to repel enemies or
insurgents attempting to sack the Palace. These
walls extended eastwards, and were called the
Gallery, or Covered Way, óf Marcian[1] in the
Byzantine histories, the accounts given by which
we can now easily understand. Near this covered

---

[1] [Διαβατικὰ ἤ περίδρομοι τοῦ Μαρκιανοῦ]. διέρχονται διὰ τῶν ἔξω διαβατικῶν
τοῦ Μαρκιανοῦ, καὶ ἀπέρχονται ἐν τῷ ἐκεῖσε εὐκτηρίῳ τοῦ Ἁγίου Ἀποστόλου
Πέτρου. Cons. P., Vol. I., p. 122. Other galleries are mentioned ; *Ibid.,*
Vol. I., pp. 84, 125, 129, 169. Τὰ διαβατικὰ σκεπαστὰ τοῦ παλατίου, G.
Kodinos, p. 135.

way were raised the two churches of S. Peter and All Saints, of which every trace had disappeared by the time of Gyllius.[1]

On the line of the projected railway, adjoining the wall, there was preserved inside a Turkish garden, a great covered Byzantine gateway supported on four pillars, which was destroyed during the operations. This was the gate Karea, sometimes called the gate of the Emperors, but seldom mentioned by the Byzantine historians. In his account of the expulsion of the tyrant Andronikos, Niketas says :—" When the mob was gathered inside the palace, having burst open the gate called Karea, Andronikos took to flight; . . ."[2] The same name was given to another gate which leads to the modern palace, near the quarter called *Ahér Kapusú*. This gate is now called *Ghiul Hané Kapusú*, sometimes *Kará Kapú* or *Kará Kapusú*, the land gate.[3]

The Covered Way of Marcian extended to the lighthouse on the shore, near the house of Justinian.

This finishes the account of these venerable relics of the Byzantines, which have never before been described. The consideration of them may put an end to the errors of many years.

If through the wall running inward, we draw a

---

1 Πρῶτα μὲν Πέτρῳ καὶ Παύλῳ νεὼν οὐ πρότερον ὄντα ἐν Βυζαντίῳ ἐδείματο ['Ιουστινιανὸς] τατὰ τὴν βασιλέως αὐλὴν, ἣ 'Ορμίσδου τὸ παλαιὸν ἐπώνυμος ἦν. Prokopios, Vol. III., p. 186.

2 P. 452.

3 G. Kodinos, p. 43.

line from the Cyclopean wall to the Eastern wall of
the Mosque of Achmet, and thence to the remains of
the Covered Way of Marcian and the gate Karea,
we have the true boundaries of the ancient Byzantine Akropolis, within which were reared the
palaces of our Emperors and the many churches
made famous by them. This wall passed behind
S. Sophia, 108 ft. from the bema, and 123 ft. from
the Mosque of Achmet. From the Covered Way to
the Cyclopean wall the distance is about 2000
yards; and the whole area enclosed is nearly
383,000 square yards.

In confirmation of this statement I will bring
forward various proofs. Above all things, I desire
to prove to every one that the Byzantine accounts
of the Palace are made much more intelligible by a
knowledge of this area.

The walls, which are now seen surrounding the
Sultan's Palace, are Byzantine structures of the
thirteenth century, built by Michael Palaiologos a
little after he ascended the Imperial throne in
1261.[1] The Crusader Emperors, who took Constantinople in 1204, lived sometimes in the palace at
Blachernai, and at other times in the Boukoleon. No
mention is made of the Great Palace which occupied
the above-mentioned area. Succeeding Emperors

---

1 Οἰκοδόμους δ' ἐπιστήσας πλείονας καὶ ἐπιστάτας ἐδιδύμου τὸ τεῖχος τῆς
πόλεως τὸ πρὸς θάλασσαν· τὸ γὰρ πρὸς τὴν γῆν δεδίπλωτο πάντως. καὶ
λαὸν πλεῖστον καὶ μάχιμον, ὅσον ἀποχρῶντα τοιαύτῃ παρασκευῇ πολέμου ᾤετο,
ἐξ αὐτῆς διέταττεν. G. Pachymeres, Vol. I., p. 364. N. Gregoras (Vol. I.,
pp. 275, 470) mentions the buildings of Andronikos, son of Michael
Palaiologos.

were unable to repair the old and already decayed
Palace so often mentioned by Porphyrogennetos,
much less to build it anew, and it is but seldom
alluded to during the last two centuries of the
Christian rule.[1] The fact that our Emperors then
lived in the palace of Blachernai, convinces me
that the old Palace of Constantine the Great was
not habitable.

In construction, the modern walls differ greatly
from the sea and land walls erected by Constantine,
Theodosios the Younger, and Herakleios. The
great towers of the land walls have wide vaulted
entrances from inside the city. In the middle a
spiral staircase of stone leads to the roof. In the
modern wall each tower has two doors, one on
either side, through which one ascends to the
ramparts by means of stone steps, most of which
are still preserved. The towers are smaller, and
some of them higher, than those on the land walls.
Anyone may examine these walls with his own eyes.
They extend from the east shore, near the present
Ahér Kapusú, and ascending between S. Sophia
and S. Irene, run down westward, till opposite the
gate *Pasha Kapusú*, and thence northward to the
shore of the harbour called *Yialé Kiosk*, anciently
the harbour of Eugenius.[2] Between the gate now
called *Kará Kapusú* and the Sublime Porte,
Bab-i-humaghiún, is preserved a fortified gate,

---

[1] J. Kantakouzenos, lib. i., cap. 54. [Vol. I., p. 273.]
[2] G. Kodinos, p. 22.

which has no name. All the site of the ancient Palace from the Covered Way of Marcian to the modern gate *Kará Kapusú* was neglected by the Emperors. Probably it was from this later place that the materials were obtained with which the modern walls were built. A considerable area was included in the new precinct, where the Sultans subsequently reared their palace.

I come now to consider the problem, for such up to this point I regard it, whether these walls were the work of Constantine and other Emperors, and to give my reasons for believing that they were not. I shall also endeavour to determine what led Michael Palaiologos to erect them after he had acquired the sovereign power.

Labarte in his book says that the greater part of the walls now visible, were built out of the ruins of the ancient walls; but by whom, and when, they were raised, he does not know. All the Great Palace, the hall of the Magnaura, the Porphyry Chamber, and the Five Chambers, remained outside these walls. His opinion is correct.[1]

Before the capture of Constantinople by the Crusaders in 1204, the northern shore of Byzantion from the Akropolis to the gate of the Drungarii, now called *Zindan Kapusú,*[2] was occupied by numerous Italian traders. The Venetians occupied the portion between the Ferry-gate, now

---

[1] *Le Palais Impérial,* p. 107.

[2] The prison gate.

Balék pazár Kapusú, and the gate of the Drungarii. They are mentioned by Ptochoprodromos.[1]

I pass over the many references of the Italians to the lodgings of the Venetians here—Βενέτικοι as they are called by Ptochoprodromos and others. The merchants of Amalfi, Pisa, and Ragusa dwelt between the Ferry-gate and the neighbouring chapel of S. Antony, on the site of which was afterwards built the beautiful mosque *Validé Djamii* or *Yeni Djamii.* Their quarter extended further to the gate *Bachtsé Kapusú,* the ancient Neôrion. From this gate eastward were the Genoese traders. How far their dwellings and warehouses extended we do not know. The number living and doing business on that long shore was considerable. Besides these, we learn that there was a Mussulman chapel called μεσγίδιον (mosque), and often μιτάτον. The Emperors wisely put the Amalfitan and Pisan settlements between the Genoese and Venetians, who were always at daggers drawn with each other.

During the whole of their stay in Byzantion, the Genoese were more friendly to the Greeks than were the Venetians. They are not mentioned as taking part in the Fourth Crusade of 1204. Though summoned, they did not take up arms with the Crusaders. During the whole succeeding Latin domination, which lasted for 57 years, they

---

[1] Καὶ διάβα κ' εἰς τὸ πέραμα γοργὸν ὡς ἐξηφτέριν,
ἐρώτησε 'ς τὸ διάβα σου ἐπὶ τοὺς Βενετίκους,
τὸ πῶς πουλιέται τὸ τυρὶν, τί ἔχει τὸ κεντηνάριν.
      Koraës, Ἄτακτα, (Vol. I., lib. ii., col. 113.)

lived in outward peace with the ruling Germans and Venetians, though indignant that all the privileges granted them by the Emperors were in the hands of the Venetians, and that they were prevented by them from enjoying the lucrative trade of the Propontis. These grievances moved Genoa to conclude a secret agreement with Palaiologos, then living at Nymphaion in Asia. A little before he made himself master of the throne in 1261, they agreed to send ships to assist him in his proposed expedition against the Latins in Byzantion. In return for this desirable aid, Palaiologos promised, if successful, to grant them their old privileges and a great many more.

Strange to say, a little after his entry into Constantinople, Palaiologos sent all the Genoese to the neighbouring town of Herakleia in Thrace, while he retained the Venetians, Pisans, and Amalfitans in their former quarters. The Byzantines had great grievances against the Germans and Venetians. During the whole period of their rule in Byzantion they had carried off many masterpieces of Greek art to Italy, plundered the shrines, and secretly or openly stolen the sacred relics venerated by the Byzantines, and preserved in their churches and monasteries.[1] Nevertheless, no reprisals were made. Palaiologos was desirous of keeping peace with the all-powerful Venetians, and held his subjects in check.

---

1 Καὶ ἐβεβηλώθησαν, οἴμοι οἴμοι, τὰ ἅγια, αἱ ἅγιαι εἰκόνες κατεπατήθησαν, ἱπποστάσια γεγόνασιν οἱ θεῖοι ναοί. G. Kodinos, p. 163.

Baldwin, the last Latin Emperor, on his expulsion, returned to Europe and stirred up the Italians, who were preparing an expedition to recover their former dominion at Byzantion. This threatened attack was a source of anxiety to Palaiologos, who knew with what ease the Crusaders had seized the Empire in 1204.

All writers, both Greek and Western, who record these events, consider the banishment of the friendly Genoese to Herakleia a most incomprehensible act. For my part, I think the reason was that Palaiologos took into his new palace all, or the greater part, of the ground on which the Genoese were formerly settled. Subsequently, owing to the complaints of the traders, and the representations of the mother city, they all returned to Constantinople, not however to their old quarters on the shore of Byzantion, but to Galata.

On this Pachymeres writes [1]:—" The Genoese . . . he first took and settled in Herakleia of Thrace ; but afterwards he thought the only safe place to let them dwell in, was right opposite on the other shore, beside the fort of Galata. The Venetians and Pisans, owing to their smaller numbers, he allowed to remain in the city."

All this apparent ingratitude, and—according to some—malevolence of Palaiologos towards the friendly Genoese, is explained by the study of these walls. Many Italians looking to the great wealth and fame of the Genoese, abuse

---

[1] Vol. I., p. 168.

Palaiologos for granting them the sheltered and
excellent harbour of Galata, which, subsequently,
gave them an overwhelming advantage over the
Byzantines across the water.[1] In his description
of the entry of Michael Palaiologos into the city,
Pachymeres[2] writes :—" In view of these events it
was resolved to raise the walls, especially those
towards the sea, which were very low because their
builder had command of the sea, and thought it
unnecessary to guard that side very strongly.   He
was Constantine, who was no less famous for his
piety than for his civil and military achievements.
And since they were pressed for time, and were unable
to complete the building with stone and lime, they resolved to heighten the walls and towers with planks
and long beams, that they might be strong to resist
attacks ; and further, that they might have a
sufficient force of defenders, to bring into the city
a body of troops from without." And again, "they
raised the walls in proportion to the towers."   The
historian also describes the preparations made by
Palaiologos for a successful attack on his enemies
in Italy, who were about to march against him.

I have made this brief recital to shew that the
real reason for sending the Genoese to Galata, was
not the clamour of the Italians, but the building
of the walls, which took the greater part of the old
Genoese quarter into the new Imperial precinct.[3]

---

1 Sauli, *Della Colonia dei Genovesi in Galata*, 2 vols., Torino, 1831.

2 Vol. I., p. 186.

3 *Geschichte des Levantehandels im Mittelalter, von Dr. Wilhelm Heyd*,
2 Vols., Stuttgart, 1879.   Vol. II., p. 208-291.

I now come to review some prior events. Manuel Komnenos (1143-1180), after the defeat of the Paeonians,[2] sent a letter announcing his success to the people. "A few days after," writes the historian, "he entered the city in a triumphal procession by the East gate, which leads to the Akropolis." This gate, now demolished, was called *Top Kapusú* by the Turks, and by the Byzantines the Gate of S. Barbara.[3] Niketas Choniates writes of this triumph :—"As befitted a great and decisive victory, he had resolved on a triumph on a magnificent scale, and had already ordered extensive preparations to be made for the procession. Every purple and gold-embroidered mantle was hung out, and the citizens, flocking together from every quarter to this procession, like water coursing down a channel, completely deserted markets, houses, workshops, vessels, and every part of the vast city. . . . On either side of the route by which the procession was to pass, stands were erected, two and three stories high, affording a view to every one, and the roofs of the houses especially were packed with a great number of onlookers all in expectation."

Before the Emperor went the magistrates and distinguished citizens. After him followed the cause of the triumph, Kontostephanos, " who went into the Great Church and praised God in presence

---

[2] N. Choniates, pp. 204, 205.

[3] Καὶ περιπλεύσας τὴν ᾽Ακρόπολιν, εἰς τὸ ἀκμαιότατον τοῦ ῥεύματος ἐλθὼν, ἐφώρμει πρὸς τὴν τῆς μάρτυρος Βαρβάρας καλουμένην πύλην. J. Kantakouzenos, lib. iv., cap. 31. *Cpolis. Christ.*, lib. i., p. 56.

of all the people, and proceeded thence to the Palace."

From this description of Choniates, who was well acquainted with Constantinople, we easily see that Komnenos entered by the Eastern, or S. Barbara's Gate, and went on to S. Sophia, through the place where the Imperial Medical School now stands. From the same authority we learn that there was here a street by which Komnenos went up to the Akropolis, with houses on either side, from which people from all quarters of the city could see the Emperor as he passed. Lofty stands were also erected, from which many more obtained a view of the procession. All this space from the Gate of S. Barbara upwards is now vacant and devoid of houses, and enclosed within the walls of the Sultan's palace. If these are the walls of Constantine the Great, or rather the ancient walls, I do not think that the Emperors could have suffered so many people to settle and trade within the Imperial Palace.

Here is another proof. After the capture of Constantinople by the Germans and Venetians in 1203, and the dethronement of Alexios, all the Crusaders took up quarters in Galata, and there awaited the promised gifts of Alexios and the Greek army, which was to join them in an expedition for the recovery of Jerusalem. All the Italian traders who until then had lived in Byzantium, and even the friendly Genoese, went over to Galata to escape the anger of the Byzantines.

On the 19th of August, 1203, some of the

Crusaders, accompanied by a few Pisans and Venetians, sailed across the harbour to destroy the Saracen mosque, which had been erected there for the use of the Mussulman traders.[1] The mosque lay on the shore near the church called S. Irene on the Shore.[2] The Praetorium, another Byzantine building frequently mentioned, was not far off. All three buildings lay to the east of the old Genoese quarter. The Crusaders, who could not tolerate Mussulman worship in a Christian city, surprised the building sword in hand, and sacked it. The Saracens made a bold defence, and were aided by the Byzantines, who gathered in from every side. The crowd, incensed against the Crusaders, sent them fleeing from the mosque, not, however, before they had set fire to the adjoining buildings. The mosque was burnt down and a disastrous conflagration raged for three days. Niketas Choniates, who was in Constantinople at the time, after describing the barbarous conduct of the Crusaders and the loss of life, says :—"Though many other fires had occurred in the city, this made them all seem mere sparks in comparison."[3] The flames devoured colonnades and market-places. Many pillars fell down. All the houses about the mosque, near the spot where Komnenos had a few years before begun

---

[1] Banduri, Vol. II., p. 49. Τῶν Σαρακηνῶν συναγώγιον. N. Choniates, p. 696.

[2] Βυζαντιναί Μελέται, p. 336.

[3] N. Choniates, pp. 730, 733. The houses in Constantinople were built of wood. N. Gregoras, Vol. I., p. 81 ; J. Kantakouzenos, Vol. III., p. 290.

his progress, were burnt to the ground. The flames were borne through the air, and assailed all the neighbouring buildings. Fanned by a strong wind, they disfigured the marbles, and reduced everything to ashes. The fire spread to the walls of S. Sophia, thence it went south as far as the Milion, the Patriarcheion, and the Senate house.[1] In another direction, the fire consumed in the evening the quarter to the west of the Hippodrome, where there were very many dwellings. South of this it extended through the hilly part of the city as far as the church of SS. Sergius and Bacchus. In a third direction it burnt many houses as far as the Ferry Gate. This conflagration is recorded by other historians.[2]

I have preferred Choniates as my authority rather than any one else, because he confirms all my previous argument. According to him the Mussulman mosque was situated in the northern part of the city, where the ground slopes down to the sea.[3] Porphyrogennetos[4] tells us that it was founded in the time of Leo the Isaurian, at the demand of Mesalma, who was advancing on the city. Niketas states distinctly that it was the adjoining houses which the Crusaders fired in several places during the sack of the mosque.

---

[1] The building beside the Patriarcheion. *Cpolis. Christ.*, lib. ii., p. 178. πρὸς δὲ τὰ βόρεια τοῦ φόρου ἐστι τὸ Σενᾶτον, ὅπερ ἐκαύθη ὑπὸ Λέοντος τοῦ τῆς Βηρίνης. G. Kedrenos, Vol. I., p. 565.

[2] Βυſαντιναὶ Μελέται, p. 188, note.

[3] N. Choniates, p. 733.

[4] Vol. III., p. 739; G. Kedrenos, Vol. I., p. 787; Ephraimios, v. 8922.

From this it would appear that up to the year 1203 the mosque near the site of the present Medical School was in the midst of a quarter which —as I have before said—could not have been inside the Palace.

We have yet another proof. In 1872 excavations for the Thracian railway were begun inside the Akropolis. Just before one comes to the present bridge, a heap of rubbish, consisting of marble slabs and columns, stones and bricks, was unearthed. Some of these remains, so long before buried under the earth, were marbles of great artistic beauty.[1] Some were used to build a fence for the railway, others were buried anew in embankments. These fragments seemed to me to be relics of the famous church of the Holy Archmartyr Demetrios, called in the vulgar Byzantine dialect Megademetrios. This church was greatly ornamented under the Palaiologoi.[2] According to the testimony of the Byzantines, it lay near the Akropolis, from which fact this spot was called the Akropolis of S. Demetrios, and according to Gyllius, the Gate of S. Demetrios.[3]

These remains were visible about 550 yards along the track of the railway, beginning at the Gate called S. Eugenius. Kodinos Kouropalates

---

1 On one square piece of marble there were sculptured vine-leaves and clusters in the best style of Greek art.

2 Ἐν τῇ σεβασμίᾳ μονῇ τοῦ Ἁγίου Μεγαλομάρτυρος καὶ μυροβλήτου Δημητρίου καὶ ἐπικεκλημένῃ τῶν Παλαιολόγων. *Acta Patriarchatus*, Vol. I., p. 42 ; Kodinos Kouropalates, p. 80.

3 *De Topographia*, lib. i., cap. 20 ; N. Gregoras, Vol. II., p. 860.

says of this famous church :—" The church of S. Demetrios within the walls was built by Bardas Cæsar, uncle of the departed Michael."

Joannes Kantakouzenos, writing about a century after the elevation of Michael Palaiologos to the throne, says :—" Coming to the church of the Archmartyr Demetrios which is in the Palace," " Coming to the chapel of the Archmartyr Demetrios in the Palace."[1] From this mention of the chapel as being in the Palace, I infer that Kantakouzenos wrote for the information of foreigners, who did not know that the chapel had some time previously been enclosed in the new precinct of the Palace. In Byzantine history the church is regularly termed the church of S. Demetrios in the Akropolis. So late as 1621, according to a French traveller, the Byzantines called the place S. Demetrios.[2] We are justly surprised that none of the Byzantine historians has recorded the building of these walls by Michael Palaiologos. I said above that till now it was not known how far east the quarter of the Genoese traders extended. In their negotiations with the Emperors, Genoese houses near the monastery of S. Demetrios are mentioned.

---

[1] These words of Kantakouzenos do not agree with the following passage from Labarte (p. 98)—Un fait de l'histoire Byzantine, que nous empruntons à Anne Comnene, va justifier la situation de Saint-Demétrius et de Saint-Georges et établir que ces deux églises étaient en dehors du Palais Impérial.

[2] *Voyage du Levant fait par le commandement du Roi en l'année 1621,* par Sr. D. C. Deuxième édition, 1629, p. 116. In the time of Gyllius, the old gate of S. Barbara was still called the gate of S. Demetrios. *De Topographia,* lib. i., cap. 20.

No church in Byzantion dedicated to S. Demetrios is known, except this one in the Akropolis,[1] and another at Balata. Probably the inhabitants of the quarter through which Manuel Komnenos' triumph passed, as well as those near the Mussulman mosque, when they were driven thence, settled in the old quarter of the Genoese, who thereupon went away to Galata.

Such is the basis of the following investigations. It is the enunciation of the problem. Next, with the aid of the Greek historians, I wish to trace the site of the ancient Palace, not merely to celebrate its grandeur and the works of art it contained, but to determine its site. We shall thus be able to understand many events of our history, which have hitherto, as I think, been extremely obscure.

In the course of my studies I have been persuaded that many remains of the Ancient Palace of Constantinople are still preserved, and that the walls now visible are the work of Michael Palaiologos, built a few years after his accession to the throne in 1261.

---

[1] Ἴστανται ἀντικρὺ τοῦ ναοῦ τοῦ Ἁγίου Δημητρίου. Cons. P., Vol. I., p. 124. This church stood within the Palace precinct. It is mentioned again, *Ibid.*, p. 170. The church in Balata is called ὁ Ἅγιος Δημήτριος τοῦ Καναβη.

CHAPTER II.

THAT we may obtain a clear idea of the site and extent of the Palace, it will be advisable for me to begin by describing the numerous buildings, so often mentioned in our history, which were situated outside of it.

THE HIPPODROME.

The Hippodrome of Constantinople was originally founded by the Emperor Severus. The site was the property of two brothers and a widow. The ground was level as far as the four-sided bronze pillar. From this point it sloped downwards, and was in some places almost precipitous. As the level ground was not sufficiently extensive, Severus built the vaults at the south end, which have survived fire and earthquake to this day, and thus extended the course to the Curve, anciently called the σφενδόνη.[1] When the seats on the east side, and the decorations of the Hippodrome had been partly completed, Severus was summoned to Italy by the news of an insurrection and disturbance in Rome.

A subsequent Emperor, Constantine the Great, added the portions which were wanting, *viz.*, the

---

[1] Σφενδόνη is also applied to a seal—Σφενδόνην, τοῦ δακτυλίου τὸ περιφερὲς, ἡ σφραγίς.—Hesychios, Souidas. This part of the Hippodrome probably derived the name from its circular shape.

stands on either side, the goals (καμπτῆρας), and the δῆμοι, or benches of the factions. He was the first " to complete the Hippodrome, and furnish it with bronzes and every kind of ornament."[1] He also instituted the races and athletic contests held in the Hippodrome on the 11th of May.[2] In his reign the sanguinary contests with wild beasts, and the disgusting spectacles of gladiators butchering one another, were banished from the circuses and hippodromes. Such sights were abhorrent to the Christian populace of Constantinople.[3] The Hippodrome had been built on the model of the. Roman circus, rather than on that of the Greek stadion or theatre. Owing to the bloodless sports engaged in on this race-course, it was not surrounded as in Rome by a strong barricade to protect the spectators from the attacks of savage and infuriated wild beasts. Sometimes, however, wild animals were exhibited to please the populace.[4] Many terms borrowed from the Roman amphitheatre remained in the Byzantine language, and may be rendered by their Latin equivalents.[5]

During the Crimean war, some officers of the

---

[1] *Chronicon Paschale*, I., p. 528.

[2] G. Kodinos, pp. 14, 19, 100, 181 ; τῇ δὲ ἐπαύριον, τὸ γενέθλιον τῆς πόλεως γέγονε, καὶ μέγα ἱπποδρόμιον, ὅτε ἡ πόλις ὠνομάσθη Κωνσταντινούπολις, p. 44 ; *Cpolis. Christ.*, lib. ii., p. 102 ; G. Kedrenos, I., p. 651.

[3] Byzantios, Κπολις., I., p. 180. The Jewish traveller, Benjamin of Tudela, mentions contests with wild beasts in the Hippodrome. He visited Constantinople towards the end of the twelfth century, in the reign of Alexios Komnenos. [Wright's *Early Travels in Palestine*, Bohn, 1848, p. 75] ; *Voyages en Asie*, par P. Bergeron, 1735, p. 12.

[4] G. Kodinos, p. 103.

[5] Cons. P., Vol. I., p. 799.

British army, then stationed in Constantinople, made excavations round the bases of the three ancient monuments preserved in the Hippodrome, built walls round them, and protected them with iron railings.[1] The ancient pavement of the Hippodrome was then discovered about ten feet below the modern level. On the way from the Bronze Column through the Ottoman School of Arts towards the Curve, where the Museum of the Janissaries is now built, there is a flight of many steps reaching as far as the Curve, on which the soil has not accumulated.

In addition to these discoveries, on the erection, in 1848, by the architect Fusati of the splendid building *Dar-el-Funún*, behind S. Sophia, the ancient pavement laid with long flags was discovered about eight feet below the surface. All this extensive quarter is now about ten feet above the ancient Byzantine level.

Four Factions (δῆμοι) are mentioned in Byzantine history in connection with the Hippodrome—the Blue, the Red, the Green, and the White.[2] These divisions were borrowed by the Byzantines from Rome. In course of time the Red joined with the

---

[1] Before this the first lines of their inscriptions were barely legible. See the Patriarch Constantius, 'Ελάσσονες συγγραφαί, Constantinople, 1866, p. 374, note. The inscriptions were quite distinct in the time of Gyllius.

[2] *Onuphrii Panvinii Veronensis, de Ludibus Circensibus libri xi., de Triumphis liber unus, quibus universa fere Romanorum veterum sacra ritusque declarantur*, Parisiis, 1601, pp. 47, 48, 92, 96 ; πύλαι χαλκαῖ τῶν τεσσάρων μερῶν. G. Kodinos, p. 50. They had their stables in the neighbourhood of S. Anastasia Pharmakolytria. Leo Grammaticus, p. 170.

Blue, and the White with the Green, so that latterly only two factions, the Green and the Blue, are spoken of.[1] Both are frequently alluded to by Constantine Porphyrogennetos in his accounts of the customary civil and ecclesiastical ceremonies of the Palace, and all the historians record the feuds and sanguinary riots in which these factions engaged. From their narratives it appears that the Blues were the followers of the Emperor,[2] while the Greens, recruited chiefly from the populace, championed the people and supported their claims. The name δῆμοι is sometimes also applied to the places in the Hippodrome allotted to these societies.[3]

I mention these facts beforehand because the factions figure largely in the history of the Hippodrome in Byzantine times.

The Hippodrome lies north and south with the Curve or semicircular end at the south. South of this stands the church of SS. Sergius and Bacchus, now used as a mosque under the title of Little S. Sophia.[4]

Three ancient monuments, the Egyptian Obelisk, the Three-headed Serpent, and the four-sided Bronze Column, stand in a straight line down the middle of the Hippodrome, and divide it into

---

[1] Cons. P., Vol. I., pp. 12, 13.

[2] Ἐπεὶ δὲ ἠκηκόει πολλῷ πρότερον Ἰουστινιανὸν βασιλέα χρώματος τοῦ Βενέτου, ὅ δὴ κυάνεόν ἐστιν, ἐκτόπως ἐρᾶν. Prokopios, Vol. I., p. 203; *Chron. Pasch.*, Vol. I., p. 592.

[3] G. Kodinos, p. 19. For the officers of the Hippodrome see Constantine Porphyrogennetos, Vol. I., p. 799.

[4] *Kiutchuk Agia Sophia.*

two equal parts. From the north end to the Egyptian Obelisk the distance is 300 paces, from the latter to the Three-headed Serpent 47, from this to the Bronze Column 47 more, and thence to the Curve 245. The total length is therefore 639 paces, or 639 cubits [320 yards], for for my pace is equal to a cubit. The middle point of the length is 23½ paces to the south of the Obelisk.

We know from the historians that these monuments stood down the middle of the Hippodrome. After the capture of Constantinople in 1453, the Turks, during the reign of Suleiman the Great, built mosques and houses on the course, so that the space on either side of them was much reduced. In addition to these, there have been built within the Curve the Museum of the Janissaries, the School of Arts, and some religious buildings in connection with the adjacent mosque of Sultan Achmet. Owing to the building of so many edifices on what was once the site of the Byzantine Hippodrome, some writers have been unable to determine the distance between the side walls and the centre.

The Curve, however, owing to its greater solidity, has been preserved. It is 158 paces in diameter. From each of its ends lateral walls extended to the north. Accordingly, the Obelisk is 79 paces distant from each of these walls, and the total breadth of the Hippodrome is 158 paces [79 yards]. It was in the Curve that the heads of malefactors were cut off. "They at once ordered their heads to be cut off in the Curve." "They were taken red-handed and arrested, and were beheaded in the Curve." [1] The bodies of these criminals were buried at the cemetery of Pelagios, outside the land walls, in the Kosmidion.

On the eastern side the mosque of Sultan Achmet was built, and its spacious courts extended 35 paces into the Hippodrome. It has been encroached upon to the same extent on the western side. The whole space has thus been reduced in length and breadth. Taking the length as 320, and the breadth as 79 yards, we get about 25,280 square yards as the area of the ancient Hippodrome. The space now unoccupied, from the north end to the School of Arts, is barely two-fifths of this, namely, 216 by 44 yards.

These measurements are not exact. In default of better, I have given them to indicate how largely the original area has been encroached upon. The whole thing could be easily settled by a regular survey of the Hippodrome by the Government Engineers, or others, as was done in the case of the land walls of Constantinople.

I subjoin the figures of other writers, with which mine may be compared. Peter Gyllius states that the length of the Hippodrome exceeds two stadia, and that the breadth equals one.[2] There were various stadia in use among the ancients. In Greece

---

[1] Theophanes Continuatus, pp. 791, 658, cf. 122, 823 ; G. Kedrenos. I., p. 544, II. p. 281 ; *Chron. Pasch.*, I., p. 558.

[2] Hippodromi longitudo duo stadia excedit, latitudo stadium æquat. *De Opoleos. Topogr.*, lib. i., cap. 7.

the Olympian stadium was employed.[1] From long and careful measurements on the Roman roads, especially the Via Appia, we know that it was equal to one-eighth of a Roman mile, i.e., to 202·25 yards. The length, therefore, would be over 404½ yards, and the breadth 200. Labarte accepts these figures as sufficiently correct, and adds that the Bronze Column stood in the centre of the Hippodrome.[2] An earlier writer than Gyllius, the Florentine Buondelmonti, who visited Constantinople in 1422, states that the length of the Hippodrome is 690 ells, and the breadth 134.[3] Taking the Florentine ell, which Buondelmonti in all likelihood used, this would make it about 408½ yards long and 79 yards broad, or less than half Gyllius' measurement.[4] Skarlatos Byzantios,[5] in his account of Constantinople, mentions, in addition to these, the English traveller Thomas Smith, who gives the length of the Hippodrome as 550 paces and the breadth as over 120 [458 by 100 yards];[6] and Tournefort, who saw the Hippodrome in 1702, and

---

[1] Le stade Olympique servait à determiner les distances dans le Peloponnèse et dans l' Attique.   J. Labarte, p. 20.

[2] *Ibid.*

[3] Nikephoros Bryennios, p. 180.

[4] J. Labarte, p. 20.

[5] Byzantios, Κπολις, Vol. I., p. 231.

[6] Lechevalier gives the same dimensions. Il est long d' environ cinquante pas ordinaires, et large d' environ six vingt.—*Voyage de la Propontide et du Pont-Euxin.*   Paris, 1800.   Vol. I., p. 128.   See also *Voyage de Dalmatie de Grèce et du Levant,* par Wheler, traduit de l' Anglais, Anvers, Vol. I., p. 139.   ["It is about five hundred and fifty ordinary paces long, and about an hundred and twenty broad." *A Journey into Greece,* by Geo. Wheler, Esq., etc.   London, MDCLXXXII., p. 183.   The pace here is the usual 30 inches.   Tr.]

writes that the length is 400 paces and the breadth 100 [333 by 83 yards]. The k. Byzantios concludes that, " according to the latest measurements the length is now about 250 paces and the breadth 150, so that from these different measurements it is plain that the dimensions have been steadily reduced as the surrounding buildings spread." I quote this to show that the majority of writers copy one another. The k. Byzantios' 250 paces are not even half of the total length of the Hippodrome, and less than the distance from the north end to the Egyptian Obelisk.

At the northern end, or rather side, of the Hippodrome, beside the great street called *Diván Yiulú*, which according to many writers is the Byzantine Main Street (μέση ὁδός) preserved almost as it was in ancient times, a café with a garden was erected a few years ago. On the south side of the garden there appeared in several places foundations of Byzantine buildings, constructed as usual of large bricks. On this spot the Emperors of Byzantion—Constantine the Great according to some[1]—built the Imperial Stand called the Kathisma, or the Palace of the Kathisma, in imitation of the Podium in the Roman circus.[2] This, I should think, occupied all the north end of the Hippodrome. Connected with it, they built a church

---

[1] Τὰ δέ παλάτια τοῦ Ἱππικοῦ . . . ὁ μέγας ἀνήγειρε Κωνσταντῖνος. G. Kodinos, p. 100. ἤγαγεν αὐτὸν ἐν τῷ καθίσματι, p. 134, cf. 183, 190 ; καὶ παλάτιον μέγα ποιήσας πλησίον τοῦ αὐτοῦ Ἱππικοῦ. *Chron. Pasch.*, I., pp. 528, 610.

[2] Remains of a similar stand are visible at the east end of the Athenian stadion.

dedicated to S. Stephen, which is frequently noticed by Porphyrogennetos.[1] From this church the Emperors proceeded to the Stand to witness the games in the Hippodrome. On either side of the Emperor were ranged the members of the household, the patricians, generals and distinguished citizens. Under the palace were a number of vaulted porches, where the chariots, horses and competitors waited. These porches were called μάγγανα, and by the Romans *carceres*.[2] They were closed by strong fences to prevent the competitors starting before the signal was given. In the first porch there was a small oratory, of which Porphyrogennetos writes—" and entering into the Hippodrome, they proceed to the chapel of Our Lady, which is in the first porch, and pray." On the same page he mentions a fourth porch. When describing another festival held in the Hippodrome he says, " at the doorpost of the great gateway."[3] The superintendent of the Mangana was called the Manganarios.[4] He had charge of the contests and gave the necessary orders. The name Mangana was also given to the arsenals in the Akropolis. A stair called κοχλίας[5] from its spiral form, led to the Stand. Kodinos describes it as

---

[1] Λειτουργοῦσι ἔξω εἰς τὸν Ἅγιον Στέφανον τοῦ Ἱπποδρόμου, Vol. I., p. 175. Καὶ ἀπέρχεται εἰς τὴν ἐκκλησίαν τοῦ Ἱπποδρόμου εἰς τὸν Ἅγιον Στέφανον, p. 251.

[2] G. Kodinos, p. 60.

[3] Cons. P., Vol. L, pp. 334, 341, 310.

[4] *Ibid.*, pp. 310, 312 ; Meursii *Glossarium, s.v.* Μαγγανάριος.

[5] Cons. P., Vol. I., p. 304.

dark.[1] The *Chronicon Paschale* says[2] of Constantine the Great—"And he made a great palace beside the same Hippodrome, and the ascent from the palace to the stand of the Hippodrome was by means of the stair called ' the spiral.' " " And he [Armatus] was killed on the spiral stair at the gate of Decimus."

From this short review of our authorities, it is evident that the seats of the spectators in the palace could not have been more than 20 feet above the ground. I think that on the top of the lower porches there was a balcony supported on marble pillars. It was in existence when Buondelmonti visited the city in 1422. In the centre of it was the Emperor's throne, and on either hand lower seats for the courtiers and generals.[3] Stones were sometimes thrown at the Emperor by the populace and the factions[4] assembled in the Hippodrome. The Emperor, when he addressed the people in the Hippodrome, stood before the throne and spoke first to the populace, and then to the Blues and Greens. The palace was two-storied. In the upper story the Emperor robed, and in the lower he was congratulated and crowned, when successful in a

---

[1] pp. 92, 112.   [2] Vol. I., pp. 528, 562.

[3] Συνόντος αὐτῷ τοῦ ἀρχιεπισκόπου Ἰωάννου καὶ τῶν λοιπῶν ἀρχόντων τῶν εἰωθότων εἰσέρχεσθαι εἰς τὸ κάθισμα. Cons. P., Vol. I., p. 428 ; N. Choniates, p. 156.

[4] Ἐλθόντες ἐπὶ τὸ κάθισμα ἔρριψαν λίθους κατὰ τοῦ βασιλέως Ἀναστασίου. Chron. Pasch., Vol. I., p. 608 ; προκύψαι οὖν ἀπὸ τοῦ ἐν τῷ ἱπποδρομίῳ καθίσματος, καὶ δημηγορῆσαι πειραθεὶς πρὸς τὸν λαὸν . . . ὕβρεσί τε πανταχόθεν πλυνόμενος καὶ λίθοις κάτωθεν καὶ τόξοις βαλλόμενος. G. Kedrenos, Vol. II., p. 538 ; J. Malalas, p. 394.

chariot-race.[1]   Mention is also made of a cell (κλουβίον) in the Stand.[2]

Along either side of the Hippodrome from the Imperial stand to the Curve, were benches supported on marble pillars.[3] Behind them was an unroofed promenade, from which a vast crowd could view the contests.[4] The benches were at first made of wood ; but, as they were an easy prey to fire, the Emperors subsequently made them entirely of stone.[5] Many of the pillars supporting them were preserved when Buondelmonti visited the place in 1422, especially those in the Curve, which were thicker and stronger on account of the steep slope of the ground to the back. It is impossible to say how many spectators could be accommodated on the benches, for no writer has thought of describing their situation and number.

With regard to the churches in the Hippodrome mentioned in the histories, I am inclined to think that they were built, not within its walls, but alongside of, or near to them.[6]

In studying the Hippodrome, and the adjacent

---

1 Cons. P., Vol. 1., pp. 308, 316.

2 *Ibid.*, p. 360.

3 The sedilia in the Roman circus are described by Panvinius, pp. 24, 25.

4 'Ο κοινὸς λαὸς ἀνῆλθον καὶ ἐπληρώθησαν τὰ βάθρα. Cons. P., Vol. I., p. 305 ; ὁ δὲ δῆμος ἵστατο ἐν τοῖς βάθροις καὶ εὐφήμει. *Ibid.*, p. 423.

5 Banduri, Vol. II., p. 565 ; *Chron. Pasch.*, Vol. 1., p. 715.

6 G. Kodinos, p. 74. In the records of the Patriarchate (1402), Vol. II., p. 495, there is a document of the Holy Synod concerning 'Αγίου Ἰωάννου περὶ τὸν ἱππόδρομον, lying to the west of it, περὶ τὸν ἱππόδρομον . . . εἰς ὃν ἄνθρωποι πρότερον ᾤκουν, . . . ἔρημον τῶν οἰκούντων, τῇ τοῦ καιροῦ ἀνωμαλίᾳ καταστάντα. Many of our historians record the destruction of the houses about the Hippodrome and S. Sophia.

Augustaion and Palace, we are driven, for want of drawings and exact descriptions, to derive all our information from the historians, many of whom had not an accurate knowledge of the places which they described. Not only had many of the famous civil and religious buildings in Constantinople been destroyed or altered during the thousand years of empire, and new buildings raised on the site of those of the older Emperors, but the historians describe buildings which were repaired by the Emperors, as entirely rebuilt. All this helps to bewilder us when studying Byzantine history.

Many of our historians have described S. Sophia; not a few have inspected it; and yet after great labour we are unable to explain all the passages in which they refer to it. If our knowledge of S. Sophia be so imperfect, what can we say about the Hippodrome, the desolation of which we so justly deplore?

Fortunately, a picture of the Hippodrome has been preserved for us by Onuphrius Panvinius, a native of Verona, who lived about the middle of the sixteenth century. Writing of the games and equipment of the Roman Circus, he gives in passing a description of the Hippodrome, which he has borrowed wholly from Gyllius.[1] But where he got the drawing, and who the artist was, he does not say. That indefatigable student of Byzantine antiquities, Banduri, has reproduced it in his *Imperium Orientale*, p. 664. Under the picture is the follow-

---

[1] *De Ludibus Circensibus*, p. 144.

ing inscription :—" The ruins of the Circus or Hippodrome of Constantinople, as they were a hundred years before the capture of the city by the Turks." Its date, accordingly, is about 1353. This picture gives a very confused view of the surroundings of the Hippodrome. The sea-wall of the Akropolis is brought very close, and behind the Curve the sea almost washes its foundations. The picture, though crude, and inaccurate in many particulars, bears out the accounts of several of our writers, and throws light on some narratives, which without it would be obscure. The marble columns which stood on the outside of the Curve are shewn, and in front of them is a strong wall, on which were built the benches so often mentioned. The Imperial Stand, the Chapel of S. Stephen,[1] and the Mangana, are represented. On the right side of the picture— i.e., to the west of the Hippodrome — appears a densely - crowded quarter, consisting chiefly of one-storied houses and a few domed churches. This district, populous even in the time of Niketas Choniátes, was burnt down when the Saracen mosque was attacked, as narrated in the last chapter. This picture is the only representation which we have of Constantinople before the capture.

Gyllius gives a long account of the Hippodrome and the structures which were then preserved in

---

[1] " Et primo versus Sophiam est ecclesia cum muro magnifico et innumerabilium fenestrarum ornatu, ubi dominæ et juvenculæ cum matronis, suos prospiciebant dilectos." Buondelmonti apud N. Bryennium, p. 180. Women did not accompany the Emperor and his suite to the Kathisma.

it.[1] After describing the Egyptian obelisk and
the other monuments in the middle of the
Hippodrome, he states that when he came to
the city, there were seventeen pillars of white
marble, with their bases, capitals, and epistyles,
on the outside of the Curve towards the
Propontis. They were built upon the strong
vaulting of the Curve. The bases were 2 feet
8 inches in height, and 5 feet 6 inches broad. The
shafts were nearly four feet in diameter and 28 feet
in length. The total height was over 35 feet.
"To-day"—continues Gyllius—"the pillars with
their bases and capitals have been taken down, and
lie on the earth to build the mosque of Suleiman
the Great. I was sad at their fate; not so much
because they lie on the ground, but because some
of them have been cut into slabs to pave the
floor of the baths, and because capitals in the
ancient style have been hewn into barbarous
forms, or hollowed for mortars, and shafts and
capitals are now broken up and built into walls."
The distance between the columns was eleven
feet. The capitals were all of Corinthian de-
sign. Iron rings hung from the tops of the
pillars by which the awnings were suspended. A
short time after the taking of Constantinople by
the Turks, there was in existence yet a second
row of pillars above this. After describing this
and other decorations of the Hippodrome, with
which we are acquainted from the narratives of

---

[1] *De Topographia Cpoleos.*, lib. ii., cap 11, *et seq.*

our historians, this painstaking writer adds—"But now the Hippodrome of Constantinople is desolate, stripped of all its ornaments, and they have lately begun to build on it : at the sight of it I was filled with grief."[1]

I have quoted these particulars, because they are peculiar to Gyllius. Our historians tell us of the pillars and benches of the Hippodrome, but none of them give their height, breadth, and thickness. According to Gyllius, the columns in the first row were about 35 feet high. If we suppose the height of those in the upper row to have been 21 feet, we have about 56 feet as the height of the walls on which the seats for the spectators were built. These would accommodate about 60,000 spectators. We can imagine what a magnificent spectacle the chariot races must have presented when the Hippodrome was in its splendour.

I have yet to describe the monuments in the interior of the Hippodrome, which, as I mentioned, have survived to this day.

The axis or centre of the Hippodrome was called by the Romans the *spina*, from its dividing the course into two equal parts, as the spine divides the body. Down the centre of the Roman Circus, was a wall of bricks, about 4 feet high and 12 feet broad. At either end sufficient space was left for the chariots to turn with freedom and safety. It is probable

---

[1] Lib. ii., cap. 13. Bien loin d'édifier aucune chose pour embellir de plus en plus leur capitale, ils [les Turques] laissent tomber en ruines les antiquités . . . le Palais de Constantin dont il ne reste plus qu'une masure. *Theatre de la Turquie,* par Michel Févre, Paris, 1686, p. 335.

that the wall in the Byzantine Hippodrome was built in the same manner.[1] It was in existence in the time of Buondelmonti, as he himself records. By the Byzantines it was sometimes called *spina*, as I have already mentioned. At other times they designated it by the usual Greek term νύσσα.[2] The two ends of the spina were rounded and were called the corners (καμπτῆρες, καμπτοί).[3] The south end was known as the Green corner, and the north as the Blue.[4] How far they were from the Curve and the Imperial Stand respectively we do not know. The space between the Stand and the northern corner was called the stama (στᾶμα). At great races the prisoners of the Prætorium had their station below the seats of the Green faction. Prisoners of war also stood there in chains, when the Emperor ordered their presence at the celebration of a triumph.[5]

In the writings of Constantine Porphyrogennetos, the course through which the competitors went is sometimes called the Π.[6]

---

[1] Panvinius, p. 79.

[2] Con. P., Vol. I., p. 344.

[3] G. Kodinos, pp. 19, 54; *Chron. Pasch.*, Vol. I., p. 594; Cons. P., Vol. I., pp. 343, 344, 352, 353, 613, 614.

[4] Τοῦ τῶν τετρώρων ἐῴου καμπτῆρος, ὃς ἐπεκέκλητο τοῦ 'Ρουσίου, (which was afterwards amalgamated with the Blue faction). N. Choniates, p. 865; ἀπὸ τοῦ μαγγάνου μέχρι τοῦ καμπτοῦ τοῦ Βενέτου—καὶ κάμπτουσιν τὸν τοῦ Πρασίνου καμπτόν. Cons. P., Vol. I., pp. 613, 614.

[5] Cons. P., Vol. I., p. 615; G. Kodinos, pp. 17, 40, 168; N. Choniates, p. 866.

[6] 'Ανέρχεται μέχρι τῆς φίνας ἤγουν τοῦ Π—ἔρχεται εἰς τὸ στάμα ἤγουν εἰς τὸ Π. Cons. P., Vol. I., pp. 310, 338, 352, 590, 614.

On the spina, as I have already mentioned, three monuments are still preserved,—the Egyptian obelisk, the three-headed serpent, and the four-sided bronze column. On the base of the obelisk are two inscriptions, one in Latin the other in Greek, which were first published by Gyllius. On the four sides of the base are engraved representations of the machines and cables, by means of which the obelisk was set up on its four bronze cubes. On another side were represented the horse races and the obelisk itself.[1] These rude sculptures represent contemporary events in the reign of Theodosios the Great, who caused the obelisk to be erected (390 A.D.). They afford some indications as to the position of the Emperor and State officials during the races. The throne in the Imperial Stand, and some steps are represented. Full and particular accounts of all these matters are to be found in works on the topography of Constantinople.

South of the obelisk is the three-headed serpent, a work of great beauty. It originally consisted of three huge serpents coiled on one another.[2] According to old accounts, the three heads with their gaping jaws were flattened on the top to form a support for the tripod of—say some—the Oracle of Delphi.[3] It was brought thence by Constantine

---

[1] Ὁ ἐν τῇ Μεγάλῃ Ἐκκλησίᾳ Δεσποτικὸς Θρόνος, ὑπὸ Γ. Χρυσοβέργη. Ἀθήνῃσι, 1861, p. 79. G. Kedrenos, Vol. I., p. 297.

[2] Du Cange quotes from an unknown author, Καὶ τίς ἀνδριὰς ἵστασθαι ἐλέγετο τρισὶ διατυπούμενος κεφαλαῖς. *Cpolis. Christ.*, lib. ii., p. 104.

[3] Ἔστησε δὲ [Κωνσταντῖνος ὁ Μέγας] κατά τι τοῦ ἱπποδρόμου μέρος καὶ τὸν τρίποδα τοῦ ἐν Δελφοῖς Ἀπόλλωνος, ἔχοντα ἐν ἑαυτῷ καὶ τὸ τοῦ Ἀπόλλωνος ἄγαλμα. Zosimos, p. 97.

the Great, and placed in its present position. In the vicissitudes which the city has since experienced, the heads have been destroyed, with the exception of one which is now preserved in the Church of S. Irene. It is well known that the names of all the Greeks who fought together against the Persians at Plataia, were inscribed on the pillar. When it was uncovered by the English, as I mentioned above, many scholars, both here and in the West, published versions of this inscription.[1] Both the pillar and the inscription have given rise to much discussion, and much has been written about them. Skarlatos Byzantios,[2] discussing the question of this column, sums up the opinions of others by saying, "It is perhaps the identical pillar of Delphi, and consequently is second to no piece of Greek handiwork in antiquity and historic interest." When and by whom the heads were taken off we do not know.[3]

South of this stood the four-sided bronze pillar, so called because it was formerly entirely covered with bronze plates, as is still shewn by the nails driven into the stone. I have no doubt that the plates have, like many more valuable works in bronze, been melted down for coining.[4] Private citizens, no matter how daring, would hardly have

---

[1] This inscription has been published recently by Mr. Grosvenor, Professor of History in Robert College, Constantinople.—[See Rawlinson's *Herodotus*, Vol. IV., p. 452 *note*, and note A, p. 483. Tr.]

[2] Κπολις, Vol. I., p. 243.

[3] The heads were in existence in Buondelmonti's time.

[4] Niketas Choniates, pp., 856, 857, 858,

ventured to strip so conspicuous a pillar. It was erected before the arrival of Buondelmonti in 1422. It is remarkable that the earthquakes, so frequent and destructive in Constantinople, have not thrown it down.

The later historians mention other monuments as standing on the spina. Buondelmonti[1] describes a great cistern of clear water, called φιάλη by the anonymous author of the *Patria*. In it stood a statue of Irene of Athens, erected by her son Constantine VII. (Porphyrogennetos).[2] Gyllius saw here seven marble pillars of great size. One measured eighteen feet in diameter, and bore on the top a bronze statue of Herakles.[3]

The picture given by Panvinius shows three small obelisks to the north of the Egyptian obelisk. The Bronze Pillar is not represented. From the picture it is clear that the races had then long before ceased; the marble benches were fallen, and private houses were being built upon the course. All goes to prove the neglect of the buildings by the later Emperors, who had long before abandoned the Palace in the Akropolis, and taken to the lofty halls of Blachérnai.

Many writers, and Porphyrogennetos in particular, mention the so called Euripos. At Rome this was a ditch full of water which surrounded the arena, to prevent the wild beasts from reaching the spectators. In Constantinople, where no such danger

---

[1] N. Bryennios, p. 180 ; Banduri, Vol. II., p. 668.
[2] G. Kodinos, p. 124.   [3] *Ibid.*, p. 39.

existed, it was a flagged course in front of the benches on either side.[1] At the festival held in the Hippodrome on the 11th of May (the Dedication of Constantinople) herbs and cakes were placed along the Euripos,[2] while fish were scattered among the people.

The Hippodrome, bounded by the Curve on the south, the Imperial Stand on the north, and the marble benches on either side, had four gates guarded by towers.[3] The gate or porch to the right of the Imperial Stand belonged to the Blue faction, which was specially favoured by the Emperor. The opposite belonged to the Greens, and from these positions they watched the competitors in the Hippodrome.[4] Near the latter gate was a small gate known as the gate of Decimus.[5] In the eastern end of the Curve was another gate called νεκρὰ, in imitation of the Roman *porta mortua*,[6] by which dead bodies were removed.

1 Cons. P., Vol. I., pp. 338, 344, 345, 363 ; *Cpolis. Christ.*, lib. ii., p. 104; ἐν τοῖς εἰς τὸν Εὔριπον τοῦ ἱππιδρομίου χαλκοῖς ἀνδριάσιν. Theophanes Con , p. 650; τοῦ ἵππου τρέχοντος ὅσον ἐδύνατο κυκλῶν ἐπῄει τὸν Εὔριπον τῆς Ἱπποδρομίας. G. Kedrenos, Vol. II., p. 343.

2 Καὶ κατελθόντες ἵσταντα ἐν τοῖς καμπτῆρσι καὶ ἐν τοῖς προειρημένοις λοιποῖς τόποις τοῦ Εὐρίπου, ἔνθα αἱ σταβαὶ τῶν λαχάνων καὶ τῶν πλακούντων εἰσίν. Cons. P., Vol. I., pp. 345, 363.

3 Τὴν τοῦ ἱπποδρόμου πύλην καταλαμβάνουσιν . . . ἐντὸς τῶν τοῦ ἱπποδρόμου πυλῶν ἀνῃρέθη. Theophanes Con., p. 382.

4 Ἀνέμου δὲ βιαίου καὶ σφοδροῦ καταπνεύσαντος Δεκεμβρίῳ μηνί, οἱ λεγόμενοι ἐν τῷ ἱππικῷ δῆμοι κατέπεσον, οἱ ἀπ' ἐναντίας τοῦ βασιλικοῦ θρόνου ἐτύγχανον. Theophanes Con., p. 431.

5 *Cpolis. Christ.*, lib. ii., p. 104 ; ἐν τῷ ἀνέρχεσθαι αὐτὸν . . . θεωρῆσαι διὰ τοῦ Κοχλίου κατὰ τὴν θύραν τοῦ λεγομένου Δεκίμου. *Chron. Pasch.*, Vol. I., p. 562 ; Theophanes Con., p. 431.

6 G. Kodinos, p. 124. ὁ τόπος ὃς καλεῖται τὰ νεκρά. Kodinos is wrong in stating that it received its name from the Nika riot. ἐκ τῆς λεγομένης νεκρᾶς πόρτας. *Chron. Pasch.*, Vol. I., p. 626.

Probably there was another gate in the opposite end, which has not been noticed by the historians. I think it is the one indicated by Constantine Porphyrogennetos in his account of the procession of the Emperor from the Palace to S. Sergius. He went through the Skyla into the Hippodrome, and passed through it and the ancient Asecreta to the church of S. Sergius.[1] There were also the mangana or carceres by which the competitors entered.

An hippodrome in the Palace is mentioned, and another near the church of SS. Sergius and Bacchus.[2]

The reader of Byzantine history wonders what was the fate of the numerous works of art and statues of every kind collected from all Hellenic countries and brought to this city,[3] which Niketas has described in his account of the capture of Constantinople by the Latins in 1204.[4] The Hippodrome and the adjacent Baths of Zeuxippos were filled with Greek works of art, of which, with the exception of the three monuments we described, nothing remains but the four horses which now adorn the front of S. Mark's, Venice.[5] Such a catastrophe has overtaken the city that, with all our labour, we can scarcely recognise the

---

1 Cons. P., Vol. I., pp. 87, 90.

2 Κατέρχονται εἰς τὸν ἱππόδρομον τοῦ Ἁγίου Σεργίου οἱ δύο δήμαρχοι κτλ. Cons. P., Vol. I., p. 337 ; G. Kodinos, p. 101.

3 G. Kodinos, pp. 52, 53, 183. In *Cpolis. Christ.*, lib. ii., p. 106, Du Cange enumerates all the writers who describe the statues in the Hippodrome.

4 Pp. 854, *sqq.* G. Kodinos, p. 183.

5 *Ibid.*, p. 53. Kodinos Kouropalates,́ p. 192.

site on which our Emperors built their Palace. Amidst the destruction of so many works of art and magnificent buildings, only S. Sophia and the Hippodrome have been spared, though wrecked and shorn of their splendour, to stand out like beacons to guide us in our troubled voyage amid the dark history of the Byzantine Empire. Lamentable wrecks as they are, they have always been full of interest to lovers of religion or lovers of shows. All the palaces of the Akropolis and Blachernai are insignificant, when compared with these invaluable historical monuments of the Emperors of Byzantion.

As I said in the previous chapter, it is not my intention to describe those ancient buildings of Constantinople, which others, such as the k. Byzantios, have described with great felicity. The reader therefore must not expect me to dwell on them, except in so far as they relate to the subject of the Palace.

The Insurrection of the Nika.

After this short account of the Hippodrome, it will be well to say something about the insurrection and massacre which took place in the Hippodrome in the reign of Justinian the Great. It is commonly known as the insurrection of the Nika, from the watchword of the rioters—Nika.[1] The best account of it is to be found in the pages of Prokopios.[2]

---

[1] "La sedition des Victoriata." J. Labarte, p. 14.
[2] Vol. I., pp. 119, 149 ; *Chron. Pasch.*, Vol. I., p. 620.

In January,[1] in the fifth year of Justinian's reign, a riot broke out in Byzantion which resulted in great injury to the people and the factions.[2] The prefect of the city condemned some of the rioters to death. The factions, usually at variance, made common cause, and rescued them from the prison, and released others also who were in custody. In an outburst of fury the rioters slew many of the prefect's officers without cause. Numbers of the citizens fled to the opposite shore of Anatole ; others set fire to a large part of the city, and so broke into open rebellion. The church of S. Sophia, founded by Constantine the Great,[3] the Baths of Zeuxippos, a portion of the Palace, and the houses of many of the wealthier citizens, fell a prey to the flames. Much property was destroyed in this conflagration. Justinian, with his wife Theodora and several courtiers, fled, and took refuge in the Palace. The object of the people's animosity was the Prætorian Prefect, John of Cappadocia, an ignorant and vicious creature, who feared neither God nor man, and was a glutton and extortioner. Tribonian, another of Justinian's advisers, was avaricious, and skilled only in wringing money from the citizens. For some time the rioters fought with one another, and committed no act of sedition. At length the Greens fraternised with the Blues, and together they rushed through

---

1 G. Kodinos, p. 131.

2 ἐν τῷ ἱπποδρομίῳ πολλοί φόνοι καὶ κακὰ γεγόνασι καί μάλιστα ἐν τοῖς πρὸ ἡμῶν. G. Kodinos, p. 184.

3 Ἔκτισε δὲ τὴν Ἁγίαν Σοφίαν ξυλόστεγον. G. Kodinos, pp. 16, 73, 131.

the city, reviling Justinian, and maltreating or killing all they met. They gave the pass-word Νίκα, from which this insurrection has derived its name. Justinian was anxious to stop the tumult. Deeming that it was due to resentment against John of Cappadocia, and Tribonian, he deprived them of their offices, and appointed in their stead Phokas, a patrician, and Basileides, a man of good reputation. Notwithstanding, the insurrection grew more serious.

Towards evening on the fifth day of the riot, Justinian ordered Hypatios[1] and Pompeius, nephews of the late Emperor Anastasios, to retire within the Palace. He was apprehensive that they might join the rioters and take part against him. They obeyed his orders and went inside the Palace.

Very early the next morning the mob learnt that, unknown to Justinian, the two had escaped from the Palace. They ran to Hypatios, and, deaf to the shrill cries and passionate protests of his more prudent wife Maria, proclaimed him Emperor. For lack of a crown, or any other Imperial trappings, they placed a torque[2] of gold upon his head, and thus decorated he was, against his will, proclaimed Emperor. Many of the populace and those of the councillors who had not gone with Justinian into the Palace, proposed to take it by storm. Should they be unsuccessful, they had

---

[1] Πατρίκιον καὶ δήμαρχον μέρους τῶν Βενέτων. G. Kodinos, p. 131.

[2] Στρεπτὸν δέ ἐστιν ἐληλάμενος χρυσὸς, ἐκ τριῶν πεπλεγμένος σχοινίων, ὅπερ ἐφόρουν ἐπὶ τραχήλου. Kodinos Kouropalates, p. 50.

others—the Palaces of Flacilla and of Helen.[1] From the words of Prokopios, it is evident that the palace, in which Justinian and his councillors had taken refuge, was so well fortified and guarded that the rioters could not take it.

While this horrible disturbance was devastating Constantinople, Justinian and his councillors were discussing measures for their safety, whether to remain in the Palace or to take flight by sea.[2] At this point Theodora, by her nervous and manly eloquence, abashed the cowardly courtiers and encouraged the wavering Justinian. She concluded by saying—"For my part, an old saying consoles me, 'A throne is a glorious sepulchre.'"

According to Prokopios, the Emperor's troops proved untrustworthy and waited the result of the insurrection. Justinian could depend on none of his generals, except Belisarius and Mundus, both of whom had fought on many fields. Belisarius had lately returned from the Median war with a devoted army. Mundus, too, brought tried men from Illyria.

Meanwhile the mob, shrieking and frantic with delight, bore Hypatios into the Hippodrome, and set him on the throne in the Imperial stand, from which the Emperors were wont to view the races. Mundus and his men left the gate of the Palace and proceeded to the dark spiral staircase, the

---

[1] The palace of Helena or the Heleniaca in the district Psammathia. Banduri, Vol. II., p. 690.

[2] From the harbour of the Boukoleon, beside the palace of the same name, whence they could cross to Anatole.

entrance to the Imperial Stand. Belisarius followed him, and arriving at an apartment where a guard of soldiers was stationed, ordered them to open the door immediately.[1] The soldiers, unwilling to commit themselves before they knew which was the winning side, did not obey. Alarmed at the clamour of the mob, and the uncertain attitude of the soldiers, the generals returned to the Palace, and reported the temper of the soldiers to Justinian. After a little Belisarius again left the Palace and went "through ruins and half-burnt houses" to the Hippodrome. From the account given by Prokopios, it is evident that he went out of the Palace behind the Curve, and entered the course on the right side by the gate of the Blues—"which is on the right of the Imperial throne—" and that he did not come from the neighbourhood of S. Sophia. He passed through blocks of buildings, burnt, as I have said, at an early stage of this sanguinary disturbance. Belisarius' first intention was to attack Hypatios, who still remained in the Imperial Stand. There, there was a small gate locked on the inside and guarded by soldiers. His fear was, lest the mob should attack him and his men, and then proceed against Justinian in the Palace. Reflecting that it was essential to fall on the mob and the factions, who stood crowding one another in the Hippodrome, he drew his sword, and ordered his men to do the

---

[1] This guard-room was probably beside the gate of the Hippodrome, on the left-hand side of the Imperial stand.

same. Then, with a shout, they charged at a run through the Gate of the Blues, on to the crowd. When the mob, who were standing loosely about in conversation, suddenly caught sight of Belisarius and his cuirassed veterans, plying their swords ruthlessly, they started to run out by the gates of the Hippodrome. But Mundus stood by the Gate of the Dead waiting Belisarius' attack on the mob.[1] Seeing him already engaged and the rioters fleeing in panic, he at once charged into the Hippodrome. The rioters, attacked in front and rear, met a violent death. They could not escape from the Hippodrome, and their companions outside could not make their way in to help them. While this was going on, Boraïdes and Justus, nephews of Justinian, ascended to the Imperial Stand, and without encountering any opposition, took Hypatios and his brother Pompeius, and handed them over to the Emperor. Upwards of 30,000 perished in the Hippodrome on that day.[2] Such was the insurrection of the Nika.

I am inclined to think that as Belisarius advanced from the Palace to the gate of the Blues, he was not seen by the people collected within the Hippodrome, because its lofty benches hindered their view. Thus, all the gates being securely closed, he was able to pass unobserved to the gate of the Blue faction, without the slightest suspicion on the part of the people.

---

1 The *Chronicon Paschale* (Vol. I., p. 626) also mentions Narses.

2 35,000 according to G. Kodinos, p. 131. μηδένα τῶν πολιτῶν ἢ ξένων τῶν εὑρεθέντων ἐν τῷ ἱππικῷ περισωθῆναι. *Chron. Pasch.*, loc. cit.

In the following chapter I intend to describe the Byzantine buildings discovered in the extensive space between the eastern wall of the Hippodrome and the walls of the Palace, a place known in the histories as the Augustaion.

CHAPTER III.

THE AUGUSTAION.

BETWEEN the eastern wall of the Hippodrome and the landward limit of the Imperial Palace, there is a considerable area extending south from S. Sophia. It measures about 144 yards from east to west, and from north to south over 550. This extensive four-porched market-place,[1] as Zozimos calls it, though often mentioned in Byzantine history, has not as yet been clearly defined. And what I now propose is to describe as far as possible the churches and other buildings which were erected within it, as well as the examples of Greek art which were collected by the Emperors from all parts of Greece and Asia, and deposited here. Although the work, as it seems to me, is difficult and thankless, and my conclusions differ greatly from those of many esteemed writers, I shall, nevertheless, as always, venture to submit my own views, and hope by so doing to throw light on some parts of the topography of Constantinople.

At the present day the whole space is occupied

---

1 Οὔσης δὲ ἐν τῷ Βυζαντίῳ μεγίστης ἀγορᾶς τετραστόου. Zosimos, p. 97 ; Simocatta, 1 10 scribit esse : ἀνάκτορον ἐν τῷ μεγάλῳ θαλάμῳ τῷ πρὸς τῃ μεγίστῃ τῶν βασιλείων αὐλῇ, Αὐγουσταῖος δ' ἄρα οὗτος κατονομάζεται. G. Kedrenos, (annot.) Vol. II., p. 800.

by the mosque of Sultan Achmet—vulgarly *Alté Minarelé*, the splendid Turkish building *Dar El Funún*, erected only a few years ago, and a small Turkish quarter with its crooked and sunless streets. The square, richly-wooded park to the south of S. Sophia, stands as it was in Byzantine times.

By the Byzantines this space was called the Augustaion,[1] sometimes the Forum, and sometimes the Forum of the Milion, or of Constantine. Owing to their ignorance of its boundaries, the accounts of it in later writers are vague and often unintelligible.[2]

THE HOSPITAL OF SAMPSON.

In the Nika insurrection, described in the last chapter, a building known as the Hospital of Sampson,[3] situated between S. Irene and S. Sophia, was burnt. The historian Prokopios,[4] who was a contemporary of Justinian, makes certain remarks which I shall follow closely, because they explain

---

[1] Αὐγουσταιών, Αὐγουστεῖον, Αὐγουστεών, Αὐγουστεὶς, etc. Cons. P., Vol. I., pp. 23-33 ; II., p. 59 ; Meursii, *Glossarium*, *s. v.* Αὐγουστεών.

[2] Ἐπὶ τούτων τῶν ὑπάτων προήχθη ἐπαρχος πόλεως Θεοδόσιος· καὶ ἔκτισε τὸ Αὐγουσταῖον ἐκ πλαγίων τῆς μεγάλης ἐκκλησίας. *Chron. Pasch.*, Vol. I., p. 593. Le grand Forum connu sous le nom d'Augustæon, resta célèbre pendant tout le moyen age. *L'Art Byzantin*, par Ch. Bayet, p. 19. διαφόρων ἁγιωτάτων πατριαρχῶν προσταξόντων, ἀπό τε τοῦ αὐγουστεῶνος, καὶ τῶν προσεχεστέρων μερῶν τῷ προνάῳ τῆς ἁγιωτάτης τοῦ Θεοῦ μεγάλης ἐκκλησίας, τοὺς τραπεζίτας διωχθῆναι. J. Meursii, *Glossarium*, *s. v.* Αὐγουστεών. Concerning this name, see *Cpolis. Christ.*, lib. iii., cap. 23. In the time of Gyllius the very name of the Augustaion was forgotten, and all the buildings in it had disappeared. *De Topographia Cpoleos.*, lib. ii., cap. 17.

[3] G. Kedrenos, Vol. I., pp. 647, 679 ; *Chron. Pasch.*, Vol. I., p. 622 ; τὸν ξενοδόχον τῶν σαμψῶν, Cons. P., Vol. I., p. 173. Gyllius, *De Topographia*, lib. ii., cap. 8, says that it was near S. Sophia.

[4] Vol. III., p. 183.

several points in connection with the buildings around S. Sophia. This church and S. Irene,[1] which, according to Prokopios, was, next to S. Sophia, the loftiest of all the churches, had been burnt. "Now, there was between these two churches a hospital for men who were utterly broken in health and in fortune." It had been erected some time previously by a God-fearing man named Sampson, who had once attended Justinian in a serious illness.[2] This hospital and all its inmates perished in the fire. It was rebuilt on a larger scale and richly endowed by Justinian, in order that a greater number of sick and poor might be relieved.[3] It was the chief of the many charitable institutions founded in Constantinople by the Christian Emperors.

This hospital is frequently noticed in the earlier history of the Empire. Simeon Metaphrastes gives the life of S. Sampson (27th of June),[4] but unfortunately says very little about the hospital itself. Under the later Empire it is never mentioned. In

---

[1] In this church the patriarch delivered the catechetical homily to the catechumens on Good Friday (Cons. P., Vol. I., p. 179), and the Second Oecumenical Council met in 482. Near it was the church of S. Menas, among the ruins of which three porphyry coffins were found, which are now preserved in the Imperial Museum. The Patriarch Constantius, 'Ελάσσονες Συγγραφαί, p. 386.

[2] Τὸν δὲ ξενῶνα τὸν λεγόμενον τοῦ Σαμψών, ὁ ὅσιος Σαμψὼν ἔκτισε συνεργείᾳ 'Ιουστινιανοῦ τοῦ μεγάλου. G. Kodinos, p. 99.

[3] Ὠικοδόμητο λίαν φιλοκάλως καὶ μεγαλοπρεπῶς. Simeon Metaphrastes, (ed. Migne) Vol. II., p. 289.

[4] *Ibid.*, p. 247. From the following words of Joannes Malalas, p. 479 : καὶ γέγονε πατριάρχης ἐν Κωνσταντινουπόλει Μηνᾶς ὁ ἀπὸ ξενοδόχων τοῦ Σαμψών, I conjecture that the hospitals were religious houses.

the Epistles of Pope Innocent III.,[1] who lived in the beginning of the thirteenth century, the abbot and monks of the Hospital of S. Sampson in Constantinople are mentioned.

Kantukouzenos,[2] describing the wretchedness and nakedness of the Catalans, says :—" Not only the influential citizens, and the sacred colleges, and the houses devoted to the common reception of strangers—this most charitable institution of the Romans—but also very many of the people, and artisans and labourers, everybody, in short, strove to surpass his neighbour in his zeal for the sufferers." Of the Hospital of Sampson, however, he makes no special mention.

I refer to these facts because they confirm all that I said in a former chapter about the erection of the Palace walls by Michael Palaiologos. At the present day the churches of S. Irene and S. Sophia are separated by a strong wall with lofty towers. Within this wall the hospital could not have been built, for the space on either side is too small for so large a building. My own opinion is that this famous building was pulled down when Michael Palaiologos built the new Palace walls, and that in consequence no mention is made of it under the later Empire, or, to be more exact, after the reign of Michael Palaiologos.

THE BATHS OF ZEUXIPPOS.

Another noted Byzantine building which is

---

[1] *Opolis. Christ.*, lib. iv., p. 164.   [2] Vol. III., p. 227.

never mentioned by the later historians, and of which, as Gyllius himself states, no traces remained in his day, was the Baths of Zeuxippos.[1]

According to the Alexandrian poet Chrysodoros,[2] they contained a large collection of statues brought together from Greece and Asia, which included statues of Homer, Aeschines, Demosthenes, Aristotle, Hesiod, Pyrrhus, Sappho, Apollo, Aphrodite, Julius Cæsar, Plato, Menander, Isokrates, Xenophon, Virgil, and many others. They were all destroyed by fire in the Nika riot, to our incalculable loss.

I think that before the time of the great builder Justinian, the public buildings of Constantinople were, like the private houses,[3] constructed of wood. This explains why the churches of S. Sophia and S. Irene, and the Baths of Zeuxippos with their statues, fell so easy a prey to the flames. It was truly an heaven-sent inspiration which moved the architect Anthemios to raise the dome of S. Sophia

---

1 Nunc nulla Zeuxippi vestigia restant, neque aliorum permultorum balneorum. *De Topographia Cpoleos.*, lib. ii., cap. 7 ; G. Kodiuos, p. 256 ; Michael Glykas, p. 450.

2 In his Ἔκφρασις τῶν ἀγαλμάτων τῶν εἰς τὸ δημόσιον γυμνάσιον τοῦ ἐπικαλουμένου Ζευξίππου. See G. Kodinos, p. 253, Souidas, *s. v.* Ζεύξιππος, Anthology, Vol. II., p. 26. This poet lived in the time of Anastasios Dikoros. Τότε δὴ ἀνεπρήσθη . . . καὶ τὸ λοετρὸν τοῦ Σεβήρου τὸ καλούμενον Ζεύξιππος, ἐν ᾧ ποικίλη τις ἦν θεωρία καὶ λαμπρότης τεχνῶν, τῶν τε μαρμάρων καὶ λίθων καὶ ψηφίδων καὶ εἰκόνων. G. Kedrenos, Vol. I., p. 647.

8 The numerous fires which occurred in Constantinople under the Byzantine Emperors convince me that the dwelling houses were built of wood. It is unfortunate that the historians should give us so little information on this point. Kedrenos (Vol. I., p. 648) tells us that there was destroyed, καὶ ὁ ἐκ τῶν φώτων τῶν κατὰ τὰς ἑσπέρας λαμπτήρων ἐπικαλούμενος οἶκος, ἅτε τὸν ὄροφον καὶ αὐτὸς ἐκ ξύλων ἔχων.

high above its neighbours, and thus teach his countrymen how to secure their glorious civil and religious buildings against fire.

Originally built by Severus, the Baths were renewed after the fire by Justinian, and adorned with a variety of marbles and statues. Kodinos [1] writes that they were built by Severus. He further states that they were sometimes known as the Baths of Severus, and that they were erected about the same time as the Hippodrome. In the " Short Scenes " by an unknown author, printed along with his *Excerpta,* they are mentioned in connection with the statue of Philippikos, and called the oldest baths in the city.[2] It would appear that in course of time fresh presents of statues were made by citizens.

These splendid Baths, which, at the time of the capture by the Turks, had fallen through age, or had been demolished by the Emperors,[3] lay in the

---

[1] G. Kodinos, pp. 36, 38. Ἐκ τε τῶν βασιλείων τό τε βαλνεῖον ὁ Ζεύξιττος, Prokopios, Vol. III., p. 202. Συζεύξας αὐτῷ καὶ λουτρὸν ἐν τῷ ἱερῷ τοῦ Διός, Souidas. Their site, according to Joannes Lydos (p. 265), was originally a market-place. *Chron. Pasch.,* Vol. I., p. 494 ; J. Malalas, p. 291.

[2] G. Kodinos, pp. 188, 191 ; C. Manasses, *v.* 2265 ; G. Kedrenos, Vol. I., p. 442 ἔδοξε τῷ βασιλεῖ (Philippikos, 697) . . . λούσασθαι εἰς τὸ δημόσιον λουτρὸν τοῦ Ζευξίττου. Theophanes, Vol. I., p. 587. According to Nikephoros Kallistos (lib. ix., cap. 9), these baths : Νουμέρων ἔσχε κλῆσιν εἰσέπειτα. Byzantios, Κπολις., Vol. I., p. 260.

[3] Nunc nulla Zeuxippi vestigia restant, neque aliorum permultorum balneorum. Gyllius, *De Topographia Cpoleos.,* lib. ii., cap. 7. According to Niketas Choniates (p. 460), the monastery of Ephoros was built beside these Baths, in a very low-lying place, παρά τινι κατωτάτῳ τόπῳ. At labenti Graecorum imperio, Zeuxippi appellatio ut et balnei usus desinit. *Cpolis, Christ.,* lib. x., cap. 27. I do not know what authority the distinguished Patriarch Constantius has for his statement, that the marbles of the Baths were removed by the Turkish conqueror to his mosque.

Augustaion to the east of the Hippodrome. The
Byzantine historians in their account of the erection by Severus of the vaults supporting the
Curve, state that south of the four-sided Bronze
Pillar the ground was steep and in some parts very
precipitous. Such to this day is the character of
the ground on either side of the Curve, which is
itself very strongly constructed. I have more than
once carefully gone over this ground. The crooked
alleys of the Turkish quarter on the east side all
slope steeply down to the south. One road alone
is level, that which runs east and west along the
south side of the mosque of Sultan Achmet, almost
opposite to the four-sided Bronze Pillar. If the
Baths had been built on the east side of the Hippodrome, I think we should have found the remains
of the strong walls or vaults, by which a level
foundation was formed for them. But nothing of
the sort exists at the present day, nor does any
trace of level ground appear in this neighbourhood.

Our information accordingly comes to this, that
the Zeuxippos was originally built in the Augustaion, burnt in the Nika riot, and rebuilt on the
original site, on a larger and more splendid scale.
We have the authority of Kodinos for stating that
it lay along the Palace wall.[1]

Between the Baths and the Hippodrome stood

---

[1] Τότε ὁ Σεβῆρος . . . ἔκτισε δύο λουτρὰ, ἔσωθεν μὲν τῆς πόλεως καὶ
πλησίον τοῦ παλατίου ἔν, τὸ καλούμενον Ζεύξιππον, pp. 13, 14. These
words of Kodinos have led Labarte astray in his account of these Baths,
Vol. II., p. 230.

a house, an epigram on which, by Leontios, has fortunately been preserved.[1]

Εἰς οἶκον κείμενον μέσον τοῦ Ζευξίππου καὶ τοῦ ἱππικοῦ.

Ἐν μὲν τῇ, Ζεύξιππον ἔχω πέλας ἡδὺ λόετρον,
ἐκ δ' ἑτέρης, ἵππων χῶρον ἀεθλοφόρων . . .

From this epigram it appears that the Baths were not connected with the Hippodrome. Our view that they were erected beside the Palace wall is further confirmed by an epigram in the Anthology,[2] presumably by the same Leontios, "To a little Bath beside the Zeuxippos" :—

Μὴ νεμέσα Ζεύξιππε, παραντέλλοντι λοετρῷ,
καὶ μεγάλην παρ' ἄμαξαν ἐρωτύλος ἡδὺ φαείνει, κτλ.

I think that this bath, which is not mentioned by any other writer, lay to the south of the Baths of Zeuxippos.

It is possible that some may consider this disquisition altogether superfluous. I wish, however, to give all the reasons which have led me to decide on the position of the Baths, as well as of other notable Byzantine buildings, in the belief that they will convince others. Moreover, both Greek and Western writers have frequently sought for the site of these Baths, in which, as I have said, so many ancient works of art perished. They were, indeed, a veritable open-air museum. Labarte in

---

[1] *Opolis. Christ.*, lib. i., p. 91; Gyllius, *De Topogr.*, lib. ii., cap. 7. The rents of some houses which stood near the Baths were devoted to their maintenance.

[2] Vol. I., p. 221 [Gyllius, *loc. cit.*].

his excellent book [1] places them to the north of the Hippodrome, behind the Imperial Stand. Byzantios [2] simply says that they were near the Palace; but where, he does not determine.

Having thus placed the Baths of Zeuxippos in the south end of the Augustaion, I shall now proceed to consider other buildings in this place of which mention is frequently made, in order that we may fix their sites with some degree of certainty. The architecture and dimensions of these buildings are but scantily described by the historians.

Referring to the Augustaion, Prokopios [3] writes: "There was an agora before the Senate-house, now the Byzantines call the agora Augustaion;" and again, "There is an agora with a peristyle in front of the Palace; the Byzantines call it Augustaion." The part of this extensive space adjacent to S. Sophia was called the Milion or the Forum of the Milion. Part of it still exists in the square mentioned above, south of S. Sophia, and opposite to the Turkish building *Dar El Funún.*

According to Kodinos,[4] the Augustaion was called Gousteion in addition to the names given

---

1 Plate II.

2 Κτολις, Vol. I., p. 260.

3 Vol. III., pp. 181, 202.

4 Pp. 15, 28. In his note on the latter passage, Lambecius (p. 232) quotes from Joannes Lydos, p. 124: ἐν τῷ γουστείῳ οἷον τῷ ὀψοπωλείῳ εἰς τιμὴν Τιβερίου οἱ σεβαστοφόροι ἐχόρευον, τὸν δὲ τοιοῦτον τόπον οἱ ἰδιῶται αὐγουστεῶνα καλοῦσιν.—τῇ εʹ τοῦ Ὀκτωβρίου μηνὸς οἱ ῥεγεωνάρχαι καὶ σεβαστοφόροι ἐχόρευον ἐν τῷ Αὐγουστείῳ οἷον ἐν τῷ ὀψοπωλείῳ εἰς τιμὴν τοῦ Τιβερίου, Souidas, s. v. Αὔγουστος.

above. Before the erection of S. Sophia by Justinian, there was a market there, where the common people often feasted and danced. It was then called Gousteion. Justinian cleared the place, and sent the market traders elsewhere. He also paved it with marble, from which it was sometimes called the Pavement ($\pi\lambda\alpha\kappa\omega\tau\delta\nu$).[1] According to our map, on entering or leaving the Palace we should have to pass through the Augustaion. Constantine Porphyrogennetos says this in so many words, "and going through the middle of the Milion and the Augustaion,"—"and going through the Augustaion he enters the Palace," etc.[2] From these passages it is clear that the Emperor, whether going into or out of the Palace, always went through the Augustaion.

Kodinos Kouropalates[3] writes :—" It is the custom to scatter purses of money ($\dot{\epsilon}\pi\iota\kappa\delta\mu\beta\iota\alpha$)[4] in the space before the doors of the Great Church, that is in what is called the Augusteion, the person throwing the money standing above on the steps of the Augusteion."

Before describing the structures in the centre of

---

[1] Ἐν τῷ πλακωτῷ τοῦ Μιλίου. Cons. P., Vol. I., pp. 84, 106.

[2] Cons. P., Vol. I., pp. 63, 128, 132, 143, 159, 415; Prokopios, Vol. III., p. 304.

[3] P. 88 ; N. Choniates, pp. 308, 309.

[4] Byzantios, Κπολις, Vol. III., p. 184. They were sums of money tied up in napkins, given to the nobles, and sometimes thrown among the people. See Kodinos Kour., pp. 355, 356. Ea erant, quæ Imperator festo coronationis vel nuptiarum die spargebat in populum.—Meursii *Gloss.*, s. v.; J. Kantakouzenos, Vol. I., p. 203. They were sometimes called ἀπόδεσμοι, G. Pachymeres, Vol. II., p. 197, and σπόρτυλα, Cons. P., Vol. I., p. 261.

the Augustaion, it will be well that we first consider the remarkable and historical buildings situated there, as I did in the case of the Hippodrome. These splendid buildings, of which no vestige is now preserved, are often mentioned by the historians. From the careful perusal of their narratives we can determine at least their sites.[1]

Owing to their ignorance of the boundaries of the Augustaion, those who have described Constantinople have fallen into mistakes, and their want of knowledge of the various localities has rendered their descriptions unintelligible. Skarlatos Byzantios, in his account of Constantinople, quotes as correct Buondelmonti's statement that the Augustaion lay to the south of S. Sophia. A few pages farther on, forgetting the correct observation of the Italian, who had seen the city before the capture by the Turks, he writes :—" The site of this extensive square of the Augustaion is now in all probability occupied on the eastern side by the first court of the Seraglio, and the buildings adjoining the *Babi-humaghiún.*"[2]

THE SENATE HOUSE.

In the Augustaion there formerly stood a building of great antiquity, called the Senate House.[3]

---

[1] About the end of last century there was a menagerie between S. Sophia and the Mosque of Achmet, probably among the then extant Byzantine buildings. Le Chevalier, *Voyage de la Propontide et du Pont-Euxin*, Vol. II., p. 228.   [2] Κπολις., Vol. I., pp. 440, 448.

[3] Σύγκλητος, βουλευτήριον, Σενᾶτον, φόρος τοῦ Σενᾶτου, αἱ Σύνοδοι. G. Kodinos, p. 40. βασιλικὸς οἶκος τῆς συγκλήτου γερουσίας. Opolis. Christ.,

It was among the first buildings re-erected by Justinian after the Nika riot. According to George Kodinos, "The Senaton, as some say, was originally the place where wills were deposited, for thither the Patricians took them in the time of Constantine."[1] I have no doubt that the building called the Senaton was originally erected by Constantine the Great in his imitation of Roman forms. Kodinos goes on, "and this Emperor built the chambers of the Senate, and called the place Senaton."[2] Sozomenos writes of Constantine: "and the great council which they call σύγκλητον, he established afresh with the same procedure, honours, and festivals as obtained among the ancient Romans."[3] A certain Eleutherios was the architect of this palace. The president of the Senate sat on the Chrysotriklinos.[4]

Prokopios gives an accurate account of the site and appearance of the building after its re-erection by Justinian. " Here [i.e., in the Augustaion] on the east side of the Market-place, the Senate House is built. By reason of its costliness and its whole construction, it is the finest work of the Emperor Justinian. Here the Roman Senate meets at the beginning of the year, and holds its annual festival in veneration of the everlasting ordinances of the

---

lib. ii., p. 145 ; N. Choniates, p. 733. ἐν τῷ τοῦ φόρου σενάτῳ. Cons. P., Vol. I., p. 169. ὁμοίως δὲ ἐκαύθη καὶ τὸ Σενάτον, ὅπου ἐστὶ τὸ λεγόμενον Αὐγουσταῖον. *Chron. Pasch.*, Vol. I., p. 621.

[1] Pp. 40, 169, 174.   [2] *Ibid.*, p. 16.

[3] Lib. ii., cap. 3; *Opolis. Christ.*, lib. ii., p. 145. In addition to the active senators there were honorary members called ἄπρακτοι, Cons. P., Vol II., p. 160.   [4] G. Kodinos, p. 63.

State. Six pillars stand before it. One pair flanks the middle division of the western front, and the remaining four stand further forward. In colour all are white, and for size the greatest, I think, in the whole world. They form a portico surrounding a roof in the form of a dome, and the upper parts of the portico are all adorned with marbles equal to the pillars in beauty, and with a great number of statues standing above these."[1]

From this account of Prokopios, whose acquaintance with Byzantine buildings I have always valued highly, we learn that the front of the Senate House faced the west, that six pillars supported a domed portico, adorned with marbles and wonderful sculptures. All his statements are confirmed by the *Chronicon Paschale*,[2] which, however, attributes to Constantine the Great all that Prokopios ascribes to Justinian. My conjecture is, that Justinian rebuilt the Senate House exactly as it stood before the Nika riot. Even before this time, it had fallen a prey to the flames,[3] when the people of Constantinople, breathing out threatenings at the banishment of S. John Chrysostom, and refusing to receive any other bishop, secretly set

---

[1] Vol. III., p. 202. Constantine Porphyrogennetos (Vol. I., p. 440) has much to say about the Senate and its President ; Gyllius, *De Topographia*, lib. ii., cap. 17.

[2] Κτίσας ἐγγὺς καὶ βασιλικὴν ἔχουσαν κόγχην, καὶ ἐξ [ἔξω text] μεγάλους κίονας στήσας καὶ ἀνδριάντας, ἥνπερ ἐκάλεσε Σενάτον, καλέσας τὸν τόπον Αὐγουσταῖον. Vol. I., p. 528. Zosimos (p. 139) writes of Julian : ἔδωκε μὲν τῇ πόλει γερουσίαν ἔχειν ὥσπερ ἐν τῇ Ῥώμῃ.

[3] George Kedrenos (Vol. I., p. 610) mentions the burning of the Senaton in the great fire in the reign of Leo Makelles.

fire to the Great Church, and destroyed all the buildings adjoining it. The flames seized on the Senate House, which stood in front of the Palace, and was adorned with many marbles and statues. From this it would appear that numerous works of art of the greatest merit adorned this Senate House from its first erection. I infer from all the accounts, particularly from that of Prokopios, that the flames scorched, but did not totally destroy the building, which was built of stone, and adorned on every side with marble pillars of the finest workmanship.

According to Sozomenos, the site of the Senate House was to the south of S. Sophia. He says : "The flames devoured the great Chamber of the Senate which lies beside it on the south."[1] Kedrenos writes : "In the north end of the Forum is the Senaton, which was burnt in the days of Leo, the son of Berene."[2] According to Constantine Porphyrogennetos, the council room called Senaton lay beside the Column of Justinian. On the festival of the Annunciation the Emperor ascended the steps of the Column, to enter the Church of S. Constantine. "The senate stand on the left side of the procession, towards the Senaton." This same writer frequently applies the name Forum ($\phi \acute{o} \rho o \varsigma$) to the whole Augustaion. "They proceed to the Senate House of the Forum."[3] Mention is made of statues of the Augusti Honorius and Theodosios,

---

[1] Lib. viii., cap. 22 ; Cons. P., Vol. I., p. 169.
[2] Vol. I., p. 565.
[3] Cons. P., Vol. I., pp. 28, 164, 169.

and of a golden statue of Theodosios the Great.[1] In the time of Leo a great fire took place, which Kedrenos has described.[2] Of the Senate House he writes : "The fire destroyed a magnificent and singular building in the Forum of Constantine, called the Great Senate House,[3] adorned with bronze statues, and porphyry stones, where the members deliberated, and the Emperor entered when he assumed the consular robe. It also destroyed the Nymphaion, which lay opposite the Senate House. Here were celebrated the marriages of those who had not houses." Zosimos is the only writer who mentions this Nymphaion.[4]

In front of, or near the Senate House, Arius breathed his last. " There Arius died a vile death, twenty-nine palms from the Chamber of the Senate."[5]

In similar studies, whether of Byzantine history or of the topography of Constantinople, I have repeatedly stated that I am guided solely by the narratives of our historians. It is beyond doubt

---

[1] *Chron. Pasch.*, Vol. I., pp. 571, 573.

[2] P. 610. On p. 281, he describes the statues in this building. ἐνέπεσε δὲ τὸ πῦρ καὶ εἰς τὸν εἰωθότα δέχεσθαι τὴν γερουσίαν οἶκον, πρὸ τῶν βασιλείων ὄντα, εἰς τὰν κάλλος καὶ φιλοτιμίαν ἐξησκημένον. Zosimos, p. 280.

[3] Cons. P., Vol. I., p. 169 : καὶ ἀνέρχονται ἐν τῷ τοῦ φόρου σενάτῳ, etc. *Cf.* G. Kodinos, p. 169 ; Agathias, p. 294.

[4] Gyllius, *De Topographia*, lib. iii., cap. 4.

[5] G. Kodinos, pp. 40, 241 ; M. Glykas, p. 468 ; Souidas says : ἐν γὰρ τῷ τῆς πόλεως φόρῳ . . . ἀποκλίνας εἰς ἀπόπατον ἀπεβίωσε, *s. v.* Ἀρειανός. Cons. P., Vol. I., p. 440 ; Kedrenos, Vol. I., p. 518. ἐν τῷ φόρῳ πλησίον τοῦ λεγομένου Σενάτου ἐγένετο. *Chron. Pasch.*, Vol. I., p. 525. Le Beau's account of the death of Arius is very confused. *Hist. du Bas Empire*, Vol. I., p. 590.

that the buildings which are described by them as standing in the early Empire, were not in existence in the later periods. During the last two centuries of power, only the memory of many ancient buildings was preserved. After the capture by the Turks, the surviving inhabitants and their descendants forgot the very names of the more notable among them.[1] At the present day, excavations would throw light on many points. Nevertheless, those engaged in such studies reap rich rewards. I would beseech all engaged in such work, first of all to go over with great care the whole site of the Palace, relying not on the so-called topographers, Greek or Western, but on the Byzantine historians, who are, as a rule, most trustworthy guides.

Thus studying the buildings about the Palace, under the guidance of our historians, we learn that the noble Byzantine building, the Bouleuterion or Senate House, was originally built by Constantine the Great, in imitation of the Roman Curia ; and was burnt in the Nika riot, and rebuilt anew with greater splendour by Justinian. It lay in the Forum or Augustaion, to the south of S. Sophia,[2] was adorned with six marble pillars, was domed, and faced the west. Accordingly, I place it along-

---

[1] Sic enim quotidie vastantur ut senex nesciat quae puer vidit, neque modo aedificia antiqua deleta, sed etiam locorum nomina, quae illa tenebant amissa sunt, aliaque barbara successerunt. Gyllius, *De Topographia*, lib. iv., cap. 11.

[2] Ὁμοίως δὲ ἐκαύθη καὶ τὸ Σενᾶτον, ὅπου ἐστὶ τὸ λεγόμενον Αὐγουσταῖον. *Chron. Pasch.*, Vol. I., p. 621.

side the walls of the Palace, to the north of the
Baths of Zeuxippos.[1]

We now come to another notable Byzantine
building, which was situated near the Senate House.
Our previous study enables us also to fix the site of
this. The Patriarcheion lay outside the precinct of
S. Sophia,[2] close to the Senate House on the one
hand, and to the church on the other, in accordance
with the order of the Council of Carthage that
bishops should reside beside their cathedrals.[3] The
Thomaïtes, a hall in the Patriarcheion, is frequently
alluded to by the historians. At the coronation
of the Emperor, he first made confession of his
faith, and then, accompanied by the Patriarch and
the Holy Synod, he " proceeds to the hall called
Thomaïtes, which faces the Augustaion, where the
populace and military stand."[4]   Choniates also
mentions the Thomaïtes.[5]   Another hall, called
Thettalos, in the Patriarcheion, is mentioned in the

---

[1] In ii., 17, Gyllius writes of the Senate House : Adhuc extant muri
Senatus, ab angulo Sophiæ intuenti Meridiem.

[2] Cons. P., Vol. I., pp. 565, 612, 616.

[3] *Cpolis. Christ.*, lib. ii., p. 143 ; Cons. P., Vol. I., p. 435.   Olim sedes
patriarchatus CPtani. penes eam [S. Sophiam] erat, *ibid.*, II., p. 636.

[4] Kodinos Kour., p. 88 ; N. Choniates, p. 327.   καὶ ἀναφέρουσιν αὐτὴν
εἰς τὸ μητατώριον ἐπὶ τὸν Θωμαΐτην, Cons. P., Vol. I., p. 260.   προκαθημένου τοῦ ἁγιωτάτου ἡμῶν δεσπότου καὶ οἰκουμενικοῦ Πατριάρχου Νικολάου
ἐν τῷ Θωμαΐτῃ. Leunclavii, *Jus Græco-Romanum*, Francfort, 1596,
Vol. I., p. 216.

[5] Ἀπὸ τοῦ ἀνδρῶνος τοῦ καλουμένου Μάκρωνος εἰς τὸν Αὐγουσταιῶνα προ-
νεύοντος καὶ τοῦ συνημμένου τούτῳ Θωμαΐτου δόμου, p. 309 ; Byzantios, Κπολις,
Vol. I., p. 517.

Continuation of Theophanes—" And in the Thettalos, a hall so named in the Patriarcheion, he was
lying upon a couch." [1]

As to the Thomaïtes, the writings of Zonaras
are of great value. [2] " A fire broke out, in which
the great banquetting hall, called Thomaïtes, in the
episcopal palace, fell a prey to the flames, when it
is said that the drafts of the exegeses of Holy Scrip-
ture, written by S. John Chrysostom, which were
preserved somewhere there, were burnt." Kedrenos'
account is almost identical. " There was a fire, and
the hall in the Patriarcheion, called Thomaïtes, was
burnt, together with the chambers beneath it, in
which lay the whole of the scrolls of S. John Chrysostom's interpretations of the Scriptures." [3] In the
Thomaïtes was the so-called Patriarchal Library,
from which Theophilos demanded books, that he
might silence the Image-worshippers. [4] In this
library were preserved all the important and
authoritative documents of the Holy Synods. On
Orthodoxy Sunday, the Emperor, after the Liturgy
in S. Sophia's, proceeded to the Patriarch's palace,

---

[1] Pp. 150, 648. καὶ δὴ ὅσα πρὸς ἀψίδα νένευκε τοῦ Μιλίου καὶ τῷ ἀνδρῶνι
συνῆπται τῷ Μάκρωνι καὶ τῷ λεγομένῳ αἱ Σύνοδοι. N. Choniates, p. 732;
G. Pachymeres, Vol. II., p. 196.

[2] *Opolis. Christ.*, lib. ii., p. 143.

[3] Vol. II., p. 25;

Καὶ πυρκαϊᾶς συμβάσης ὀλεθρίας
ἀνακτόρων κέκαυτο τῆς ἐκκλησίας
Θωμαΐτης κάλλιστος ἐκλαμπρος δόμος.

Ephraimios, *vv.* 1887-9.

[4] Τὴν κατὰ τὴν πατριαρχικὴν ἐν τῷ Θωμαΐτῃ κατὰ τήνδε τὴν θέσιν κειμένην
βιβλιοθήκην—τὴν τὲ καλουμένην βασιλικὴν, ἐν ᾗ ἀπέκειτο βιβλιοθήκη ἔχουσα
βίβλους μυριάδας δώδεκα, G. Kedrenos, Vol I., p. 616; II., p. 115; Theophanes Con., p. 105.

and breakfasted with him.[1]　Labarte places the Thomaïtes near the metatorion of S. Sophia, forgetting that there was also a metatorion in the Patriarcheion.[2]

The Patriarcheion is very seldom mentioned by the historians—less often, in fact, than any other of the buildings in the Augustaion.[3]　Within it were two rooms, called *Secreta*, the greater, and the less, in which the Patriarch and the Holy Synod tried all ecclesiastical cases.[4]　The court, composed of metropolitans and archbishops, which sat with the Patriarch, was also called *Secretum*.[5]

THE CHAPEL IN THE PATRIARCHEION.

From the following words of Porphyrogennetos, it is plain that there was a church, or rather chapel, in the Patriarcheion.　He is describing the ceremony on the third day of Lent.　" The Archbishop of Constantinople invites the Emperor and his senate to his holy and magnificent palace, and when the Holy Liturgy is finished, a banquet

---

[1] Cons. P., Vol. I., pp. 160, 191.

[2] *Le Palais Impérial*, p. 30.

[3] Cons. P., Vol. I., pp. 530, 531. Ὅσα δεῖ παραφυλάττειν ἐπὶ χειροτονίᾳ πατριάρχου Κωνσταντινουπόλεως, ibid., p. 564. . We learn little from these passages.　The Patriarcheion was burnt by the. Latins in 1203 ; καὶ δὴ ὅσα πρὸς ἀψῖδα νένευκε, τοῦ Μιλίου καὶ τῷ ἀνδρῶνι συνῆπται τῷ Μάκρωνι . . . εἰς ἔδαφος κατερράγγησαν· N. Choniates, p. 732.

[4] Σέκρετον dicitur locus in quo judices conveniunt et causas audiunt, Lambecius in G. Codinum, p. 234. ἐφίστανται τῷ καθ' ἡμᾶς ἱερῷ συνοδικῷ δικαστηρίῳ, Acta Patriarchatus, Vol. I., pp, 276, 279. καθίζονται οἱ σύγκλητοι . . ἐν τοῖς τοῦ Πατριάρχου σεκρέτοις,. Cons. P., Vol. I., p. 532.

[5] Ὁ κλῆρος τοῦ σεκρέτου τοῦ πατριάρχου. Cons. P., Vol. I., pp. 208, 209, cf. 616, 761, 771 ; παπάδας τοῦ σεκρέτου τοῦ πατριάρχου λς', ibid., p. 755.

(κλητώριον) is set in the greater secretum of the Palace." (Vol. I., pp. 760, 761). Kedrenos mentions the lesser. " In the same year Niketas the false Patriarch destroyed the mosaics in the little secretum, and the other pictures in the whole of the Patriarch's palace." (Vol. II., p. 16.) That the secretum was a large room, is evident from the following words of Porphyrogennetos. On Orthodoxy Sunday, the Emperor, coming from the festival celebrated in Blachernai, " proceeds to the very magnificent and spacious secretum in the Patriarcheion."[1] The whole assembly, consisting of the Emperor and many courtiers, feasted together in the secretum. The above accounts are in agreement with that given by the Patriarch Nikephoros. " The chambers which the Romans call *secreta*, the smaller and the greater chambers, and the pictures of the Saviour and the saints, executed in mosaic and encaustic panels, he destroyed." (P. 85.)

That the Patriarcheion was not inside the Imperial Palace, is evident from the words of Porphyrogennetos, in his account of the " Ceremonies to be observed at cutting the hair of a son of the Emperor." " The Emperor commands the Patriarch to be present, and the praepositus goes and summons him, and he enters the Palace, attended, as is his wont, by his secretum, and the Metropolitans and Archbishops."[2] The Patriarcheion occupied the same site until the final capture."[3]

---

1 Vol. I., p. 761 ; 'Αρμενοπούλου ἡ ἐξάβιβλος, Athens, 1872, p. 195.

2 Vol. I., pp. 531, 621 ; G. Kedrenos, Vol. II. p. 16.

3 G. Pachymeres, Vol. I., p. 385. The scholarly k. M. J. Gedeon, of

The Synodical Courts mentioned in the *Acta Patriarchatus*, were these secreta in the Archbishop's Palace.[1] After the assumption of power by Michael Palaiologos, the Holy Synod met sometimes in the south catechumeneia of S. Sophia, and sometimes in the cells of the Patriarch's church of S. Theophylaktos. It is probable that on the Emperors abandoning the Palace, which lay immediately behind the Patriarcheion, it, or part of it, was also deserted. The Patriarch was always elected in the south catechumeneia of S. Sophia.[2]

These, then, are a few particulars concerning the Byzantine Patriarcheion, which is extremely seldom mentioned in history. Constantine Porphyrogennetos says nothing about its internal arrangements. The pictures and mosaics which adorned it, we know only from the Image Controversies. Labarte says nothing about it, but mentions the Thomaïtes, which, as I have said, he unwarrantably places at the south-east corner of S. Sophia.

The oratory of S. Theophylaktos, which Constantine Porphyrogennetos mentions,[3] appears to me to have been the church or chapel of the Patriarch, situated inside the Patriarcheion. I said above

---

Constantinople, has given us much information about the Patriarcheion and the Secreta in his Χρονικὰ τοῦ Πατριαρχικοῦ οἴκου καὶ τοῦ ναοῦ, 1884, pp. 15, 51.

[1] *Acta Patriarchatus CPtani.*, Vol. I., p. 382; IV., p. 315,

[2] Cons. P., Vol. I., p. 565.

[3] Καὶ δούλκιον ἐποίει ὁ κύριος Θεοφύλακτος ὁ πατριάρχης ἐπὶ τὸ μέρος τοῦ εὐκτηρίου τοῦ ἀγίου Θεοφυλάκτου, καὶ οἱ δεσπόται ἀπήλαυον τοῦ δουλκίου μετὰ τῶν μαγίστρων, Vol. I., p. 160. Concerning this Patriarch Theophylaktos, son of Romanus, see *ibid.*, p. 635,

that, according to the *Acta Patriarchatus*, the Holy Synod met sometimes in the catechumeneia of S. Sophia, and sometimes in the cells of S. Theophylaktos.[1] In the account of the ceremonies to be observed on Orthodoxy Sunday, the shrine of S. Theophylaktos is mentioned in such a manner as to convince every reader that it was within the Patriarcheion.[2]

The Russian monk Antony, who was in Constantinople in 1203, makes the following remarks on the Gardens of the Patriarcheion. "In the garden of the Patriarcheion, grow pulse of every kind, melons, apples, and pears. They are kept hung down wells in baskets, and when the Patriarch breakfasts, they are brought up exceedingly cool. The Emperor also partakes of such fruits. The baths of the Patriarcheion are in the Palace. The water is conveyed through conduits, and there is also rain-water at hand." It is probable that this garden separated the Patriarcheion from the Senate House. The baths Antony mentions were in the gardens, or else inside the Patriarcheion, and not, as he states, in the Palace grounds.[3]

---

1 Καθίσαντες ἐν τοῖς δεξιοῖς κατηχουμενείοις τῆς ἁγιωτάτης τοῦ Θεοῦ μεγάλης ἐκκλησίας. *Acta Patriarchatus*, Vol. II., p. 2. Προκαθημένου τοῦ παναγιωτάτου ἡμῶν δεσπότου τοῦ οἰκουμενικοῦ Πατριάρχου κὺρ Ἡσαΐου ἐν τοῖς κατὰ τὸν Ἅγιον Θεοφύλακτον κελλίοις αὐτοῦ. *Ibid.*, Vol. I., pp. 98, 99, 102, 104, 106, 107, 111, 132, 135, 136, 140, 143, 144, 149, 151, 155, 156, 164, 594; IV., p. 379.

2 Cons. P., Vol. I., p. 160. The cells of the most holy Patriarch Arsenios are also mentioned, where the Holy Synod sat, *Acta Patriarch.*, Vol. I., p. 475. During the Latin domination, the Papal legate occupied the Patriarcheion, Riant, *Exuviæ Sacrae*, Vol. I., p. 171.

3 G. Pachymeres, Vol. II., pp. 258, 454; Byzantios Κπολις, Vol. I., p. 519.

OUR LADY IN THE COPPER MARKET.

North of the Patriarcheion, and near to S. Sophia, lay a church dedicated to Our Lady, styled in the Copper Market.[1]   Kodinos says, "In the Chalkoprateia in the time of Constantine the Great the Jews had been living for a hundred and thirty-two years, and sold copper vessels.   Theodosios the younger expelled them, and having cleared the site, built thereon the church of Our Lady."[2] According to Kedrenos, "he then built the church of Our Lady where a Jewish synagogue formerly stood."[3]   From all accounts, and especially those belonging to the earlier centuries of the Empire, it appears that beside S. Sophia there was an extensive market, where domestic utensils and food of every kind were sold.   The place was cleared after the conflagration in the Nika riot.   The church in the Copper Market had, according to Constantine Porphyrogennetos, a women's gallery and a chapel on each side of the altar.[4]   It also had three doors in the narthex, for he writes, "The Emperor enters the Church of Our Lady in the Copper Market, and

---

[1] 'Η Θεοτόκος τῶν Χαλκοπρατείων, Cons. P., Vol. I., p. 30 ; Theophanes Con., p. 829.

[2] P. 83.

[3] Vol. I., p. 602.   Joel, *Chronographia*, p. 40.

[4] Cons. P., Vol. I., pp. 30, 31, 165.   In all probability there were anciently copper-smiths' workshops beside the market-place on which, as the Byzantine historians tell us, Constantine the Great built S. Sophia. This Church of Our Lady had a shrine containing relics of its patron, εἰσέρχεται εἰς τὴν ἁγίαν σορόν, Cons. P., Vol. I., pp. 166, 339; II., p. 136 ; G. Kodinos, pp. 113, 275; G. Kedrenos, Vol. II., p. 18.   In his account of this Church, Du Cange writes 'Αγιοσυρίτασσαν instead of 'Αγιοσωριότισαν.

entering into the narthex, sits there awaiting the Patriarch. The citizens and the inferior clergy enter by the right door of the royal doors." [1] This church was heightened and adorned by Basil the Macedonian. [2]

I mention these facts because they shew distinctly that this was a large church, and not a mere chapel. It was sometimes called shortly the Chalkoprateia. "On the 8th of September, a procession is held in honour of the nativity of our most blessed Lady, the Mother of God, the ever-virgin Mary, and the Emperors go with great pomp, accompanied by all the Senate, to the Church of Our Lady in the Copper Market." [8] A procession was also made to the church on the 15th of March.

This church did not lie close beside S. Sophia, for it was in all probability surrounded like all the other churches by an extensive close; but rather opposite to it on the south-east side, where the Turkish building *Dar-el-Funún* was built a few years ago. [4]

Labarte would place the Church of Our Lady near, or rather along the south side of S. Sophia. [5] The *Acta Patriarchatus* mention a small monas-

---

1 Vol. II., p. 139.

2 Theophanes Con., p. 339 ; Anna Komnena, Vol. I., p. 278.

8 Cons. P., Vol. I., pp. 169, 781 ; Theophanes Con., p. 676.

4 Chalcopratiana quae Sophianae perinde aedi proxima fuit. *Cpolis. Christ.*, lib. iv., p. 85 ; Cons. P., Vol. I. p. 190. Gyllius states that an unknown writer, in describing ancient Byzantion, places the Chalkoprateia not far from the Milion. *De Topogr.*, lib. ii., cap. 21.

5 Labarte, Plate II. According to him the axis of S. Sophia is not exactly west and east as in other Christian churches, but inclines considerably to the south. p. 17.

tery behind the east end of the most great and sacred church of the Divine Wisdom, which is dedicated to Our Lady, called the Varangian. Unfortunately, nothing further is said about its site.[1] It is probable that this was the name given towards the close of the Empire to the Church of Our Lady in the Copper Market.

THE COVERED STAIRCASE.

Many, no doubt, have read that the Emperor sometimes went up to the Catechumens' Gallery in S. Sophia by a wooden staircase. It is extremely difficult to understand how the Emperor could go from the Palace to the galleries of S. Sophia, a distance of some 40 yards, by means of a wooden staircase of such length. The situation of this church in the Chalkoprateia, near S. Sophia, explains the difficulty. Let us consider the words which Porphyrogennetos uses in describing the ceremonies in the churches, and the adoration of the Emperor in the Church of Our Lady in the Copper Market. "Having saluted the sacred table, and gone round it with a censer, he goes out, and after praying in the south chapel, he places his offering on the holy table and leaves it, and ascends by the wooden staircase to the catechumens' gallery, where he takes part in the Holy Liturgy." (I., 166.) "He passes through the Magnaura, and the galleries above it, and enters

---

[1] Vol. I., p. 423.

the catechumens' galleries of the Great Church by the wooden staircase." (I., 125.) "Ascending by the wooden staircase, he enters the catechumeneia of the Great Church." (I., 157.) To prevent any-one imagining that the Emperor went by this stair-case to the catechumeneia of the Church of Our Lady, he expressly adds that the Emperor took his stand in the catechumeneia, "when the Liturgy was finished." This done, the Patriarch came up beside the Emperor, and after embracing each other, they went each his own way, the Patriarch to his own residence, and the Emperor, by the usual and well-known route through S. Sophia, to the Palace.

This wooden staircase was "the covered gallery of the Palace," which Justinian made "that he might cross over as often as he wished."[1] It passed through the Church in the Copper Market, and not through the Palace walls.

In the south catechumens' gallery of S. Sophia, for the aisles[2] on the ground-floor below are also called catechumeneia, there is still preserved in the eastern wall, a wooden door, about as high as a man, fast closed, and never now-a-days opened, which leads to no balcony, or passage. This, I think, is the door to which the Emperor ascended by the wooden staircase, that rested against the north wall of the catechumens' court in the Church of Our Lady.[3] This staircase was covered in, and

---

[1] G. Kodinos, p. 135.

[2] On p. 138 Kodinos calls the galleries, δεύτερα κατηχούμενα.

[3] De l'extremité orientale des Catéchumènes superieurs de la Grande-Église, l'empereur pouvait passer dans son palais par un escalier de bois.

those ascending or descending by it could not be seen.   The little door is just above the single eastern door of S. Sophia, through which they enter as formerly by some steps.

We now enter S. Sophia that we may examine some fragments neglected in other accounts of this church, though frequently mentioned by Constantine Porphyrogennetos.   Without them the account of the Palace will, in many places, be unintelligible.

METATORION IN S. SOPHIA.

In the church in the lower south catechumeneia, there was a chamber called Metatorion.   It was built by Justinian, "that he might go there with his court and often eat." [1]   Behind the bema was a narrow passage, called the passage of S. Nicholas, through which the Emperor always went in passing from the north to the south catechumeneia. [2]   On the great festivals, those called δεσποτικαί, the Emperor, who had his place at the altar in S. Sophia, received the censer from the hand of the Patriarch, and burnt incense before the crucifix of S. Constantine, [3] which stood on the south side of the

---

Labarte, p. 32.   According to our view, in Theophanes, Vol. I., p. 697: ἡ βασίλισσα Εἰρήνη ἀνῆλθεν διὰ τοῦ ἀναβασίου τῆς Χαλκῆς εἰς τὰ κατηχούμενα τῆς ἐκκλησίας μὴ ἐξελθοῦσα εἰς τὴν μέσην τοῦ ἐμβόλου, we should read Χαλκοπρατείων instead of Χαλκῆς.   In the time of Gyllius, the inhabitants thought that pillars used to support the stair by which the Emperors went from the Palace to S. Sophia.   *De Topogr.*, lib. ii., cap. 18.

[1] G. Kodinos, p. 135.
[2] Cons. P., Vol. I., pp. 182, 184.
[3] *Ibid.*, pp. 5, 565, 636.

bema, or rather, in the southern chapel. After this, the Emperor and the Patriarch entered into the chapel which stood before the metatorion, and thence into the metatorion.[1] Its position is clearly indicated by Constantine Porphyrogennetos in the words, " on the right hand side of the bema, before the metatorion." In this chamber the Emperor occasionally ate with the Patriarch and the leading and most intimate members of the Senate.[2]

There was another metatorion in the catechumens' gallery above this, as may be inferred from the words of the same writer. " The Augusta," he writes, " comes out from the metatorion which is in the catechumeneia."[3] That he does not mean those on the ground-floor is evident from what follows. " The Augusta rises up and enters the metatorion with her personal attendants, and the rest of her train go down to the Emperor." In his description of Orthodoxy Sunday, he writes, " going to the catechumeneia by the spiral staircase behind the apse, he enters the metatorion." The way from the lower metatorion to the catechumens' gallery was

---

[1] *Ibid.*, pp. 16, 17, 27, 64, 65, 133.

[2] Καὶ ἀναστὰς ὁ βασιλεὺς ἀπὸ τοῦ κράματος, *ibid.*, pp. 68, 135, 185. Monks often ate together in the church. See Kodinos Kour., p. 327.

[3] Vol. I., pp. 67, 68. Paul the Silentiary writes of this chamber, in his description of S. Sophia—

Δήεις καὶ νοτίην βορεώτιδι πᾶσαν ὁμοίην
μηκεδανὴν αἴθουσαν, ἔχει δέ τι καὶ πλέον ἦδε·
τείχει γάρ τινι χῶρον ἀποκρινθέντα φυλάσσει
Αὐσονίων βασιλῆϊ θεοστέπτοις ἐν ἑορταῖς.
ἔνθα δ' ἐμὸς σκηπτοῦχος ἐφήμενος ἤδάδι θώκῳ
μυστιπόλοις βίβλοισιν ἐὴν ἐπέτασσεν ἀκουήν.

vv. 580-585.

by this spiral staircase which he calls μητατωρικός. There was also a metatorion called the Patriarch's in the Patriarcheion.[1] Others are mentioned in the church of SS. Sergius and Bacchus, and at Blachernai.[2] Farther on, in his account of the promotion of the Zosta Patricia,[3] he writes that after the ceremony in the church, the cubicularii and silentiarii conduct her to the metatorion at the Thomaïtes.[4]

THE HOLY WELL.

Beside the metatorion was a chamber with three doors. Two of them were in the inside, and communicated with the metatorion and the choir of the church. The other led outside to the Augustaion. " And having saluted the Holy Well, they enter by the door which leads thence into the church." " And their majesties going out by the outer door of the Holy Well . . ." and, a little further on, " the Emperor and Patriarch having kissed each other, the Emperor goes out, and takes his stand outside the gate of the Holy Well, which

---

[1] Καὶ ἀπέρχονται οἱ δεσπόται εἰς τὸ μητατώριον τοῦ πατριάρχου. Cons. P., Vol. I., p. 160.

[2] Ibid., pp. 88, 157, 158.

[3] [Erat Patricia Zosta foeminei comitatus Augustae princeps, eique proxima comes et amica, sic forte dicta non quod cingeret et comeret Augustam, sed quod cingulum seu baltheum, honoris indicium, adipisceretur in sua promotione et gereret. Ibid, Vol. II., p. 166. Tr.]

[4] Ibid., Vol. I., p. 260. The word μητατώριον is from the Latin meta, metatum, Cf. ibid., p. 393. [Du Cange, s. v. metare]. A curtain separated it from the Holy Well. εἰσέρχεται ἔνδον τῆς κορτίνας τῆς κρεμαμένης ἐν τῷ ἁγίῳ φρέατι, ibid., p. 68, etc.

leads to the portico, and receives the Blue faction there." [1]

This chamber was known as the Holy Well, because the stone mouth was "brought from Samaria, and was the one on which Christ sat talking to the woman of Samaria." [2] The Byzantines held this well in great reverence. In the chamber beside the Holy Well the Emperor and the Patriarch often kissed each other.

I shall quote some passages from Constantine Porphyrogennetos that we may have the assistance of one so thoroughly acquainted with Constantinople. Describing the festival of the Annunciation, which occurs on the Sunday of the Middle Week, he says :—" The Emperor, entering by the door of the Holy Well, lights candles, and prays. The Patriarch receives the Emperor at the door leading from the Holy Well into the church, and having kissed and embraced one another, they go into the church." The same writer mentions another holy well in the Palace, and also the metatorion of the Magnaura. [3]

I have followed with great attention all Porphyrogennetos' descriptions of the civil and ecclesiastical ceremonies. No account, ancient or modern, of S. Sophia, throws light on so many dark corners of this great church. The metatorion, between which and the bema was the southern chapel, containing the well, does not now exist. From it, or rather its

---

[1] Cons. P., Vol. I., pp. 27, 34, 68, 135.
[2] G. Kodino*, p. 142 ; Cons. P., Vol. I., pp. 18, 19.
[3] *Ibid.*, pp. 163, 583.

site, one enters by the eastern door of S. Sophia, the only one in this wall.[1] The well exists in the site so distinctly indicated by Porphyrogennetos, and is pointed out by all the clergy of the mosque. The numerous processions to it, from the neighbouring square of the Milion bear further witness to the truth of his statements. It is, however, fenced all round with boards, and covered with carpets.[2] It lies in the middle of the southern lower catechumeneia. I do not know whether the famous mouth, about which so many enquiries have been made, is still preserved.[3]

To the right of the well the Turks have built a chamber, protected with rails, containing MS. and printed service-books. The well itself is between the great porphyry pillars and the wall. The door which leads out of it to the Forum of the Milion is still preserved just as described by Porphyrogennetos.

THE SPIRAL STAIR.

In the description of the palace in the Imperial Stand, I mentioned the dark spiral staircase by

---

[1] Στὰς πρὸς ταῖς μεγίσταις πύλαις [of S. Sophia] ὡς δ' ἔμελλε διὰ τῆς κατ' ἀνατολὰς πύλης ἐξέρχεσθαι, κτλ. G. Pachymeres, Vol. I., p. 270.

[2] I think that Byzantios is wrong in writing "equally indeterminable is the place once called the Holy Well." Κπολις, Vol. I., p. 498.

[3] The porphyry omphalion in front of the holy doors, mentioned by Porphyrogennetos (Vol. I., p. 15), is somewhat oval, and about seven feet in diameter. It is adorned with variegated marbles, and is quite intact, but hidden under mats and carpets. In the south end of the narthex were the font and the often-mentioned Athyras. *Ibid.*, pp. 156, 158, 164, 185.

which the Emperor and his suite gained access to the stand. The word κοχλιὰς was commonly used by Byzantines of all spiral stairs in the Palace and the churches.[1] There was the great spiral stair in S. Sophia, by which the Emperor descended to the Didaskaleion, where the Paschal cycles were inscribed,[2] and another behind the bema.[3] George Kodinos mentions the pillars of S. George the wonder-worker, and that of S. Basil, on the north and south side respectively of the women's gallery.

All the spiral and other staircases in S. Sophia have been preserved, with the exception of the one from the metatorion into the catechumens' gallery, which I have not been able to discover. It is probable that it was destroyed along with the metatorion and the chamber of the Holy Well. The present stair by which visitors ascend to the north galleries, does not resemble the others. It was the stair used in common by all the female congregation. The spiral stair from the holy well to the south galleries, is a stair with stone steps, and is closed by a wooden door.[4] Another stair, now closed up, similar to this, is to be seen in the east wall of the southern catechumens' gallery. Pro-

---

[1] Cons. P., Vol. I., p. 77. The door of the spiral stair is mentioned, in the Church of the Holy Apostles (*ibid.*, p. 100), of S. Mokios (*ibid.*), of the Life-receiving Spring (p. 109) in Blachernai (pp. 257, 542) and in S. Christina (p. 214).

[2] *Ibid.*, p. 126.

[3] *Ibid.*, p. 160.

[4] Ἀνέρχονται διὰ τοῦ κοχλιοῦ τοῦ πρὸς τὸ μέρος τοῦ ἁγίου φρέατος ἐν τοῖς πρὸς ἀνατολὰς δεξιοῖς μέρεσι τῶν κατηχουμενείων. *Ibid.*, p. 182.

bably this is the spiral stair behind the bema, mentioned by Constantine Porphyrogennetos.[1]

In the south end of the second or inner porch there is a vaulted passage closed at the outer end by a Byzantine door of great antiquity. In this passage on the right hand side there is an ancient door, now shut up. A stone stair inside it leads up to the south catechumens' galleries. Constantine Porphyrogennetos mentions this stair in his account of the Imperial ceremony on the 14th of September. The loggia, or rather vaulted passage, below, was called the διδασκαλεῖον. "The Emperor," he writes,[2] "accompanying[3] the holy cross, descends by the great spiral stair, and turning to the left, crosses through the Didaskaleion where the Paschal cycles are inscribed." This part of S. Sophia is unfortunately little referred to, and the accounts of it are very vague.[4]

I have given these few particulars about S. Sophia, though there are perhaps many for whom they contain nothing new, to prepare the way for the following accounts. We have yet to study other buildings in the Augustaion, which, though not, it may be, of great size, bulked largely in the history of the Empire.

---

[1] Beneath the south catechumeneum there is a small chamber where the Turks keep vessels belonging to S. Sophia. It is quite different from the ancient sacristy.

[2] Vol. I., p. 126, 167 ; cf. Byzantios, Κπολις., Vol. I., pp. 464, 517.

[3] Ὀψικεύων, ὀψίκιον, obsequium. See Meursii *Glossarium*, s. v. ὀψικεύειν.

[4] Concerning the right of asylum of S. Sophia, see the *Acta Patriarchatus*, Vol. I., p. 232.

CHAPTER IV.

In the preceding chapter I have described some buildings in the Augustaion, which are often mentioned by the Byzantine topographers and historians. More conspicuous than their neighbours, and continually occurring in connection with political and ecclesiastical history, they aid us in forming a correct idea of the other and smaller structures in the Augustaion. Readers of the voluminous narratives of these writers are soon convinced that it is no easy task to make out the site of buildings from them. Though no doubt of great value, their accounts are far from harmonious. They are careless in describing their situation, and our difficulties are increased by the fact that the last ruins of the buildings themselves, which had endured until the final capture of the city, were utterly demolished by the Philistine conquerors.

Prokopios states that there was a market-place in front of the Senate House, which the Byzantines called Augustaion, and also that it was in front of, and not far from the Palace. His account harmonises entirely with all that I said about its situation being in front of the Palace.[1]

---

[1] Ταύτης δὲ τῆς ἀγορᾶς οὐ πολλῷ ἀποθεν τὰ βασιλέως οἰκία ἐστί. Vol. III., pp. 181, 202, 203.

The Augustaion was, as I have said, oblong[1] and adorned with noble buildings and works of art from all parts of Greece and Asia. It was bounded on the north by S. Sophia, on the east by the Palace, and on the west by the eastern wall of the Hippodrome. Of the boundaries on the south side no account is given. At the present day this side is entirely covered with Turkish houses, small mosques, and enclosed gardens. It is probable that here, among the extensive gardens of the Turks, all access to which is denied, remains are preserved which may indicate the boundaries at this end.

The breadth of the Augustaion from the Palace walls to the Hippodrome is, as I said, 177 paces or about 133 m. [150 yards]. The length from S. Sophia to the conjectured southern boundary is about 688 paces[2] or over 500 m. [about 570 yards]. The area of the whole is 73,150 sq. m.[3] Regular measurements by experienced persons will give more exact figures. The utter want of interest, and the entire ignorance displayed by the Turkish officials respecting the famous buildings that anciently stood here, convince me that we shall never be able to learn more about the dimensions of this market-place, the boundaries of which have years since been obliterated. The adornments and

---

[1] Λέγουσι δὲ περὶ τοῦ φόρου ὅτι εἰς μίμησιν τοῦ Ὠκεανοῦ ἐκτίσθη κυκλοειδής, καὶ ψεύδονται οἱ τοῦτο λέγοντες. G. Kodinos, p. 76.

[2] [Here Dr. Paspates appears to take the βῆμα at the usual measurement of 2½ feet, and not as in the chapter on the Hippodrome at 1½ feet. Tr.]

[3] [From Dr. Paspates' figures this should be 66,500 sq. m., or 85,500 sq. yds.—Tr.]

remains have long ago been destroyed, or used for other buildings since the Ottoman capture of Constantinople. The place itself is now covered over with ill-lighted evil-smelling workshops, and strange public and private buildings, which Greek and Western visitors alike regard with irritation and anger. Should they venture to make investigations among them, they are stoned by the children of the place, while the light-headed inhabitants look on, and mock them.

THE STATUE OF EUDOXIA.

Opposite the Senate House, which lay, as I said, south of the Patriarcheion, anciently stood the Statue of Eudoxia consort of Arcadius (395-408) of which so much is said in the life of S. John Chrysostom. According to Theophanes, the statue was of silver, and stood in a place called the Pittakia, near the Church of S. Irene.[1] The choruses and dances of the Pagan worshippers disturbed Chrysostom, and prevented him celebrating the Divine Liturgy in quiet, in the neighbouring church of S. Sophia, for the tumult "often interrupted them whilst singing." Manichaios, the pagan prefect of the city incited Eudoxia against Chrysostom, representing that he was piqued at the honour paid to her statue. At the same time Chrysostom preached in the Cathedral a sermon against evil women, which

---

[1] Τούτῳ τῷ ἔτει (398) ἡ βασίλισσα Εὐδοξία ἀργυραίαν στήλην ἰδίαν ποιήσασα, ἔστησε ἐν τόπῳ λεγομένῳ τὰ Πιττάκια πλησίον τῆς Ἁγίας Εἰρήνης, Vol. I., p. 123 ; G. Kedrenos, Vol. I., p. 563.

certain enemies of the faith reported as if levelled at Eudoxia and the words uttered round her statue by the frenzied crowd. The hostility of this woman and those . like-minded with her was the cause of the banishment and death of the courageous Bishop.[1]

Amid the frequent encounters between the citizens and the soldiers who guarded the Palace walls, this piece of silver work, and its pedestal which was covered with silver fell an early prey to the mob, or to the opposing factions of the Hippodrome. How long it stood here, or when it disappeared we do not know. According to the Patriarch Constantius, and after him the learned Byzantios, the pedestal was discovered in 1848, during the excavations in the Augustaion, for the new Ottoman University.[2] It is now preserved in the Imperial Museum. The Patriarch also mentions the two inscriptions, Latin and Greek on the pedestal. The Greek inscription is damaged through time. It is thus restored by him—

---

1 Ἀνθίσταται τῇ βασιλίσσῃ Εὐδοξίᾳ, πάσχει πολλὰ διὰ τοῦτο δεινά. M. Glykas, pp. 479, 480 ; Zosimos, p. 278. Ἐπεὶ δὲ αὖθις συνέβη τὰ κατὰ τὴν ἀργυρᾶν στήλην τῆς Εὐδοξίας, καὶ πάλιν μῖσος, καὶ πάλιν ὀργή . . . οὗ ἡ ἀρχὴ Πάλιν Ἡρωδιὰς μαίνεται. G. Kedrenos, Vol. I., p. 581.

2 Ἐλάσσονες Συγγραφαί, p. 481 ; Byzantios, Κπολις., Vol. I., p. 461. The learned Patriarch, who has told us so much about Constantinople, writes of this square :—"About the base of this pedestal of the pillar of Eudoxia, was uncovered the pavement of the once magnificent square of the Augustaion. It consists of large black stones one geometric foot in length, and a half in breadth, very well laid." Ἐλάσσονες Συγγραφαί, p. 383. None of the remains recently disclosed has escaped the eyes of this widely-learned hierarch. His words were completely borne out by the operations of the English engineers, to which I alluded above (Chapter II.)

—ΟΝΑΠΟΡΦΤΡΕΗΝΚΑΙΑΡΓΤΡΕΗΝΒΑΣΙΛΕΙΑΝ
ΔΕΡΚΕΟΕΝΘΑΠΟΛΗΙΘΕΜΙΣΤΕΤΟΤΣΙΝΑΝΑΚΤΕΣ
ΟΝΟΜΟΛΑΔΕΙΠΟΘΕΕΒΙΣΕΤΔΟΞΙΑΤΙΣΔΑΝΕΘΗΚΕΝ
ΣΙΜΠΛΙΚΙΟΣΜΕΓΑΛΩΝΤΠΑΤΩΝΤΟΝΟΣΕΣΘΛΟΣΤΠΑΡΧΟΣ

[Κἰ] ονα πορφυρέην καὶ ἀργυρέην βασίλειαν
Δέρκεο, ἔνθα πόληι θεμιστεύουσιν ῎Ανακτες.
Ὀνομα δ' εἰ ποθέεις, Εὐδοξία· τὶς δ' ἀνέθηκεν ;
Σιμπλίκιος μεγάλων ὑπάτων γόνος ἐσθλὸς ὕπαρχος.[1]

DN. AEL. EVDOXIAE SEMPER AVGVSTAE
YG. SIMPLICIVS PRAEFC. VRB. DEDICAVIT

Dominae Aeliae Eudoxiae semper Augustae
YG. Simplicius Praefectus Urbis dedicavit.

The great Ottoman University[2] is at the northern end of the Augustaion, where in Byzantine times the Church of Our Lady in the Copper Market, and the Patriarcheion with its garden stood. The east front adorned with marble pillars, is built upon the eastern wall which divided the Augustaion from the Palace. If the statute of Eudoxia was, as Theophanes and Byzantios say, near the Pittakia and S. Irene, how did the pedestal come to be found in the excavations for the University? According to Sozomenos the Pittakia stood in front of the house of the Great Council, *i.e.* the Senate House,[3] and south of S. Sophia, near S. Irene. This is a manifest

---

[1] Praefectus urbis modo ὕπαρχος modo ἔπαρχος appellatur. Reiske in Cons. P., Vol. II., p. 37. ["Behold an imperial pillar of porphyry and silver, where the princes of the city deliberate. If thou desirest the name 'tis Eudoxia; and who erected it? Simplicius the noble scion of mighty consuls, the prefect."]

[2] *Dar-el-Funin*, or House of the Sciences.

[3] Concerning the Pittakia, see G. Kodinos, pp. 35, 186. The term σύγκλητος is applied by Porphyrogennetos to the members of the Senate : μηνύεται πᾶσα ἡ σύγκλητος ἵνα προέλθη μετὰ ἀλλαξίμων, Vol. I., pp. 236, 237.

contradiction because S. Sophia lies between the Augustaion and S. Irene, so that the pillar could not have been south of S. Sophia, and at the same time near S. Irene, which lies further north. Moreover the Hospital of Sampson lay between the two churches.

Near S. Irene, where the Emperor and the Patriarch sometimes attended church together, there was another ecclesiastical building, known as the Church of the Deaconess, or Deaconesses.[1] Remains of it still exist, I think, in the huge underground vaults of Byzantine construction which once formed a foundation for the building on this sloping site,[2] and on which the Turks have now erected their Archæological Museum, and School of Fine Arts. That these were the foundations of a church seems to be the case from the crosses still to be seen on the great pillars buried in the depths of the vaults. On the whole, it appears to me improbable that the Byzantines should have erected a statue beside so many well known churches. Besides, the sound of the mob's dancing and orgies in a place so far removed from S. Sophia would not disturb the

---

[1] The Patriarch Kyriakos built this Church of the Deaconess, while still a deacon, in the reign of the Emperor Mauricius (582-602) ; G. Kodinos, p. 105. There was another church of this name ; Cous. P., Vol. I., pp. 75, 85, 590 ; G. Kedrenos, Vol. I., p. 699.

[2] Byzantios, Κπολις, Vol. I., p. 155. Kedrenos (Vol. I., p. 679) mentions two cells of ascetics (ἀσκητήρια) beside S. Irene, which were burnt in the Insurrection of the Nika. The Byzantine writers give very vague accounts of them. After a certain festival in the Hippodrome, the Green faction went in procession to the Church of the Deaconess, probably to this spacious crypt. Cons. P., Vol. I., pp. 357, 590.

choristers there. From all these circumstances, the truth of which any one may test for himself by inspecting the spot, I conclude that the statue of the vain-glorious Eudoxia stood in the Augustaion, not before the Patriarcheion but before the Senate House.[1] The pedestal found in the excavations for the Ottoman University certainly belongs to this statue. It may be that after the death of Chrysostom, the statue was torn down by the mob in its anger against Eudoxia, and the pedestal cast far from its original place. The intervention of other buildings, the Milion and the Church of Alexios, precludes the idea of its being erected nearer the Church of S. Sophia. Besides, a broad and open space, where a large concourse could collect without hindrance, was favourable to shouting and orgies enough to disturb the singers in S. Sophia, and Chrysostom as he officiated.

Here we may refer to the account of the life of Chrysostom by Simeon Metaphrastes,[2] whose knowledge of the topography of Constantinople is of great value. "A certain silver statue of the Empress stood on a pillar somewhere near the church called Sophia. At it the children of the city were wont to gather. This the great man judged to be in contempt of the Church, owing to their making reply in a disorderly and unseemly fashion to the sacred hymns which were being sung. When after much admonition, he had failed to

---

1 Gyllius, lib. ii., cap. 9.

2 Migne's *Patrologia Graeco-Latina,* Vol. CXIV,, cap. 47,

induce them to cease, he assailed with his tongue those who allowed the nuisance to go on." From this we see that the cries of those who paid homage to the statue disturbed the people worshipping in the church of S. Sophia. The statue disappeared after the death of Chrysostom and of Eudoxia, for no mention of it is found in the subsequent history of the Empire.

A little lower down[1] Simeon mentions a fact which confirms all that I have already said about the site of the buildings in the Augustaion, and especially the Senate House. The same day as Chrysostom was exiled, "a heaven-sent fire, kindled by no human hand, broke out at the throne on which he was wont to sit and pour out his holy teaching, and sprang up to a great height. Then, having eaten through the roof, it spread along the top of the venerable chambers. The wind carried the flames, and bore them to the Senate House, which was far from the centre of the fire, sparing like a rational creature the buildings between, so that no one might ascribe the occurrence to the proximity of the buildings. And in the space of three hours a building of great size, which had taken a long time to build, of most costly materials, and most beautiful appearance, was totally destroyed, and reduced to nothing. Thus this fire of divine origin, crept round in a circle, and on its return spared only the little building, where the bulk of the sacred vessels were kept."

---

[1] Cap. 50.

From this narrative I am persuaded that between S. Sophia and the Senate House stood the Patriarcheion, and the connected buildings, in which the sacred vessels were preserved.

The buildings erected by Justinian in the Augustaion after the bloody insurrection of the Nika, were erected on the sites of those burnt down, for the Augustaion, bounded by the walls of the Palace and the Hippodrome, could be neither extended nor lessened. A clear and circumstantial account is given by Prokopios.[1] Justinian acquired a considerable piece of ground and some houses beside it belonging to private owners for the new Church of S. Sophia. The strong walls of the Palace and the Hippodrome, on either side of the Augustaion, remained as they had been erected by Severus and Constantine the Great. In short, Justinian re-erected the same buildings on the same sites, only more magnificent than those burnt in the insurrection.

From the testimony of many writers about the site on which S. Sophia was built by Constantine the Great, it appears that all the place was then called Gousteion. According to some, this was a corruption of Augusteion. The place was more probably the Provision Market. Such is the opinion of Kodinos. " The place was styled Augustaion. It was formerly called Gousteion, that is the Provision Market."[2] On the authority of

---

1 Vol. III., pp. 167, *et seq.*

2 G. Kodinos, p. 28. Ἐν τῷ Γουστείῳ ἤγουν τῷ ὀψοπωλείῳ ; Meursii, *Gloss.*, *s. v.* Γουστεῖον.

many more writers, I should conclude that it was originally a market, and that the name, like many other words in the vulgar Byzantine dialect, was employed by later generations of inhabitants, ignorant, or forgetful of its derivation from the Latin.

The eminent Byzantios very properly writes : " One can only conjecture, that before S. Sophia was built, this square was probably the Provision Market, which may have been subsequently removed elsewhere." [1]

After the time of Constantine the Great, the buildings here, S. Irene, the Hospital of Sampson, and S. Sophia, with the adjoining buildings, covered all this extensive market place, which, as I said, is sometimes mentioned in accounts of the ancient city before the-time of Constantine the Great. It is however evident that it extended further south of S. Sophia, to the place where the Milion or great Milestone stood.

THE MILION.

The Milion [2] was a building which stood to the south of S. Sophia, near the Hippodrome. It was known as the apse or chamber of the Milion, [3] some-

---

[1] Κπολις, Vol. I , p. 441 ; Meursii, *Gloss.*, *s. v.* Αὐγουστεών.

[2] The name is from the Latin. Μίλιον, μέτρον γῆς, Souidas. It was also called Μιλίαριον, and, incorrectly, Μιλιαρίσιον—τὸ τοῦ νομίσματος δέκατον, Sonidas. Μιλιαρίσιον, Miliarense, nummi genus, duodecima pars solidi, G. Kedrenos (annot.), Vol. II., p. 921.

[3] Πλήσιον τῆς ἀψίδος τοῦ μιλίου, G. Kodinos, p. 38, *cf.* 35. δοχὴ θ' ἐν τῷ φουρνικῷ τοῦ Μιλίου—δέχονται οἱ τοῦ μέρους τῶν Βενέτων ἐν τῇ καμάρᾳ τοῦ μιλίου, Cons. P., Vol. I., pp. 32, 51, 56, 106, 375. Φουρνικὸν, Furni instar habens, laqueatum, cameratum, J. Meursii, *Gloss.* Gyllius, lib. ii., cap. 9.

times as the rostrum (ἔμβολος) of the Milion.[1] The name of the building was also applied to all the northern part of the Augustaion as far as S. Sophia. How far south the space so-called extended, is not clear. According to Constantine Porphyrogennetos, the northern part of the Forum was called the Milion, and the southern the Marble Walk (τὸ μαρμαρωτὸν) or the Pavement (τὸ πλακωτόν).[2]

The Milion was originally a simple column. In course of time a square building resting on seven marble pillars was built in place of the column. Steps led up to a raised floor, from which sprang an upper range of pillars supporting a domed chamber—the Chamber of the Milion. This chamber is mentioned very frequently by all the Byzantine historians, especially by Constantine Porphyrogennetos in his account of the public ceremonies and processions of the Emperor to S. Sophia, the route of which lay through the Milion. At it he used to receive the courtiers, and the chiefs of the factions.[3] It is difficult to understand the plan and dimensions of the building from the historians. According to Kodinos, it contained the monuments of Constantine the Great and S. Helena, of Sophia the wife of Justin the Thracian, Arabia his daughter, and his niece Helena.[4] That it stood

---

[1] Διελθόντες τὴν μέσην ἕως τοῦ μιλίου εἰσῆλθον διὰ τοῦ ἐμβόλου τοῦ μιλίου. Cons. P., Vol. I., p. 502.

[2] *Ibid.*, p. 84.

[3] *Ibid.*, pp. 51, 56, 63, 168, 185, 375.

[4] G. Kodinos, pp. 28, 35.

opposite the south door of S. Sophia is shewn by the following passage : "At the Milion the members of the Senate dismounted from their horses, and made their way on foot before the Emperor, to the Holy Well in S. Sophia." [1] Certain criminals were sent there to beg. [2] The building was square, and had four arched doorways, by which one could pass from side to side. From the large number of courtiers and prominent citizens who collected there at some processions, I should infer that it was a building of considerable size. The Patriarch Constantius says that in the excavations in 1848 they observed some remains apparently of a triumphal arch, but this " object which resembled an arch was a very large vault with arches supported on seven marble pillars which lay in the so-called Milion." [3] In the time of Gyllius, remains of the building were preserved. On a pillar he read, Ἐν τούτῳ νίκα. [4] Taking all things into consideration, I should place it opposite the south door of S. Sophia—the Horologion—and west of the Patriarcheion.

The heads of decapitated malefactors were exposed on this building. " He ordered his head to be cut off in the Kynegion of the city, and to be hung in mid-air from the place called the Milion." " They beheaded Baktageios in the Kynegion, and

---

1 Cons. P., Vol. I., p. 506.
2 Theophanes Con., p. 680.
8 Ἐλάσσονες Συγγραφαί, p. 384.
4 Lib. ii., cap. 18.

hung his head in the Milion for three days."[1] Constantine Porphyrogennetos says nothing about this custom. Possibly it was observed only during the latter days of the Empire.

THE STATUE OF JUSTINIAN.

South of the Milion was the splendid erection, upon which stood the colossal statue of Justinian. It is alluded to by most of our historians. Gyllius' account is, that some time previous to his visit the barbarians had stripped the statue of Justinian, and had removed all the bronze ornaments. Thirty years previously, the statue and all the column above the pedestal had fallen. What remained had been converted into a fountain, and the statue carried off, and kept in some part of the Sultan's palace, whence it was taken to a foundry where military engines were made. The leg of Justinian was greater than Gyllius' stature. The nose measured more than nine inches long. The feet of the horse, which lay stretched on the ground, he could not measure, but he succeeded in measuring one of the hoofs without the knowledge of the Turks. It was nine inches long.[2]

I know of no other writer who gives the dimensions of this work of art, of which the Byzantine writers often speak in the highest terms. Before Gyllius' visit, Buondelmonti had seen the statue

---

1 Nikephoros Patr., p. 84. Theophanes, Vol. I., pp. 647-8.
2 Lib. ii., cap. 17.

standing.[1] Prokopios gives by far the best description of the column and the statue, and other writers have been content to copy from him.[2] "There is a market-place in front of the Palace. The Byzantines call this market-place Augustaion. Here no fewer than seven courses of stones are set together in a square. Each recedes, and is so much less than the one below it, that it does not project so far, and thus stages are formed, on which the men gathered there sit as on steps. On the summit of the stones stands a pillar of marvellous height. It is not, however, a monolith, but is composed of great stones set in circles, dovetailed at the joinings, and fitted into one another by the art of the stone-cutters. The finest bronze, cast into the form of bas-reliefs and wreaths, covers the stone all over. In colour, the bronze is fairer than pure gold, and in value is very nearly equal to silver. On the top of this pillar stands a bronze horse of immense size, facing the East, truly a notable sight. It seems to be going bravely forward. On this horse sits the statue of the Emperor like a colossus. He is shod in half-boots, and his legs are without greaves. He is cuirassed like a hero, and a helmet guards his head, giving the impression that he is commanding. He looks to the rising sun, riding, I

---

[1] Extra ecclesiam ad meridiem in platea columna septingentorum cubitorum alta videtur. Apud N. Bryennium, p. 180. Labarte (p. 36, note) correctly changes "septingentorum" into "septuaginta." The same correction was already pointed out by the editors of Nikephoros Gregoras (Vol. II., p. 1221).

[2] Vol. III., p. 181 ; G. Kodinos, pp. 28, 69 ; N. Gregoras, Vol. II., p. 1217 ; G. Kedrenos, Vol. I., p. 656.

think, against the Persians. In his left hand he holds an orb, by which the artist shews that all the earth and sea are subject to him. He has neither sword nor spear, nor any other weapon, but on the orb there is a cross, from which, indeed, proceed both his empire and his success in war. Holding forth his outstretched hand to the East, he commands the barbarians there to stay at home, and advance no farther."

According to Constantine Porphyrogennetos,[1] there was in the building where the colossus stood, a colonnade (κιονοστασία), and steps leading up to a broad flat platform, on which the members of the Senate took their stand at great Imperial festivals in the Palace. The interior was called κιονοστασία. The metropolitans and archbishops ascended by the left hand flight of stairs. In this same building there was a chapel of S. Constantine connected with the statue.[2] After service there, the Emperor went to the neighbouring church of Our Lady of the Copper Market. Kodinos[3] calls this statue the Pillar of Theodosios, and places it in the great Milion. In the same passage he describes it as having eight columns. In another passage he states that Justinian erected an equestrian statue of himself on a pillar;[4] his description of it is the same as Prokopios'.[5] A statue of Theo-

---

1 Vol. I., pp. 28, 609, 610.

'Ανέρχεται ἐν τῷ εὐκτηρίῳ τοῦ αὐτοῦ κίονος, ἤγουν τοῦ Ἁγίου Κωνσταντίνου. Cons. P., Vol. I., p. 30.   3 P. 69.   4 P. 28.

5 Sir John Mandeville writes of this pillar—" And before the Church is the image of the Emperor Justinian, covered with gold, and he sits

dosios anciently stood on this pillar, whence the confusion in the accounts of the historians, some calling it the pillar of Justinian, others the pillar of Theodosios. Beside it were six great marble columns. According to Nikephoros Gregoras, the pillar stood before the doors of the great church of the Wisdom of God.[1] Pachymeres writes :—" A ring of public buildings was anciently built round about the church of S. Sophia, in the midst of which is the Augusteon, that is, the pillar of Justinian Augustus, erected in his honour soon after he had undergone the toils of the campaign against the Persians." His next words, " which may be seen on the left hand by those entering the church," shew that the statue stood to the south of S. Sophia. Pachymeres must mean the south or Horologion door, for persons entering by the Great Porch could not see it. In his description of the earthquake which destroyed half of Cyzicus, Kedrenos writes :—"All the pavement about the Bronze Pillar was of golden tiles, forming the entrance to the Palace of Constantine the Great, which is still called the Bronze Gate. This pillar is the one called Augusteon." [2] From these words of Kedrenos, we see that the site of the often mentioned Bronze Gate of the Palace was opposite this statue.

---

crowned upon a horse . . . This image stands upon a pillar of marble at Constantinople." Wright's *Early Travels in Palestine,* p. 130. This traveller visited the city in 1333.

[1] Vol. I., p. 275.

[2] Vol. I., p. 656 ; Theophanes Con., p. 808.

The pillar and its statue lay to the north of the Milion. Constantine Porphyrogennetos, detailing the ceremonies on the Feast of the Annunciation, says that the Emperor comes out of S. Sophia, and proceeds to the Milion. Thence he passes through the middle and goes up the Forum as far as the pillar where the Church of S. Constantine is built.[1] From his words we get an explanation of the obscurity caused by the historians giving the name Forum to the space about the column of Justinian, commonly called the Augustaion. In this Church of S. Constantine there were two altars or chapels, one to S. Constantine, and the other to S. Helena.[2]

The Milion and the statue of Justinian were built not in the middle of the Augustaion, but more towards the walls of the Hippodrome. There was thus a clear space between them and the opposite buildings, the Senate House, and the Patriarcheion. This was called the Middle ($\dot{\eta}$ $\mu\acute{\epsilon}\sigma\eta$.) The same name was also given to the thoroughfare running from S. Sophia, behind the Imperial Stand in the Hippodrome, which still exists under the name of *Diván Ghiulú*.[3] " Germanus then, arrived at his own house by the thoroughfare which is vulgarly called the Middle."[4] It must, however, be

---

[1] Cons. P., Vol. I., p. 164.

[2] Probably situated on either side of the great column, for such structures were not erected on churches. *Ibid.*, p. 534.

[3] *I.e.*, the Public Road.

[4] Theophylaktos, p. 320. The name $\mu\acute{\epsilon}\sigma\eta$ was also given to the road leading from the Golden land-gate to S. Sophia and the Palace. I think, however, that they are mistaken who apply this name to the thoroughfare between S. Sophia and the land-gate of Adrianople.

understood that these buildings—the Milion, and the statue of Justinian, were not connected with the wall of the Hippodrome, where such serious, and often fatal brawls and riots between the factions took place. This I hope to shew later on.[1]

THE PITTAKIA.

The Pittakia, or according to some Byzantine writers the Pittakes, are mentioned as being in the Augustaion. Our historians give but little aid in determining its site. The only writer, Greek or foreign, who does so is Kodinos who merely says, "There, at the steps of the column." In the chapter on the Hippodrome, I quoted an epigram on a house in the Augustaion, between the Hippodrome and the Baths of Zeuxippos. This house lay opposite the Baths, and consequently at the south end of the Augustaion. Probably there were other houses alongside it. Kodinos'[2] account of the Pittakia is that the Pittakes was the pillar of the great Leo Makeles, which his sister Euphemia erected, because "her house was there, and every week the Emperor used to resort to it, because she was prudent, and a virgin." All who had any grievance presented their petitions (πιττάκια) there. Every morning the Emperor sent a gentleman in waiting[6] to collect the petitions, and gave his answers

---

[1] G. Kodinos, p. 169, 241 ; Theophanes Con., p. 645.

[2] Pp. 35, 186. These and other passages of the same writer are not clear.

[6] Ἑβδομαδάριοι or ἐβδομάριοι was the name given to the weekly attendants in the Emperor's bed-chamber. ὄπισθεν δὲ τοῦ βεστιαρίου, ἢ τοῦ

early the next morning. From this short account we learn little or nothing about the site of the building. It is evident that the place commonly called the Pittakia was in the Augustaion, probably near the statue of Justinian, and opposite the Bronze Gate leading into the Palace. According to the passage quoted from Kodinos, the pillar was built near the house of the sister of the great Leo Makeles. Possibly it was a domed building, through a window in which, the petitions were thrown. I should think that it lay south of the statue of Justinian. The contradictory statements of Byzantine writers proceed sometimes from their ignorance, sometimes from the overthrow and disappearance of the buildings during the thousand years of Byzantine rule.[1]

There remain yet other buildings often mentioned in the valuable work of Constantine Porphyrogennetos, which describes the Imperial festivals, public ceremonies, and processions to churches at some distance from the Palace. All these buildings, which are not described, but merely alluded to by him, were in existence in the brighter days when he was Emperor. The student of the topography of the Palace and the surrounding buildings must be guided mainly by him. Many

---

φύλακος, καὶ καθεξῆς κοιτωνιτῶν καὶ ἑβδομαρίων καὶ λοιπῶν διακονούντων οἰκείων τῇ βασιλικῇ ὑπηρεσίᾳ, I. Meursii, *Glossarium ;* ἀποστέλλει σελεντιάριον τὸν ἔχοντα ἑβδομάδα ἐν τῇ προελεύσει τοῦ ἱπποδρόμου—τῷ σιλεντιαρίῳ τῷ ὄντι ἑβδομαρίῳ. Cons. P., Vol. I., pp. 273, 274.

[1] Τω λς' ἔτει [τοῦ 'Ιουστινιανοῦ] γέγονε πάλιν στάσις δημοτικὴ ἐν τοῖς Πιττακίοις, καὶ πολλοὺς αὐτῶν ὁ βασιλεὺς ἐτιμωρήσατο. G. Kedrenos, Vol. I., p. 679.

later writers have described them, not from any distinct knowledge, but merely from recollection or tradition. The destruction of the majority of them, which took place on the accession of Michael Palaiologos in 1261, I will subsequently relate in the few extant words of our historians. No one thought of restoring the falling palaces, for the State was poverty stricken, and the Emperors were living at Blachernai.

THE HOROLOGION.

The Horologion is frequently mentioned by Constantine Porphyrogennetos, who describes the Emperor as passing from the Palaces through the Middle of the Milion and the Augustaion, and entering by the Horologion of the Great Church.[1] The Emperor Nikephoros at his proclamation, "went on foot from the Forum and entered S. Sophia in the procession of the Holy Cross, and stood at the Horologion to receive the acclamations of both the factions."[2]

In the south side of S. Sophia, underneath the women's gallery, was the chamber of the Holy Well, where certain rites were performed when the Emperor and Patriarch visited the place in the course of the Imperial ceremonies. An arched exit

---

[1] Vol. I., p. 38, 63, 415.

[2] *Ibid.*, p. 439; G. Kodinos, p. 136. For information about this horologion and others in Byzantion, see the learned notes of Reiske, Cons. P., Vol. II., p. 559. Ὁ φιλόσοφος Λέων ὁ Θεσσαλονίκης γενόμενος πρόεδρος, τῷ βασιλεῖ Θεοφίλῳ συμβουλεύσας, ὡς ὡρολόγια ἐποίησεν δύο ἐξ ἴσου κάμνοντα. Theophanes Con., p. 681.

from the Well to the square of the Milion is still preserved. This door led directly to the Augustaion, and by it the Emperors usually went to and from the Church. The Horologion, which the historians mention without any further description, was over this door. "And he goes out through the side of the Church as if to the Metatorion, and so to the Horologion."[1] That it was attached to the south wall, is evident from the following passage in Constantine Porphyrogennetos' account of the proclamation of the Emperor Leo, "And he goes into the Church, passing through the Augustaion opposite the Horologion."[2] Kedrenos calls it the Horologion of the Milion.[3] The k. Byzantios justly remarks that it is not clear whether it was a sundial or a clepsydra or both.[4]

S. JOHN'S, THE BAPTISTERY.

From the words of Kodinos,[5] "and he built the Church of S. John, called the Baptistery, which is beside the Horologion," there can be no doubt about the site of this building. Constantine Porphyro-

---

[1] Cons. P., Vol. I., pp. 14, 268.

[2] Vol. I., p. 414.

[3] Vol. I., p. 650.

[4] Κπολις, Vol. I., p. 449. A sun-dial would be useless in the sunless winter of Constantinople. Constantine Porphyrogennetos mentions another horologion in the Church of SS. Sergius and Bacchus, Vol. I., pp. 526, 535, 536, 580, 605, 622. See also the epigrams εἰς ὡρολόγιον in the Anthology, Vol. II., pp. 258, 259, and the notes of the learned hierarch of Imbros on one found in that island. *Proceedings of the Philological Society of Constantinople*, Vol. XIII., 1880, p. 4.

[5] P. 135.

gennetos [1] often mentions it, sometimes as the Church of S. John, sometimes as the Baptistery. Another Baptistery in the Palace is mentioned. The numerous explicit statements of the site of the Horologion which this writer gives, help us to fix the real site of this Church. [2]   The k. Byzantios writes, "At the north-east corner of the Cathedral there is an octagonal building, which I take to be the Church of S. John the Forerunner, called the Baptistery or the Great Baptistery, perhaps also used as a sacristy." [3]   Here he is manifestly at variance with Kodinos, who places the Baptistery beside the Horologion, on the south side of S. Sophia.   Du Cange identifies it with the building at the west end of S. Sophia, not far from the Narthex. [4]

The font of S. John Baptist was probably the great oval marble basin now contained in the enclosure of the Mosque *Zeineb Sultan*, which lies to the west of S. Sophia, opposite the Palace Gate known as *Soouk Djesmé Kapusé*. [5]   The fact that this immense font has been conveyed from its original position, convinces me that the Church of the Forerunner has been destroyed.

It is, as I said just now, very often noticed by

---

1 Vol. I., pp. 14, 192, 415.

2 *Ibid.*, Vol. II., p. 559.

3 Κπολις, Vol. I., p. 506.

4 Paulus Silentiarius, p. 149.

5 Gate of the Cold Spring.   In the precincts of the Mosque Kotza Mustapha Pasha, a Byzantine Church of SS. Peter and Paul, there is another smaller font.   These are the only. two known.   See Βυςαντιναl Μελέται, p. 317.

Constantine Porphyrogennetos.[1] "At the baptism of a male child of the Emperor . . . at the Emperor's command, the magistri, proconsuls, patricians, generals, commanders, commanders of cavalry, officials, and all the Senate, take their rank and proceed to the Great Baptistery of the Cathedral, and their Majesties go in front, attended by their body guards as is the custom on great festivals." The sons of the Emperor were always baptized in this Baptistery.[2] From the concourse of so many people the size of the church must have been considerable. It is useless for writers to seek this building on the north side of S. Sophia. The south side, which looks directly to the Augustaion and the Milion, where so many ceremonies were performed, and through which the Emperors came and went, could not have been blocked up by so large a church. A building such as S. John the Baptist's built near this side of S. Sophia was destroyed by the Turks.[3] To justify this remark, I may state that in 1876, while clearing the ground to the west of S. Sophia, which was then occupied by work-shops, and poor Turkish dwelling-houses, two colossal marble pillars were uncovered on the south-west side supporting a brick arch. Some months later the pillars fell,

---

[1] Vol. I., pp. 619, 413.

[2] Καὶ εὐξαμένη [ἡ βασίλισσα] πρὸ τῆς εἰσόδου τοῦ ἁγίου θυσιαστηρίου, μετῆλθεν εἰς τὸν μέγαν βαπτιστῆρα. G. Kedrenos, Vol. I., p. 792.

[3] On the Baptistery was inscribed νιψορανομηνηματαμημονανοψιν, which can be read either backwards or forwards. Byzantios, Κπολις, Vol. I., p. 464. According to the Patriarch Constantios ('Ελάσσονες συγγρ.), this iambic was written round the edge of the tank (φιάλη) in the Narthex.

were broken to pieces, and disappeared. The passage under this arch was called the Anethas.[1] Salzenberg gives representations of the Baptistery in the sixth plate of his great work; but the building represented is not the true one.[2] S. Sophia has suffered many changes at the hands of the Turks.

The Baptistery had the right of sanctuary. Prokopios, for instance, telling of Theodora pursuing Photios, writes :—" And the second time he came into the sanctuary of S. Sophia, and suddenly sat down somewhere on the sacred font itself, which the Christians are wont to observe with special veneration."[3] The *Chronicon Paschale*[4] writes of Basiliskos pursued by the Emperor Zeno : "Basiliskos, taking his wife and children, fled for refuge to the great church of Constantinople at the great font "—φωτιστήριον, as the Byzantines sometimes called it.

For want of the guidance of Constantine Porphyrogennetos, Du Cange, like other writers, has fallen into error in his description of Constantinople, especially of the Palace and the buildings contained in it. He and Banduri have been slavishly followed by the majority of later writers, whence the many glaring errors in the accounts of the topography of the city.

---

1 Τὴν καμάραν τὴν λεγομένην τὸν Ἀνηθᾶν.   Cons. P., Vol. I., p. 583.

2 J. Labarte, p. 30.

3 Vol. III., p. 28.

4 Vol. I:, p. 601,

THE CHURCH OF S. JOHN, OR THE DÏIPPION.

Before his accession, Nikephoros Phokas erected in the Augustaion a church without a roof dedicated to S. Phokas. After his proclamation, he placed two statues of horses near it, and called the place Diippion. "There he also set four pictures in gold mosaic of Constantine and Helena." The Church, which was renewed by Basil the Macedonian, stood at the entrance to the Palace called the Mono-thyros.[1] In Byzantine history it is usually termed the Diippion. "On the 26th of September, the memory of S. John the Divine is celebrated, the Emperor and his train going to his venerated church in the Diippion."[2] At the chariot races, which took place on the 11th of May, they led in the horses through the Diippion and the first porch of the Mangana.[3]

In the riot which took place in the Augustaion, on May 2nd, 1182, the followers of the Emperor Alexios went out by the gate Monothyros[4] of the Palace, entered the Church of S. John, and then fought against the soldiers of the Caesar John, who were stationed in the Milion. A large body of soldiers came out of the Palace and blocked up the

---

[1] Theophanes Con., p. 336.

[2] Cons. P., Vol. I., p. 562. εἰσίασι τὰ πρῶτα τὸν τοῦ Θεολόγου Ἰωάννου ναὸν, ᾧ τὸ ἐπίκλην Δίιππιον, N. Choniates, p. 307.

[3] Cons. P., Vol. I., pp. 341, 376. καὶ ἀποκινεῖ ἐκ τοῦ δίιππίου, ibid., p. 366. τότε δὲ καὶ τοῦ Μιλίου ἡ καμάρα χερσαία πόρτα ἦν, καὶ εἰς τὸ δίιππιον ἦν ἡ ἀλλαγή. G. Kodinos, p. 51.

[4] This gate was near the Numera, and led from the Palace to the Augustaion.

streets leading to the Augustaion, thus cutting off those in the Milion from all help. Towards evening the followers of the Caesarissa were driven out of the Milion. The followers of Alexios erected the standards of the Emperor upon the building, and from the Palace of the Milion and the Church of S. John, they fought against those in the Augustaion with stones and darts, as well as "from the statue called Makron, which commanded the Augustaion, and the Thomaïtes which is connected with it."[1] From these words of Choniates it is evident that the darts discharged from the Church of S. John hit the enemy in the Milion.

In the ancient Augustaion, which, as I said, is now full of Turkish buildings, there is to the south of the Ottoman University, a little lane called *Medresé Sokaghi*.[2] In it are preserved strong walls of Byzantine build, with little low doorways, plain to every passer by. The owner of this building would never give me permission to inspect the interior. I think that these are the ruins of the Church of S. John. For it was in this quarter that the historians say it was built, and there I have placed it. The Patriarch Constantius is in error when he says that after the capture of the Turks it was used as a menagerie.[3]

---

[1] N. Choniates, p. 307-9. I have mentioned this Makron in the account of the Patriarcheion.

[2] School Street.

[3] Tournefort (Vol. II., p. 193) says—'A quelques pas de-là (S. Sophia) se voit une vieille tour, que l'on prétend avoir servi d'Eglise aux Chrétiens ; on y nourrit plusieurs bêtes et c'est comme un petite ména- gerie du Grand Seigneur.' The tower was not this church. Perhaps it

THE CHURCH OF ALEXIOS.

This church is spoken of in the above-mentioned narrative of Choniates. He writes :—"When the hour of fighting drew near, about the third hour, when the market place was crowded, these soldiers distressed not a little the supporters of the Caesarissa who were fighting from the Arch of the Milion, and the Church of Alexios." From these words it appears that the church was beside the Milion, and between it and the statue of Justinian. I do not know whether this church is mentioned by other historians.

THE BATHS OF ACHILLES.

Near the Gate of Meletios, which lay to the north of the Church of Our Lady in the Copper Market, were the Baths of Achilles, which most probably gave the name to the Passages of Achilles. They lay to the north of the Gate. Constantine Porphyrogennetos writes :—" The fifth reception is at the place called Achilles near the Great Gate of Meletios." "Thence they hold a reception, opposite the Achilles at the Gate of Melete."[1] In these baths stood a statue of Achilles, whence their name. The *Chronicon Paschale*[2] says :—" In

---

was part of the Patriarcheion. See the Patriarch Constantius' Ἐλάσσονες συγγραφαὶ, p. 383. Until the end of last century wild animals, chiefly lions, were kept in the Augustaion, whence the name *Arslán Hané ;* but I do not think they were kept in this church. See Byzantios Κπολις, Vol. I., p. 450.

[1] Vol. I., pp. 37, 56 ; II., p. 143.
[2] Vol. I., p. 582.

the fourteenth consulship of Theodosios Augustus, and that of Maximus, a great fire broke out in the dockyard, and the granaries and the public baths of Achilles were burnt." It may have been a building either wholly of wood or roofed over with wood.

THE PASSAGES OF ACHILLES.

The few words Prokopios uses when describing the architectural achievements of Justinian, throw great light on the topography of the Augustaion. "There is an agora with a peristyle before the Palace. The Byzantines call this agora Augustaion."[1] The Byzantine Emperors never erected any public or private buildings directly connected with defensive or military walls. On the land walls no structure so connected appears. The crowded cemeteries of the Turks at all the land gates are fifty yards and more from the trenches. From the treaties between our Emperors and the Genoese in Galata, we learn that fifty cubits' breadth of vacant ground was reserved in front of the land walls of Galata. All the walls were some distance from any private houses. The Imperial Palace, though surrounded on every side by strong walls, owing to the not unfrequent attacks on it by the people in riots,[2] was isolated even from the Augustaion by this colonnade. It is this which is mentioned by Constantine Porphyro-

---

[1] Vol. III., p. 202.
[2] See N. Choniates, pp. 12, 453 ; Leo the Deacon, p. 140.

gennetos in his account of the return of the Emperor Theophilos from a campaign.[1] After his exit from the Church of S. Sophia, he sat down upon a throne before the Bronze Gate, amid the acclamations of the populace and the magistrates. "And rising up from the throne,[2] he mounted his horse, and passed through the Passages of Achilles, and by the side of the Baths of Zeuxippos, and came into the uncovered hippodrome." What the historian calls the Passages of Achilles were, I think, built along either side of the Augustaion, and separated both the Palace and the Hippodrome from the populace who collected in this quarter.[3] Consequently all the buildings on the east side of the Augustaion, viz., the Church of our Lady of the Copper Market, the Patriarcheion, the Senate House, the Diippion and the Baths of Zeuxippos, were separated from the walls of the Palace by these passages of Achilles. From the passage referred to, it is plain that Theophilos passed behind the Senate House and the Church of S. John alone. No mention is made of the Patriarcheion and the Church of Our Lady, which lay to the north of the Bronze Gate, and were conse-

---

[1] Vol. I., p. 507.

[2] The same writer (p. 280) mentions a throne (σέντζον, *i.e.* sessum) in the Imperial Stand. Theophilos entered the Palace by the Skyla which led to the Hall of Justinian, and passed thence to the uncovered hippodrome in the Palace. Labarte places the baths of Zeuxippos beside the great Hippodrome, and says that it was it which Theophilos entered.

[3] These same passages are meant by Buondelmonti (apud N. Bryennion, p. 180): etiam de immenso palatio usque ad Sanctam Sophiam erat per milliare via columnarum binarum, per quam domini accedebat. These pillars are not mentioned by Gyllius. Probably they did not then exist.

quently behind him.   In my opinion, the whole of
this side was surrounded by a peristyle for protection to the Palace.   Of the opposite side I find
no mention in the Byzantine writers; but from
the language of Prokopios, who was well acquainted
with Constantinople, and gives a better description
of the city than any subsequent writer, I infer that
it too had a peristyle.   I am accordingly disposed
to place the buildings in the Augustaion clear of
the walls of the Palace and the Hippodrome.
What the breadth and height of these passages
were, no one has told us.

Further on, in describing the Gate Monothyros
in the Palace wall, between the Numera and S.
John's, I shall shew that the breadth of these passages of Achilles was 3·75 metres, or 5 cubits [12
feet].   Guided by this, if the buildings in the
Augustaion, viz., the Senate House, the Patriarcheion, and S. John's were 45 m. deep [146 feet],
we have the buildings on either side 90 m. [292
feet], and the passages 7·50 m. [24 feet] deep.
Deduct this from the total breadth of the Augustaion 133 m. [144 yards, 432 feet], and 35·5
m. [38·3 yards, 116 feet] is left for the broad
road in the middle.   This road at the present day
is largely occupied by the Mosque of Sultan
Achmet, and is in consequence much narrower
than formerly.

Such were the principal civil and ecclesiastical
edifices in the famous forum of the Augustaion.
Along the walls of the Hippodrome were some
private houses, the great Statue of Justinian, the

Church of Alexios, and the Chamber of the Milion.
From the numerous ecclesiastical and civil ceremonies performed there, the buildings must have
been so disposed, that in the midst of them there
was a broad space, where the ceremonies took
place, and through which the public had free passage. The Augustaion was further occupied by
great numbers of persons engaged in civil or ecclesiastical business in the Patriarcheion or Senate
House. The northern end of this spacious square
was occupied by the Cathedral of S. Sophia. On it
was the Horologion, and beside it the Baptistery or
S. John the Baptist's, the great marble font of which
is, I suspect, preserved in the mosque of *Zeineb
Sultan.* Owing to the presence of so many buildings, I do not doubt that before the erection of the
new walls by Michael Palaiologos, and the residence of the Byzantine Emperors at Blachernai, it
was frequented by the people of Constantinople
more than any of the other squares.

CHAPTER V.

In studies such as this, it is well to compare our results with the works of native writers, especially with those of Constantine Porphyrogennetos, to see whether we have been correct in our descriptions and as to the position of buildings which were demolished centuries ago, and whose sites are now entirely occupied by the mosques, squalid houses, and crooked lanes of the Turks. Constantinople contained no more famous place than this Augustaion. No other is so frequently mentioned by the historians. Owing to the total disappearance of the various buildings, no description of it has to this day been written, and the ceremonies which were performed there are imperfectly understood. The remains of magnificent civil and ecclesiastical buildings, which may yet be seen on every side in Constantinople, shed a wonderful light on the history not merely of the metropolis, but also of the whole Empire. Accordingly, I judge it advisable to check my description of the structures in the Augustaion by a sketch of some of the ceremonies of which it was the scene.

I may repeat what I said above, that it is no part of my purpose to enlarge upon the size and splendour of the buildings. This has already been done by many of our historians. My chief aim is to describe their situation, that we may understand the ceremonies performed in them. Here we could have no more trustworthy guide than Constantine Porphyrogennetos. Careful study of his writings is the more necessary, because many places noticed by him were neglected during the last two centuries of the Empire, fell in ruins and disappeared. The text, however, of his writings is often corrupt, and his vocabulary sometimes hard to interpret. His descriptions are not all equally clear, for he gives the same building now one, now another name. This confusion proves a fruitful source of error to persons who are not well acquainted with the places described.

On Whitsunday[1] " the Emperor went out by the great gate of the Palace through the middle of the Milion and the Augustaion, and entered the great Church by the door of the Horologion." On Easter Monday "The Emperor, after the Divine Liturgy is celebrated in S. Sophia, goes out by the Narthex and the Font, crosses through the Milion and the Middle, and goes up the Forum as far as the column where the Church of S. Constantine stands. There he ascends the steps and stands."[2] From this we see that the Milion was near S. Sophia, and that at the south end of it was the great building where the column with the statue of the Justinian stood. The centre of the Augustaion which contained no buildings,

---

1 Cons. P., Vol. I., p. 63.   2 Ibid., p. 74.

public or private, he calls the Middle, or the Forum. After the usual ceremony in the Church of S. Constantine, "the Emperor and his train go in procession through the Middle."[1] At Epiphany after the Divine Liturgy in S. Sophia, "the Emperor goes through the Middle and enters the Palace by the great Bronze Gate."[2] "Proceeding through the Middle on horseback as far as the Forum." The name Middle was also frequently applied by the Byzantines to the level thoroughfare which ran from the Church of S. Sophia past the Church of S. Stephen, and the Imperial Stand in the Hippodrome, up to the Golden Gate in the landward wall. In triumphs the Emperor went from the Golden Gate to S. Sophia by this road. "He goes along the Middle as far as the Church of the Holy Apostles."[3] There is no danger of confusing it with the Middle of the Augustaion.

After the return of the Emperor from the Church of the Apostles, "the members of the Green faction of the city receive him at the Pavement of the Milion. The Suburban Blue faction receive him at the Zeuxippos, and then at the Bronze Gate."[4] It is evident that the Emperor traversed the whole Augustaion from the Milion to the Baths of Zeuxippos. No one but the Emperor entered the Palace on horseback.[5]

---

1 *Ibid.*, p. 75.
2 *Ibid.*, p. 145; II., p. 167.
3 *Ibid.*, P., Vol. I., pp. 76, 188.
4 *Ibid.*, pp. 84, 439.
5 *Ibid.*, Vol. II., p. 191.

When the Emperor returned from the procession to the church of S. Mokios in Psamathia he was accompanied by the magistrates and the factions. " The Blue faction from the city accompany him as far as the chamber of the Milion. They receive him there, or in the Chamber, and escort him as far as the Marble Pavement. The Suburban Green faction receive the Emperor at the Pavement and escort him to the Zeuxippos. The Green faction from the city receive him there and escort him to the Bronze Gate. The Suburban Blue faction receive the Emperor at the Bronze Gate, when all proceed in this order on foot. The Emperor alone remains on horseback." [1]

From this description it is plain that from this thoroughfare, the Emperor went through the Milion into the Augustaion, thence to the Marble Pavement and the Baths of Zeuxippos.

According to the account of the ceremonies in the Church of SS. Sergius and Bacchus,[2] the Emperor proceeded from the Palace through the two southern gates of the Hippodrome, for the entrance to the Augustaion was at the north end, by the Milion. Hence the procession to this church was forced to pass through the Hippodrome. This confirms all that I said about the Augustaion being surrounded by lofty walls, and also my localisation of the buildings.

It may be well to state that a portion of the Middle of the Augustaion still exists to the south

---

[1] *Ibid.*, Vol. I., p. 106.   [2] *Ibid.*, Vol. I., p. 86.

of S. Sophia. The southern part is occupied by the grounds of *Sultan Achmet*, which come close up to the old Palace wall. Probably the road which runs over the ancient Middle of the Augustaion, has remained in the same condition since the period of the final capture. With the exception of those mentioned in the account of the Church of S. John at the Diippion, I have found no Byzantine remains in this place.

At the feast of the Annunciation, a ceremony took place in S. Sophia, from the description of which we learn a great deal about the buildings in the Augustaion.[1] After the Liturgy, the Emperor went out into the Milion through the Narthex and the Athyra.[2] Thence he crossed the Middle and proceeded to the part of the Forum where the Church of S. Constantine was built beside the statue of Justinian. He ascended the steps in front of the church and waited there, leaning upon the balustrade on the right side. The patricians and the Senate stood below beside the columns. Soon after the Emperor entered the church, the Patriarch followed with the usual ceremony, and the Senate took its stand on the left hand of the procession next to the Senate House. The clergy who usually accompanied the Patriarch stood below among the populace on the Emperor's left.

On the Great and Holy Sabbath (Easter Eve),

---

[1] Cons. P., p. 164.

[2] It was probably so called from the Athyra, a harbour near Constantinople, now called Bughiúk Djekmedjé. Cons. P., Vol. I., pp. 74, 156, 158 ; II., p. 177.

"The Emperor descends the steps of the Athyra, and goes out to the Milion, and passing through the Middle proceeds up the Forum, and there performs all, as has been already described." [1]

When triumphs were celebrated in the Augustaion, the Patriarch went into the Church of S. Constantine; "and the Emperor stands without. The captives stand in the Prætorium [2] or even in the Senate House. Then they are brought before the Emperor on the steps of the column." [3]

According to this account by Porphyrogennetos, the statue of Justinian was not connected with the walls of the Hippodrome; for it was through the West end, or narthex, that the Church of S. Constantine was entered. It is scarcely possible that a church or chapel visited by the Emperor should be without a narthex. We further learn that the Senate House lay in front of the statue, at some distance from the Milion. This clear account of the Church of S. Constantine helps us greatly to a right understanding of the buildings in the Augustaion.

At the obsequies of an Emperor, "the corpse leaves the Palace by the Bronze Gate, and is carried through the Middle." [4] When the Emperor went to the Hippodrome, he always went through

---

[1] Cons. P., Vol. I., p. 185.

[2] This Prætorium—there was another on the shore near the Saracen mosque—lay to the west of the Curve of the Hippodrome. It was a prison. "He straightway ordered that we were to be imprisoned in the Prætorium." Simeon Metaphrastes, Vol. III., p. 672 ; Βυʃαττιναὶ Μελέται, p. 368.

[3] Cons. P., Vol. I., p. 609.   [4] *Ibid.*, Vol. I., p. 276.

the Augustaion. " The Emperor passes through
the Arch and the Augustaion,[1] and through the
private stair, and enters the Imperial Stand."
" Accompanied by the · usual escort, he passes
through the Augustaion and the private spiral
stair, and enters the palace of the Kathisma.[2]

When the Emperor Theophilos returned from
his campaign against the Saracens of Cilicia, a
great procession took place in Constantinople.[3]
The Emperor entered by the Golden Gate, and
proceeded to the Milion amid the acclamations of
the whole people. There the Senate dismounted,
and proceeded on foot before the Emperor as far as
the Holy Well in S. Sophia. When the Emperor
came out from the church, he entered the Bronze
Gate, and sat upon a throne to receive the congratulations of the magistrates and the people.
After a little, " he rose from his seat, mounted his
horse, and proceeded through the Passages of
Achilles, by the side of the Baths of Zeuxippos.
From the language of Porphyrogennetos, it is evident that the Baths of Zeuxippos were near the
often-mentioned Bronze Gate, which probably lay
to the north of them.

In the above account of the Augustaion I have
mainly followed Constantine Porphyrogennetos.
In his lifetime, the whole of the buildings mentioned
in the writings of the Byzantine historians were
preserved in all the splendour with which they had

---

[1] He calls the Augustaion sometimes the Augusteus and sometimes the
Forum.   [2] Cons. P., Vol. I., pp. 360, 364.
   [3] *Ibid.*, Vol. I., p. 506.

been erected by the arch-builder Justinian and succeeding Emperors. In very many cases, my localisation of the principal buildings in the Augustaion explains events which happened in Constantinople, especially the ceremonies detailed by Constantine Porphyrogennetos. With the exception of Labarte, all who have hitherto attempted to describe the Palace, the Augustaion, and the Hippodrome, fail to mark the site of the buildings which they describe. Unfortunately, the laborious work of investigation among the ruins on the spot did not begin until quite recently. Many, too, who never saw Constantinople have written descriptions compiled entirely from the works of others.

The Augustaion, where it divided the Palace from the Hippodrome, was long and narrow. The south end is very seldom mentioned by the historians, and never by Constantine Porphyrogen-· netos in his account of the Imperial ceremonial. It may have been occupied by the Baths of Zeuxippos, with their many ornaments and statues. On one occasion only—in the Nika riot—Belisarius left the Palace at this end, and passed behind the Curve of the Hippodrome, that he might attack the mob gathered in it, from the opposite gate. I mentioned above, that when the Emperor went from the Palace to the Augustaion on his way to the Church of SS. Sergius and Bacchus, on Easter Tuesday, he passed through the south end of the Hippodrome.[1] It was possible to pass behind the

---

[1] Cons. P., Vol. I., p. 87.

Curve to the people standing in the Hippodrome. In all the ecclesiastical and civil ceremonies no mention is made of going or coming through the south end of the Augustaion. Whether a wall or other barrier prevented the people going from the city to the Augustaion I cannot tell. I have never discovered any trace of a Byzantine building or ancient wall. I am inclined to think that this end was closed, or else entirely occupied by the great Baths of Zeuxippos.

The chief public entrance to the Augustaion was by the Milion, that is, the northern end of the Forum, next to S. Sophia. Here the people had access to the Imperial festivals, or to the Senate and Patriarcheion on private business. No other way for Emperor or people to the Augustaion is mentioned.

The buildings which I have described above were built partly beside the Palace walls, and partly beside the walls of the Hippodrome. Between them, was left an open space of great extent called the Middle, which was thronged by the populace. Whenever the Emperor returned to the Palace after visiting any of the churches or great monasteries in the city, he entered the Augustaion through the Milion. When a chariot-race or other contest took place in the Hippodrome, he went to the Imperial Stand through the Milion, and returned the same way. The Augustaion was so much frequented that the chief entrance to S. Sophia was from the Milion, through the portico, or door, of the Horologion, and the other doors in

the south end of the church.   The Emperor very
rarely entered by the Great Narthex.

THE GATES OF THE PALACE.

I have now to describe shortly the Gates of the
Palace,[1] before proceeding to describe the Palace
itself and the many entrances to the buildings
there.   As for the gates opening on to the Augustaion, we cannot fix their position without first
studying the Palace buildings.   Owing to the
vague statements of the historians, it is a troublesome task to determine their number and situation.

In the long extent of the sea-walls there were
some small posterns which are, I think, still preserved.   Since they were of little importance in
the history of the Empire, the notices of them are
few and vague.[2]   Their Byzantine names are consequently seldom mentioned, and at the present
day they all go under Turkish designations.[3]

At the southern extremity of the Palace precincts, a land gate called Karea is mentioned.
Choniates writes, "When the mob had rushed into
the Palace, having broken open the gate Karea,
Andronikos took to flight."   Luitprand also mentions this gate in the account of his Embassy to
Nikephoros Phokas.[4]   The Turks have transferred

---

[1] N. Choniates, p. 12.   [2] Byzantios, Κπολις., Vol. I., p. 110.

[3] Τὴν βασιλικὴν εἴσεισιν αὖθις τριήρη, δι' ἧς ἐκ τοῦ Μαλουδίου πρὸς τὸ μέγα
παλάτιον ἐσαφίκετο.   N. Choniates, p. 452.   καὶ νυκτὸς διὰ παραπυλίδος
εἰσελθὼν τοῦ πρωτοβεστιαρίου Μιχαὴλ, οὔσης πλησίον ἀκροπόλεως.   Theophanes
Con., p. 719 ; Byzantios, Κπολις., Vol. I., p. 181.

[4] Pridie nonas Iunii . . .   Constantinopolin ante portam Caream
venimus.   Apud Leonem Diac.. p. 344.

the name to the gate lying beside the *Ahér Kapusú,*[1] and some barracks. It is called *Kará Kapé,*[2] or the Black Gate, sometimes *Kará Kapusú,* the Land Gate, and often *Ghiúl Hané Kapusú,* or the Gate of the Attendants at the Baths. In the middle of August, 1872, when the Turkish houses and the high walls of the numerous gardens were being demolished by the workmen on the railway, the Palace wall called the Gallery of Marcian was discovered. A great arched gateway was disclosed connected with it. It was supported on four large marble pillars. The depth of the gate was 6·05m. [19 ft. 8 in.], the breadth, 5·5 m. [17 ft. 10 in.]. Unfortunately, however, it stood in the middle of the railway, and was no sooner discovered than demolished. It had been surrounded by the walls of a large Turkish garden, and had never been previously seen. The portion of the Gallery of Marcian to the north of it was destroyed within three years. This ancient gate was about 750 paces [625 yards] from the modern *Kará Kapé.*

At the other end of the Palace precincts, where the often mentioned Tzukanisterion lay, there stood a gate, the name of which, unfortunately, has not been preserved. After the banishment of Romanus Lakapenos to the island of Proté, the people of Constantinople, learning that they were

---

1 *I.e.,* Gate of the Stables. Ὁ χορτοβολὼν ὃ ὢν εἰς τὸ Βύκινον, ἐκκλησία ἦν τοῦ Ἁγίου Ἀνδρέου . . . ὁ δὲ Καβαλλῖνος ἐποίησεν αὐτὴν χορτοβολῶνα. G. Kodinos, p. 109.

2 Byzantios calls this gate the Gate of the Negroes (Vol. I., p. 175). I think, though, that the name is borrowed from the old Karean Gate.

about to abuse, or were already abusing, Constantine and his sons, gathered in a body at the gate of the Tzukanisterion, when Constantine hastily appeared at the bars of the gate to convince the people of his safety.[1] In his account of the departure of the Saracen envoys from the Palace, Constantine Porphyrogennetos says that they went through the eastern gate.[2]

These are the only gates in the sea wall of the Palace precincts which are mentioned by the historians. They are all far from the Palace.

Five gates leading from the Palace to the Augustaion are mentioned by the historians. All these gates were under the superintendence of the Great Papias, the janitor of the Palace. They were—the Gate of the Skyla, to the north of the great Hall of Justinian, the Monothyros beside the Numera, the Greater and Lesser Bronze Gates, and the Porta Regia,[3] sometimes, I think, called the Gate of Meletios or Meletê. The two Bronze Gates are mentioned by the historians more frequently than the others, and especially by Constantine VII. in his accounts of the many ecclesiastical

---

[1] Ex ea parte qua Zucanistrii magnitudo portenditur Constantinus crines solutus per cancellos caput exposuit. Luitprand, *Hist.*, lib. ii., cap. 21. [2] Cons. P., Vol. I., p. 592.

[3] *Chronicon Paschale*, Vol. I., p. 530. Reiske in his notes to Constantius Porphyrogennetos (Vol. II., p. 367) thinks that this was an ancient designation of the Bronze Gate. Regia olim audiebat porta, quae, isto nomine abolito, deinceps Chalce dicebatur, extrema palatii in urbem educens. From a study of the Palace buildings, I have come to the conclusion that this gate was the one to the east of Our Lady in the Copper Market, opposite the east end of S. Sophia. The site of the gate is explained by subsequent passages.

and civil ceremonies. These gates and their sites will be more fully considered in the description of the Palace.

Hitherto I have described the Byzantine buildings in the Hippodrome and the Augustaion, because otherwise the study of the Palace would be difficult and frequently intelligible. The site of the buildings has seldom been examined by students of history or archæology, and the few who have inspected the place have not found heaps of ruins strewed here and there, nor shafts and capitals from which they could gain information about the palaces so often celebrated by historians and poets. With the exception of S. Sophia, time has preserved no record of any building. We walk in the dark when we try to describe the Imperial Palace. The place, which for reasons unknown to us the Emperors had entirely neglected for many years before the capture, has been entirely stripped of its numerous ornaments by the Turks who now possess the city.[1] The pillars of the halls, the white and purple marbles of the churches, all have been carted away to the Sultans' new Palace, which stands near at hand, or to the barbaric mosques of the Turks.[2]

---

[1] . . . Adde incendia, et ruinas quas cum alii barbari, tum postre-mum Turci ediderunt, qui jam centum annos non cessant funditus antiquæ urbis vestigia delere. Ita enim ab imis fundamentis ædificia prisca demoliuntur, atque in aliam formam immutantur, ut ne illi quidem qui ea viderint agnoscere queant. Gyllius, *De Topographia,* lib. ii., cap. 1.

[2] Aedes Mametanas . . . ornatae ex spoliis Christianarum ædium ; ut hae prius ornatæ fuerant ex veterum deorum spoliis. *Ibid.,* lib. iv., cap xi.

Before proceeding to study the Palace of Constantinople, called the Holy, the Great, and the God-protected,[1] let me repeat what I said at the outset—"I have never undertaken the discussion of any Byzantine problem more difficult than the present." I continued—"the reader must not suppose that I desire to unduly magnify the labour which such works involve." To explain, or rather to justify these words I quoted the words of distinguished authorities to show how many have abandoned the undertaking through impatience or discouragement at the vagueness of the historians, and the utter nakedness of the site of the Palace.[2]

We do not study these relics of our forefathers for the sake of their art alone. All the ruins of our land are clear and unimpeachable witnesses to our ancient history, which has not always been too familiar to recent generations. In my opinion, many passages of Byzantine history will be for ever obscure and unintelligible, unless we have a knowledge of the Palace, the scene of so much of our political and ecclesiastical history.

The demolition and denudation of the Palace I

---

[1] Describing the ceremony on Easter Monday, Constantine Porphyrogennetos writes—"The Emperor passes through the Catechumeneia in front of him, and through them goes to the God-protected palace which is there, and enters into his chamber." It should be understood that the larger churches had apartments where the Emperor rested. Porphyrogennetos mentions them very frequently in his accounts of the accustomed progresses of the Emperor to these churches.

[2] We are surprised to read such as this—"Le palais Imperial s'étendait entre le Senat et l'Hippodrome." Le Chevalier, *Voyage de la Propontide et du Pont-Euxin*, p. 133. Yet he stayed many months in Constantinople investigating the ruins.

shall describe in another chapter. Here I shall only quote the account given by Nikephoros Gregoras. In the course of some remarks on the Palace in 1317 he writes : "Into such poverty had the Empire then fallen, that none of the plates and cups were of gold or silver. But some were pewter, and all the others clay or earthenware. From which, those who are not unacquainted with such matters can understand what other things were also lacking. . . . On the arrival of Kantakouzenos the Imperial treasuries were completely empty, and save air and dust, and, so to say, the atoms of Epicurus, nothing was to be found in them." "Thus," he continues, " was the ancient luxury and splendour of the Roman State so swiftly and utterly quenched and undone." [1] Such was the estate, or rather the poverty, of the Palace of Constantinople, a century before the final capture.

The Florentine Buondelmonti,[2] who visited Constantinople in 1422 speaks of the shocking desolation of the buildings in the neighbourhood of the Church of S. Sophia.

Petrus Gyllius, who spent a long time in the city in the following century, says that nothing was left of the ancient Palace, and that it was most difficult to discover the site of the ancient and celebrated Byzantine buildings.[3] The learned Reiske, who

---

[1] Vol. II., pp. 788, *et seqq.*   [2] N. Bryennios, p. 178.

[3] These words of Gyllius deserve our attention. "Ex ante scriptis facilius fortasse cognosces absens monumenta antiqua, quae tradit antiqua regionum urbis descriptio, quam si sine his praesens videas Constantinopolim : quod experietur qui similia investigare post me conabitur. Lib.

has thrown so much light on the works of Constantine Porphyrogennetos, writes in his notes to the Ἔκθεσις τῆς βασιλείου τάξεως (Vol. II., p. 593)--"To tell the truth, I do not understand this passage, nor many more relating to the topography of Constantinople, which no one will ever comprehend until he has seen the places for himself. But as many of these are destroyed and utterly changed, it is clear that a great part of this book will be a mystery for ever." Such are the words of the learned commentator who, though he never saw Constantinople, has done much to elucidate the harsh and often unintelligible language of his author. Compare what the estimable k. Byzantios writes about the Palace. "To describe and accurately fix its various parts is impossible, owing to the obscurity of the historians, and their persistent long-windedness, and self-contradiction. Constantine Porphyrogennetos, for instance, busies himself over needlessly minute and inflated description of details, yet neglects to give any general sketch." [1] This is the opinion of a native of Constantinople, who has frequently inspected the existing remains. It is an instructive commentary on the hope of the learned Reiske.

Labarte's book, which we mentioned before, was published about the same time as that of Byzantios. It is still the only book which shews any advance on previous descriptions of the Palace and the ad-

iv., cap. 9. As a matter of fact the history of the Palace confirms the opinion of this excellent writer.

[1] Κπολις., Vol. I., p. 189.

joining buildings. In the conclusion he writes
(p. 220) " Of the Palace of Constantine, of the
splendid buildings connected with it, of the veritable open air museum of the Augustaion, of the
noble buildings in front of the Palace connected
with S. Sophia, nothing, absolutely nothing has
been preserved,[1] and the very ruins have vanished,
and are buried under unlovely Turkish dwellings."

Of the walls which surrounded the Palace, he
writes, (p. 107) "The walls of the Sultan's Seraglio,
extending westwards from the Karean Gate to the
Sublime Porte *Bab-i-humaghiún* were probably
erected at a period near the capture, in the same
style as the older walls though they are comparatively modern. These walls cut the residence of
the Greek Emperors in two. We find nothing
about their erection in the historians. They were
certainly built of the material derived from buildings in the neighbourhood which had been demolished." These sensible observations Labarte
occasionally forgets—as when on his map he places
buildings in this uninhabitable quarter.[2]

Guided by the Byzantine historians, and aided
by researches on the spot—now accessible to all—I
have essayed, for the sake of our history, to point
out the site of these buildings, that with this aid

---

[1] Le sort ne l'a point épargné (the Palace) et depuis longtemps, ses
ruines même ont disparu. Rayet, *L'Art Byzantin*, p. 119.

[2] Leunclavius writes that the Great Palace was built in the centre of
Constantinople, where the War-office, called *Serasksier kapusú*, formerly
Eské serai, or the Old Palace now stands. He learnt this from the mouth
of the Byzantines. *Histoire de l'Empire de Ople. sous les Empereurs françois*, Venise, 1729, Ier. Partie, p. 152.

we may render intelligible the hitherto incomprehensible records of the Byzantine writers. Now,
however, that the buildings have been destroyed,
the dimensions and construction both of the
walls and roof must remain a puzzle.[1] Those
however who are desirous of studying Byzantine
art, especially as exemplified in S. Sophia, will find
abundant material in the splendid work of Salzenberg,[2] which gives a full account of the art and
works of Byzantine artists.

Very many of the works on Constantinople and
its environs are unworthy of serious study. The
majority of writers describe the city with the help
of earlier writers, rather than go through the toil-
some task of traversing the crooked and sunless
lanes of this inhospitable city. Hence travellers
are frequently misled.

All the area within which the Palace of Constantinople was anciently built, slopes steeply to
the eastern shore. From the Gate of the Tzukanisterion to S. Sophia there is a considerable hill. On
the summit of it, after the capture, the Sultans
built halls of every size and shape, palaces,
treasuries, and kitchens. These filled the whole of
the space, which was formerly destitute of any
building of importance. The Byzantine palaces

---

[1] Τοῦ πυρὸς τοίνυν ἐπινεμηθέντος ἅπαν τὸ τέμενος (*i.e.*, the Senate House)
ὁ μὲν ἐπικείμενος τῷ τέγει μόλιβδος ἔρρει τηκόμενος κατὰ τῶν ἀγαλμάτων.
Zosimos, p. 281.

[2] *Alt christliche Baudenkmale von Constantinopel, von V. bis XII.
Jahrhundert*, Berlin, 1854; *L'Art Byzantin*, par Rayet, Paris; *Geschichte
des Byzantiner und des Osmanischen Reiches*, von Dr. Hertzberg, Berlin,
1883.

which lay near the sea-wall, such as the Boukoleon, the New Church, and other smaller ones, were entirely demolished.[1] In the reign of Severus or of Constantine the Great, extensive excavations were made, and the Palace walls, which extend from the Tzukanisterion to S. Sophia, were built. These walls which are still preserved are very strong, and retain the banks of earth behind them, which in many places rise level with the top. In some parts new and strong walls have been built to support weak portions of the older walls. Their general unsymmetrical appearance shows the patching up, which time and the strain upon them have necessitated. I have discovered no trace of a gate in this wall, and none is mentioned by the historians, nor in Constantine's account of the ceremonies. Besides, in many places, under heaps of earth, or covered over with plants of all kinds, there are signs of the foundations of the thick and strong buttresses, which were added to support and strengthen the tottering walls. All the portion of the Palace precinct to the east of this, in which Basil the Macedonian built the Tzukanisterion, is artificially levelled. Previous to the building of the wall, the hill behind it sloped down to the sea, which is here very deep. On this long and narrow strip of ground it was impossible for the Emperors to build palaces. Immediately behind them would have been a lofty hill, supported only by the walls. In addition to this, the atmosphere of the place is

---

[1] Κπολιτ., Vol. I., p. 158.

close, being confined by the retaining wall and the high sea wall so near to it.[1] Until the reign of Basil, this portion of the precinct was occupied by private houses, which the Emperor bought up.[2] Private houses in the Palace precincts at Blachernai are also mentioned.

On this level strip of ground the Sultans latterly built the women's quarters completely hidden from observation. Here, too, were the Sultan's gardens, used principally by the ladies of the Court; these were subsequently neglected, and finally destroyed during the construction of the railway.

These drawbacks moved the first founders of S. Sophia and the Palace, to build them at the southern extremity of the Imperial precinct, beside the Augustaion, where S. Sophia now stands. Here the ground slopes gently eastwards to the narrow plain through which the Thracian Railway now runs. The slope, for the most part regular, compelled the Byzantine Emperors to build the great vaults, flights of steps, and staircases in connection with the many halls and galleries of the Palace.

These few particulars about the nature of the site of the Palace will prepare us for seeking, and,

---

[1] Ταῦτα τὰ πρὸς τὴν θάλασσαν τοῦ παλατίου τείχη, παρεξέβαλε Θεόφιλος τοῦ Μιχαήλ. Theophanes Con., p. 88.

[2] Ἔπειτα εἰς τὰ βασίλεια ἐλθόντες τὸ λεγόμενον Καστέλλιον διεπόρθησαν, ἀφύλακτον εὑρόντες, καὶ διήρπασαν τῶν ἐνοικούντων οἰκίας. Βυζαντιναὶ Μελέται, p. 88. It is remarkable that Benjamin of Tudela reserves his praises for this Palace of Blachernai. Bergeron, *Voyages*, etc., Vol. I., p. 12, [ed. Wright, p. 75.]

if possible, finding the Palace buildings in the space immediately to the east of the Augustaion.

REMAINS OF THE PALACE.

After this we now proceed to the investigation of the ruins of Byzantine structures, which are preserved in this area, that with their aid we may be enabled to determine the site of the Palace buildings.

THE NUMERA.

In the first chapter I described the remains of the wall which still exists standing to the east, or at the back, of the great Mussulman mosque of *Sultan Achmet,* which is built partly in the Hippodrome and partly in the Augustaion. This wall, which is built of large, dark-coloured stones, well-hewn, and laid in alternate courses with the ordinary large Byzantine bricks, is a remnant of the ancient wall which enclosed the whole of the site of the Palace, and extended to the shore. All this quarter has been occupied by poor Turkish families, and is now called *Ak Bughiúk Mahalesi.*[1] The long narrow street in front of the wall is called *Kampá Sakál Sokaghi.*[2] The street is about 150 paces long. At the south end there is another and broader road, which cuts it in a line drawn from east to west. It is called *Arista Sokaghi.* It

---

[1] The Street of the White-Mustached.

[2] The Street of the Long-Beard. Both these designations are noticed by Byzantios, Κπολις., Vol. I., p. 67.

is strange that this Byzantine street and these strong walls should have escaped the notice of travellers and topographers till now.

All the houses built on this wall are low. ·From the street the inhabitants descend by three or four steps to the floor of their dwellings. I infer from this that the level of the road has been raised, like all the ground in the neighbourhood of the Palace. Externally, each house consists of a single very narrow domed chamber, with no communication with the road behind, which is occupied by larger houses. These domed chambers are divided into two equal storeys by a wooden floor. On the ground floor the domestic work of the poor inhabitants is performed. In the upper storey, which is lighted by small windows, are the bedchambers of the family. At the back of the lower room is a ladder leading to the upper floor.

Such is the arrangement of all the houses which I visited in company with a friendly Turk; and such, according to the neighbours, is the plan of the others. The length of the houses from the front door to the back is 9·4 m. (about 30 feet). The houses of some more prosperous tenants have been raised by an additional storey built on the domed roof. When passing through this narrow lane full of dirty children and their ragged parents, amid the mocking of the women and the abuse of the men, one finds it hard to realise from the external appearance of the street that these humble structures cover Byzantine buildings which, owing to the presence of these poor families, have remained unharmed while the greater part of the walls has been demolished. On account of this, and the rudeness of the inhabitants, these ancient buildings have remained not merely unnoticed but almost unknown. Opposite the houses a wall may be seen, which is evidently Byzantine, and some remains of arches. Possibly the road, or at least some part of it, was arcaded in Byzantine times.

I regret that I was unable to investigate these remains as I desired, for I was stoned by the children and abused by the women. I could not always secure the company of my Turkish friend.

They are, I think, the remains of the Numera which is often mentioned in history. Its site has been fixed in various places by later writers.[1] George Kodinos writes (pp. 18, 76), " The Numera and the Bronze Gate were built by Constantine the Great. Since it was otherwise useless, Heraclius and his successors made it a prison." " He also built the Palace from the Bronze Gate and the watch-towers (ἐξκουβίτων), . . . and the building now called the Numera."[2] It was therefore built at the same time as the walls of Constantine the Great. Constantine Porphyrogennetos[3] men-

---

[1] Labarte places the Numera in the Augustaion : Les Noumera étaient sur le Forum, et les Thermes de Zeuxippe en dehors, p. 32.

[2] Œcumenius in Act., c. 15 : σπεῖρα δέ ἐστιν ὃ καλοῦμεν νῦν νούμερον, quid vero σπεῖραι ; Suidas : πλήθη στρατευμάτων, φάλαγγες, νούμερα. G. Kedrenos (annot.) Vol. II., p. 793, cf. 923.

[3] Vol. I., pp. 6, 61, 524, 525, 604, 714, 728, 731, 752. τριβοῦνοι τῶν Νουμέρων—ὁ χαρτουλάριος τῶν Νουμέρων, p. 737—ὁ πρωτομανδάτωρ τῶν Νουμέρων, p. 738.

tions the domesticus and chartularius of the Numera without any observations concerning its size or site. He never, however, calls it a prison. He mentions the subordinates who went with the domesticus of the Numera when he accompanied the Emperor at festivals.[1] At the reception of the embassy from Amerimne, "Outside the bars of the Bronze Gate stood a crowd,[2] some near the Numera, others near the chamber of the Milion." In the reign of Michael and Theodora, Theophilitses mentions the Count of the Numera and of the Walls.[3]

The Byzantine writers give us no precise information as to why this series of vaults was built beside the walls of the Palace. Possibly they formed the residence of the captains of the guard ($\phi\rho ov\rho\alpha\rho\chi\epsilon\hat{i}\alpha$), or barracks for the guards of the Palace, and were built between the Bronze Gate and the Gate of the Skyla, that the guards might have a good and close view of all who went in or out of the Palace.[4] That the Numera was near the Baths of Zeuxippos is attested by Prokopios. In the Nika riot he says that the Numera was burnt down together with the Baths of Zeuxippos and S. Sophia.[5]

---

[1] Vol. I., p. 604. The Count of the walls (κόμης τῶν τειχῶν) is constantly mentioned along with the domesticus of the Numera. *Ibid.*, p. 6.

[2] *Ibid.*, pp. 6, 579; II., p. 682. Reiske explains ἕστησαν τάχωμα by : turba miscella ut videtur, faex, amurca veluti plebis nauticae esse.

[3] Theophanes Con., p. 655.

[4] Notum enim ex scriptoribus *Numeros* appellatas militares cohortes ac praesertim eorum qui imperatorum custodiae deputati sunt. *Cpolis, Christ.*, lib. ii., cap. 4.   [5] Vol. I., p. 121.

The authors of the Continuation of Theophanes say distinctly that it was a prison. " On the first day of the month, [Irene] walked on foot through the schools to visit the prisoners confined in the prisons of the Bronze Gate, the Praetorium, and the Numera, asking them one by one for what cause they were imprisoned." Of Romanus Laka-penos the historian writes :—" He ordered that at his grave they should each day distribute 30,000 loaves, and that on Wednesday and Friday they should give every man in the Praetorium and the Bronze Gate and the Numera, fifteen follis, and on Good Friday one piece of silver[1] to each prisoner." The same writer, narrating the sufferings of the Patriarch Ignatius under Michael and Theodora, says :—" Leo Lalakon struck his cheeks so that two of his teeth fell out. A few days after, they cast him in chains into the Numera." [2]

Michael Glykas, who wrote a chronicle from the death of Alexios Komnenos in 1118, in one of his poems writes of the Numera, where he was at one time confined[3] :—

"Ἄδην καλῶ τὰ Νούμερα τὰ χείρω καὶ τοῦ "Αδου
"Οσον καὶ γὰρ εἰς κάκωσιν νικῶσι καὶ τὸν "Αδην.

.   .   .   .

---

1 Φόλλις, a copper coin, 500 of which were equal to a pound of silver. There was also a larger follis—follis senatorius—varying in value from two to eight pounds of gold. The " piece of silver " νόμισμα is the Roman solidum. See Du Cange, *Dissert. de Inferioris Ævi Numismatibus*, §§. 88 (78), 100 (90), and 101 (91).—[Tr.]

2 Theophanes Con., pp. 175, 430, 668.

3 *Bibliothèque Grecque Vulgaire*, par Emile Legrand, Vol. I., pp. 21, 23.

Ἐν τούτῳ δὲ τῷ ζοφερῷ καὶ βαθυτάτῳ λάκκῳ
Οὐ φῶς παρὰ τοῖς ὄμμασιν οὐδέ τις ὁμιλία
Τὸ συνεχὲς γὰρ τοῦ καπνοῦ τοῦ σκότους ἡ παχύτης
Ἀλλήλους οὐ παραχωρεῖ βλέπειν οὐδὲ γνωρίζειν.

" Hades I call the Numera, and even worse than Hades,
For in its horror it surpasses even Hades.

.   .   .   .

In this murky and most deep dungeon
There is no light to the eyes, nor any conversation,
For the constant smoke, and the thickness of the darkness
Suffer us not to see or recognise each other."

From the two following lines it appears that the Varangians were the jailors :—

Ἀμμὴ δεσμὰ καὶ βάσανα καὶ φυλακὰς καὶ πύργους
Βαράγγους ἀλαλάζοντας καὶ ὁ φόβος ἐξυπνᾷ σε.

" But bonds and tortures, and guards and towers,
And the shouting Varangi ; and terror keeps thee awake."

The Byzantine prisons were mostly under the palaces, as, for instance, the prison of Anemas under the palace of Blachernai, and the prisons of the Boukoleon and the Praetorium.[1] The overseer of them was the domesticus of the Numera, and under him were the topoteretai, tribuni chartularii, the protomandator, vicarii, mandatores, and portarii.[2]

In the reign of Michael Palaiologos some Latin prisoners were confined in the prisons of the

---

[1] Βυζαντιναὶ Μελέται, pp. 24, 26, 113, 367 ; ἐπεὶ δ' ἔτυχεν ἐν μιᾷ τῶν ἐντὸς βασιλείων εἱρκτῇ δέσμιον ἐκ πολλοῦ κατέχουσα Παλαμᾶν, N. Gregoras, Vol. II., p. 768. The chief prisons of Constantinople have fortunately all been discovered.

[2] Cons. P., Vol. I., p. 719.

Zeuxippos.[1] These are nowhere else mentioned. As the Baths were separated from the Numera only by a wall, it is possible that after their destruction their name survived, and was transferred to the Numera. No one else in the whole range of Byzantine history calls the Baths of Zeuxippos a prison.

The Byzantine prisons were horrible places.[2] Nikephoros Gregoras writes :—"Lest he [Apocauchos] be suddenly snatched off, even thence, and cast into the Hades and darkness of the prisons."[3]

THE GATE MONOTHYROS.

A few paces to the north of this wall, there is a small arched doorway, built after the usual Byzantine fashion, of stone and brick. At the west side of this gate there were discovered, during the excavations in 1870, two marble columns with their bases and capitals, which had long been hidden under a mound of earth. Along with them were found many bricks and fragments of marble without ornament or inscriptions. The length of the pillars was 4·45 m. (about 14 ft. 6 in.), and the circumference 1·75 m. (5 ft. 8. in.). The height of an adjacent capital was 0·55 m. (1 ft. 9 in.), and the breadth 0·77 m. (2 ft. 5 in.). A base, which lay in its original position, was about 3·75 m. distant from the wall. In my opinion, these pillars

---

1 Pachymeres, Vol. I., p. 519 ; II., p. 683.

2 Constantius, Κπολις., (1846) p. 51.

3 Vol. II., p. 726.

formed a portion of the Passages of Achilles. From the situation of the base, I should suppose that the colonnade was about 3.75 m. (12 ft. 2 in.) broad, and 5 m. (16 ft. 3 in.) high. All these remains were soon after destroyed, and small Turkish houses were built upon the whole of the site. The little door was, I suspect, the gate called Monothyros. I hope that further investigation will confirm this view. I never succeeded in learning the Turkish name of the gate.

CHAPTER VI.

THE ARISTETERION.

AT the south end of this narrow road is the street running eastward, called by the Turks *Arista Sokaghi.* The name is not Turkish. My opinion is that in Byzantine times the Aristeterion,[1] or as Anna Komnena calls it, the Aristerion, stood here. Though seldom mentioned by the historians, it is very often referred to by Constantine Porphyrogennetos in his accounts of the banquets of the Emperors in the Palace.[2]

That the so-called Aristeterion was the magnificent banquetting hall of the Emperors, and the courtiers and foreigners whom they invited, appears from the following words of the latter writer:— " On the evening of the 11th day, a table is laid in the Aristeterion, and the usual guests banquet with the Emperor, viz., the magistri, the praepositi, the patricians, the officials, the generals and others who may be present, but in preference those of the blood royal."—"And when the dessert (δουλκιον)[3] is being brought in, some of those waiting

---

[1] Greek ἐστιατώριον. *Cpolis. Christ.* lib. ii., p. 121.

[2] Cons. P., Vol. I., pp. 529, 581, 597, 602, 603.

[3] The courses were termed by the Byzantines μίσσον and μίσον (Latin *missus, ferculum*). καὶ πρῶτον μισὸν ἐκξεστὸν, δεύτερον τὸ σφουγγάτον.

at table pronounce the 'Many years, etc., and both the guests at the table, and the rest of the servants standing by the table make reply."[1]— "After this, another more private table is laid in the same Aristeterion, and the old and the young Emperor, and the Augusta sit at it." On the Emperor's birthday the feast was held here. At the upper table next the Skyla the Emperor and the chief courtiers sat, and the remainder at the lower table. The mantles of the guests were taken charge of at the Skyla by the servants of the Palace.[2]

That the great festivals were held in this hall is evident from the following words of Constantine Porphyrogennetos :—" In the reign of the most religious Emperor Leo, it was determined thus : on the morrow of the Brumalia :[3] one private table

Koraës, Ἄτακτα, Vol. I., p. 5, l. 130. Three courses are mentioned by Porphyrogennetos. The first, the second called ὀπτόμινσος, (Vol. I. p. 740), and the third, δούλκιον or δούλκια, the ancient ἐπιτραπεζώματα (*ibid.*)— δεῖ ὑμᾶς προσέχειν τὸν̄τοῦ ὀπτομίνσου μίνσον (p. 748).—ἐν τῷ δευτέρῳ μίνσῳ, (p. 767).—ἐν τῷ καιρῷ τοῦ μίνσου τῶν δουλκίων (p. 751).—καὶ τὸν καιρὸν τοῦ μίνσου τῶν λεγομένων δουλκίων (p. 755).—μετὰ δὲ . . . τὴν εἴσοδον τῶν τυρεψιτῶν ζωμῶν, (p. 760).—μετὰ τῆς ἀφίξεως τοῦ μίνσου τῶν δουλκίων, (p. 768).—ἐν δὲ τῇ εἰσόδῳ τοῦ ἑνὸς ἑκάστου μίνσου ἐν τῇ τραπέζῃ ἀξιοῖ ὁ βασιλεὺς τὸν πατριάρχην πρὸς τὸ εὐλογῆσαι, (p. 96). Unfortunately he does not mention the dishes of the first course. ἐπιτελεῖται ἡ συνήθης τάξις τοῦ κλητωρίου, καὶ ἀπὸ τοῦ ὀπτομίνσου ἐξέρχονται οἱ ἀρτοκλῖναι, (p. 293). See also Vol. II., pp. 304, 600, 865. μίνσος τῶν ὀπτωμένων vel τῶν ὀπτῶν. Meursii, *Glossarium*, s.v. μίνσος ; Byzantios Kπόλις., Vol. III., p. 158.

[1] *Ibid.*, pp. 602, 603.

[2] Cons. P., Vol. I., p. 277. τοῦ τὴν ἐπιστασίαν ἔχοντος τῶν εἰς τράπεζαν κεκλημένων, ὃν ἀτρικλίνην [for ἀρτοκλίνην] φημίζουσι. Genesios, p. 31.

[3] *Brumalia* was the name given by the Byzantines to the festivals at Christmas and on S. Basil's Day (January 1), which lasted till the Feast of Lights (Epiphany).

was laid in the Aristeterion for three courses or thereby [Reiske, "pro tribus fere missibus," and compare his Note, Vol. II., p. 865], at which were present those who usually banquet with the Emperor, his most intimate friends and relatives, the magistri, praepositi, proconsuls, patrician and private protospatharioi, and some others known to the Emperor. In the magnificent Hall of Justinian, another private table was laid, for six courses or thereby, at which the young Emperor and the other magistrates, proconsuls, etc., sat in order of precedence." "The Emperor goes out and sits at his august table in the Hall of Justinian." The same writer states that games and players were sometimes introduced at the command of the Emperor.[1]

The great banquets held here were on the 11th day of the Nativity, at the Feast of Lights (Epiphany), on the day of the Annunciation (March 25.), on Easter-day, Pentecost, S. Elias' day (July 21.), The Transfiguration (August 6), S. Basil the Emperor's day (August 29), and on the 8th of September (the nativity of Our Lady).[2] I have thought it well to note the above passages from Constantine Porphyrogennetos, for from him alone do we learn any particulars about the Aristeterion. I shall speak more fully of them in a later chapter.

---

[1] Cons. P., Vol. I., pp. 604, 416, 417. On p. 581 he mentions the γρυτάριον τοῦ ἀριστητηρίου, which Reiske translates, gryparium seu pannus figuris vulturum refertus. Concerning the army of cooks 'and waiters of the Emperor Theodosios, see Zosimos, p. 205,

[2] Cons. P., Vol. I., pp. 753, 757, 762, 773, 775, 777, 779, 780, 782.

Only those who have studied the Palace of the Byzantine Emperors from the writings of native and other historians, can estimate the value of the discovery of remains by which we can fix with any degree of certainty the site of each of the buildings mentioned in history. In the opinion of some, it is impossible now, after the destruction of these Palaces and the change of so many names, to fix the site of the numerous buildings within the precincts. It is comparatively easy for any writer guided by Constantine Porphyrogennetos—as was the painstaking Labarte—to picture the dimensions and many decorations of the Palace; but such sketches are, in my opinion, little better than fanciful.

Having given some account of the Numera and the neighbouring Aristeterion, which, I have no hesitation in saying, were both within the Palace precinct, I shall describe some more remains, which have fortunately been preserved, and which guide us like beacons to a more correct localisation of the buildings. I am convinced that in this, the broadest part of the area occupied by the Byzantine Palace, there are preserved, under the Turkish houses[1] and their high-walled gardens, many more ancient remains, which might throw light upon our history, if only investigation and undistracted study of them were possible. Future writers will, I am sure, describe the place better than I have done. But unfortunately, these remains are being daily des-

---

[1] All this neighbourhood is now inhabited by the Turks.

13

troyed and sold by the poverty stricken inhabitants, under the eyes of a government which regards them with indifference.

After the Numera I shall describe other remains which illustrate very many parts of the Palace.

The above mentioned Aristeterion was within the great and famous Hall of Justinian, which as it was connected with other buildings, I shall describe in the proper place, that we may better understand its position.

REMAINS OF THE HALL OF JUSTINIAN.

The modern *Arista* road, which runs from the walls at the south side of the Numera, and continues eastwards for about 50 paces, is interrupted by some houses belonging to wealthy Turks. Near this road is a wooden house with an extensive garden behind, to which the occupants descend by a flight of steps. I often entered this house, which had for some time been under repair, and was then unoccupied, and under the considerate guidance of the architect—a Greek—I inspected all the great ruins preserved in this considerable area. On the south side of the garden there is a very thick and lofty wall, which divides the property from the neighbouring house. The masonry of this wall is Byzantine—stone and brick in alternate layers. Its direction is the same as that of the street *Arista*, that is from west to east. In the lower part of the garden, which slopes steeply, its height appeared to me to be about 15 m. (50 ft.) In the middle of it some buttresses and abutments are preserved, the remains of an ancient arch, the other side of which probably rested on a parallel wall now completely destroyed. This wall could not be seen from the road. Its length is about 30 m. (98 ft).

To the north of this wall, and under the large patched up house, is a great subterranean vault resting on square pillars. It is plastered in some places, and is clearly of Byzantine construction. This crypt has windows facing the garden, and a door on a level with the thoroughfare. On entering the house from the higher *Arista Sokaghí*, one arrives on the dome, and then descends by many steps into the vault, whence one gets on to the level thoroughfare by the above-mentioned door. The vault is at present occupied by vendors of provisions and olives.

These remains are both, as I said Byzantine, portions of the Palace. I think that the wall is a portion of the Hall of Justinian. To the vault I shall revert later.

REMAINS OF THE PHAROS.

Proceeding north-east from the Numera, one sees a great and lofty Byzantine building, on the west side of which is built a large wooden house. The eastern side, which looks to the Propontis and the opposite shore of Anatole, is entirely free from houses or other buildings connected with it. The masonry is Byzantine.[1] A small garden, which sets

---

[1] Gyllius, *De Topographia*, lib. ii., cap. 6.

off the size and height of the wall, surrounds this side. Inside it there are inscribed bricks confusedly lying together, and broken marbles of Byzantine workmanship, with unlovely designs. The strong foundations which are visible extend under the adjoining Turkish houses. A small wooden house to the north side of this garden, is also built upon the old Byzantine foundations. Only one very narrow entrance is visible near the ground leading from the garden to the recesses of these strong vaults. It is now wholly blocked up with stones and bricks. No other entrance on this side of the garden is visible. From the house access is had to the roof of the building, which is flat, and covered with tiles. Small ancient windows can be seen on the east side. The building is three-storied, and, in spite of its desolate condition, well preserved.

In this building dwells the Turkish proprietor, a cripple, who can hardly drag his swollen feet along. A small mat of rushes and some earthen cooking vessels were all his goods. For a small fee he conducted me not once, but several times, through all the nooks and corners of this mysterious building.

Under the wooden house is a great Byzantine arch, beneath which runs a broad road. The walls on either side of this covered road are rough, showing that there formerly were buildings connected with them, which have been violently pulled down. Here is the western door of the house, by which I always came and went. In the small chamber, lighted by tiny windows, where the old man lives, there is a wooden trap-door. This he raised with difficulty, and giving me candles and matches, bade me descend myself, as he could not follow on account of his crippled feet. I descended alone into the pit, which the light barely illumined, and went through dark foul-smelling passages, and vaults, full of stones and black earth. The preservation and perfect dryness of all these vaults was a marvel. It shows the excellence and uniform solidity of the Byzantine masonry. There is no sign of mortar in these vaults. At the end, the low door in the outer wall—which I mentioned above—leads out of them. This I learnt from the mouth of the old man himself. The last and deepest vault is larger than the others. I frequently went into all of them. They are at present dark, and empty, and contain no Byzantine inscription or mark. The owner never went into them, nor did he know to what use they were formerly put. He only said that they had been built in the time of Constantine. I subsequently visited these newly discovered vaults with some friends, who can bear witness to the accuracy of what I have written.

They are probably identical with those alluded to in the Continuation of Theophanes, where the writer mentions the buildings of Basil the Macedonian. "The same Emperor built the Chapel of S. John the Divine, together with the airy and sunny marble paved walk, which runs as far as the Pharos, and also the very strong houses to the east of it, one of which is a treasury, and the other serves for a wardrobe."[1] It, is however, more prob-

---

[1] P. 336.

able that they are the buildings described by Propokios. " There was a subterranean building in the Palace, secure and difficult of access, like a Hades, where she [Theodora] confined and kept in ward many of those who had offended her. Buzes was accordingly cast into this dungeon."[1] Possibly some portion of them was used as a prison in the reign of certain of the Emperors. No other such vaults are mentioned, except in the palace of the Boukoleon ; and I do not think that it was built in the time of Propokios. It was enlarged and adorned by Nikephoros Phokas.

After inspecting all this building and the vaults, I went through the house built above them, under the guidance of the old Turk. Beneath part of the vaults, there runs, as I have said, a broad road. At the entrance to the house there is a more recent vault. From the upper storey one comes on to the roof of the building through a large room, which covers a great part of it. I found nothing more of importance in this house, every portion of which I inspected under the guidance of the excellent old Turk, who was a friend of the family which occupied it. The view from the roof of the building was marvellous. All Anatole, Skoutari, Chalkedon, and the mountains as far as Olympus could be clearly distinguished. Besides, owing to the height of the house, all the vessels sailing past the Akropolis could be easily observed.

I have spoken at great length about this hither-

---

[1] Vol. III., p. 30.

to unnoticed building, for in my opinion it is the Pharos of the Palace, which is mentioned very frequently. Beside it stood the famous Chrysotriklinos, where so many ceremonies were performed, and the Emperors displayed to foreign ambassadors their untold wealth, the gold and silver vessels, and the Golden Throne. These vaults, strong and dry, were, I am persuaded, the places where these treasures were stored in safety. A public road runs through this quarter to the right side of the tower, and then turns to the left and passes through the broadest vault. This arcade was built large and solidly for a foundation to the Chrysotriklinos. So, too, in the case of Blachernai and the Boukoleon, the Emperors founded the palaces on vaults that they might overlook the sea and the plain. These vaults subsequently served as prisons. Without this arcading, the Chrysotriklinos and the Emperor's bed chamber, would have been the most insignificant of the Palace buildings, buried behind the Pharos, which for the convenience of the shipping rose to a great height. Inside a Turkish garden on the north side of this vault, where the Gallery of the Forty Saints formerly stood, there are great ruins, which I was never able to inspect.

This building, commonly called the Pharos, has been preserved till our day on account of the solidity of the walls and its strong foundations. Beside it on the right hand, lay the Church of Our Lady of the Pharos which often figures in the history of the Empire. " In the Chapel of our

most Holy Lady, which is called the Pharos."[1]   The
building was called the Pharos for the following
reason.   In the time of the Romans, when the
Saracens made an incursion from the east, a chain
of signal fires to Constantinople was kindled.   The
lights on the summit of Olympus were taken up by
Korhizos, and Moukilos, after them by S. Aux-
entios[2] called the Watch Tower, behind Chalkedon,
and then the light on the terrace of the Pharos—
or, as the Byzantines called it, Our Lady of the
Pharos—was kindled.   This practice prevailed until
the reign of Theophilos son of Michael, when, for the
reason which Constantine Porphyrogennetos gives,
it was discontinued, but only for a short time.   According to the Continuation of Theophanes, the
Pharos is so called because, "a fire is regularly
lighted at night to guide safely to the haven."
Possibly it may have served both purposes.   As a
watch-fire the Pharos was anciently needless, for
when it was built the Saracens were not in the
East.   No writer mentions its erection.   Probably
it was in the time of Severus or even earlier.   On
the terrace of the Pharos there dwelt *Dietarii,*

---

[1] Genesios, p. 7 ; Cons. P., Vol. I., p. 492. Our Lady of the Pharos
is not to be confounded with Our Lady of the Forum (τοῦ Φόρου) which
was in the Forum Boarium. See Theophanes Con., p. 339.

[2] Now *Kaïs-dagh* or the Hill of the Lash. The learned Reiske is far
wrong when he says (Cons. P., Vol, II., p. 572) that this hill was beside
Mount Olympus in Bithynia. It is four miles east of Chalkedon, now
Kadi-kioï. G. Kedrenos, Vol. II., p. 174. Anciently many monasteries
were built on this mountain, the ruins of which still exist. Μοναστὴν
. . . ὑπὸ τὴν τοῦ μεγίστου ὄρους. ἱδρυμένον ἀκρώρειαν, ὃ καλοῦσι τοῦ ὁσίου
Αὐξεντίου λόφον, Nikephoros Patr., p. 81.

watchmen specially assigned to the work,[1] keeping watch there continually, and having no connection with the Palace.[2]

Every one who has examined this building, is persuaded that the rulers of Constantinople could have selected no more suitable place with a view to the safety of their city. On the whole, it seems evident that near this building stood the Church of Our Lady of the Pharos. I cannot endorse the statement of the eminent Byzantios that "probably Theophilos demolished this church."[3] He stopped the beacons kindled on it, and that for a time only, for after this date, the Pharos and Our Lady of the Pharos are often mentioned.

REMAINS OF THE MANAURA.

Not far to the north of this building in a street called *Toprak Sokaghi,* or the Street of the Mound, there are preserved colossal Byzantine buildings so dilapidated that it is difficult to tell what purpose they served. They are two storeys high, built according to the Byzantine custom with dark

---

[1] Διαιτάριος, Atriensis διαιτάρχης—τοῖς ἐν τῷ μεγάλῳ παλατίῳ ἐπὶ τούτῳ ἀφωρισμένοις διαιταρίοις δῆλην ἐτίθη τὴν προτομήν, Meursii, *Glossarium*; Cons. P., Vol. II., p. 43. The dietarii of the Church of Our Lady, of the Manaura, of the Hall of the Nineteen Conches, and of S. Stephen in the Daphne, are also mentioned. *Ibid.*, Vol. I., pp. 800, 802, 805.

[2] Ἐν τῷ μεγάλῳ παλατίῳ κατὰ τὸ ἡλιακὸν τοῦ Φάρου, Theophanes Con., pp. 19, 197, 682; Cons. P., Vol. II., p. 43. There was another Pharos at the northern entrance of the Euxine, ἐπεὶ δε πλησίον τοῦ ἐν τῷ Εὐξείνῳ Πόντῳ φάρου ἐγένοντο (φάρος δὲ καλεῖται ἀφίδρυμά τι ᾧ πυρσὸς ἐπιτίθεται πρὸς ὁδηγίαν τοῖς ἐν νυκτὶ παροδίταις, Theophanes Con., p. 746. The dietarii ἀπὸ τῆς πόλεως καὶ τοῦ στενοῦ were exempt from military service, Cons. P., Vol. I., p. 699. Probably they had quarters in the lower rooms of the building. [3] Κτολις., Vol. I., p. 214.

narrow passages. Milch kine and their keepers live in the vaults. The floors are covered with dung and foul water. A little open courtyard where the cattle are kept contains inscribed bricks which have fallen from the walls, and some broken fragments of marble. Guided by one of the cowherds I went through all these lofty vaults. I then went by another way to the top of them. Here unfortunately poor Turkish houses are built, which I was not allowed to enter. I observed nothing of importance on this building, which is now roofless. I was convinced by a long study of the structure, especially of the underground portion, that a great Byzantine building must have been erected on these vaults; but whether it was civil or ecclesiastical my frequent examination did not inform me. Above the vaulting, level with the ground, no signs of Byzantine work are to be seen. Any structure that was once here has utterly disappeared. Buildings such as these vaults were never erected by the Byzantines except for monasteries. This, however, was not a monastery, for the vaults of such as have been preserved, have all marble pillars. It was not a church, for so great a number of narrow passages are not found in Byzantine churches. Besides, there is no sign of sanctuary or altar in them. They are strong vaults built to support a great, widespread building, forming a separate part of the Palace. I conclude that it was the famous Manaura, which was separated from the other Palace buildings by an open space very often mentioned by Constantine VII. in his account of the ceremonies. The size of the building, and its distance from the Chrysotriklinos are in complete accordance with his accounts.

One day as I was inspecting these ruins with great attention, two Turks who lived near approached me, and asked for information about the building. They told me that the ruins, in common with the entire neighbourhood, were formerly called *Dhomoúz dhamí* (the pigstye). This reminded me that Constantine Porphyrogennetos mentions a part of the Palace called Delphax. Unfortunately the passages where he notices it do not aid us much in determining the site, and the place is mentioned by no one else.

He writes :[1] " The triple door of the Onopodium is guarded and the doors of the Delphax." " Or else as the Emperor is going to the Hippodrome, he stands before the Delphax, and speaks." "And the benches having been placed before the Delphax the magistrates sat and began to consult about the candidate for the throne." " On the fourth of April in the fifth indiction, Tatian being magister, the Emperor ordered a silentium, and a convention,

---

[1] Vol. I., pp. 234, 391, 421, 433. Δέλφαξ χοιρίδιον, δελφάκιον χοιρίδιον, Hesychios. Δελφάκιον τὸ τοῦ χοίρου βρέφος ἢ τὸ γουροῦνι, Kyrillos, *Glossarium;* see Meursii *Glossarium, s. v.* γουρούνιον. Byzantios (Vol. I., p. 204) gives the name Delphax to the Aristeterion beside the Chrysotriklinos, on the authority of Du Cange. " Le Delphicum où les Empereurs prenoient leur repas appellé pour cette raison par *Anna Comnena* ἀριστεῖον." *Histoire de l'Empire de Constantinople sous les Empereurs Français,* Venice, 1729, part i., p. 152. These writers confuse the Aristeterion of the Chrysotriklinos, the private banquetting hall of the Emperor, with the Aristeterion of the great Hall of Justinian.

and the schools and all the army to gather together to the Delphax . . . not in the hippodrome but in the Delphax."

Prokopios writes :—"The Romans call the place Delphix, not in their own language, but using the ancient Greek name." "The Romans call the tripod Delphix, since it was first at Delphi and then at Byzantion, and wherever the Emperor's couch is, they call the house Delphix."[1]

Unfortunately these words of Prokopios and Constantine do not give us any precise information about the site of the Delphax. We can only say that it was beside the Onopodium and the Consistory, opposite the Manaura. Later on in our account of the Palace, I think we shall find that its site was not in the Manaura, but in a part of the Palace near it. I should think that it was a place beside the Onopodium, within the Gallery of the Lord. Unfortunately Constantine Porphyrogennetos is the only writer who gives any indication of its site. Labarte says nothing about it. Such a building as this, and so near the Palace, certainly was not a pigstye. The Turkish name is derived from the Delphax which was somewhere opposite, and clearly determines the site of the latter opposite the Manaura.[2]

---

[1] Vol. I., p. 395. I think that Prokopios is wrong in calling every couch Delphix. The Delphix has no connection with the Delphax of Constantine VII. and the Byzantines. The name Delphax, like many more Byzantine terms, has descended from an ancient building which stood there before the erection of the Palace.

[2] The Turkish names of a great number of places in Constantinople and its environs throw light on many passages of the Byzantine historians.

REMAINS OF THE BOUKOLEON.

We have now to consider other remains of the Palace which were discovered in 1872 by the excavators of the Thracian railway, that from the study of all the remains we may fill up, as far as possible, the site of the Palace.

Near the sea-wall of the Palace precincts, in a place called Intzele Kiosk,[1] the workmen uncovered vaults of great size, the arches of which were 13 metres (42 ft.) above the sea-level, and four or five metres (13 or 16 ft.) below the ground. A large and exceedingly strong wall running from west to east, divided the place into two unequal portions. From these chambers, which till then had been completely covered by a gently rising mound, a narrow underground passage led into another great vault beside the sea, still in excellent preservation. This vault is now used as a workshop by some Armenian blacksmiths. It looks more like a cave than an artificially built vault. It is accessible to all from the shore ; but the narrow passage leading to the larger vaults has been blocked up. At the north side there is another vault, which probably served as the prison for the Palace.[2]

In May 1872, when many chambers had already been demolished (for the railway, unfortunately, was to run right through them), and when the mound lying above them had been all removed, the

---

[1] *I.e.*, the Pearl Hall.

[2] N. Ch........ . ...

foundations of a large Byzantine building which
rested on these vaults, were brought to light.
These foundations were parallel with the sea wall
of the Palace. The length of either side was 98·88
metres (321 ft.) and the breadth 17 metres (55 ft.).
The western side of the foundations was slightly
recessed for a great part of its length, and opposite
it, I observed two steps lying in their original
position, 2.76 metres (9 ft.) apart. The breadth of
them was about 0·76 metres (2 ft. 6 in.). The area
of the building was about 1670·76 sq. metres, (1962
sq. yds.).

Some days after this, when the workmen had
broken up these strong and well built walls with
pickaxe and gunpowder, they discovered a great
heap of heavy hewn marbles in the northern
extremity of the vaults. They consisted of marble
slabs, and fragments of every shape and size, which
had fallen from the building above, as if it had
experienced a severe earthquake, and the walls and
the marbles had fallen into this hole, which had
been afterwards covered by the ruins of the arches.
In this pit four large, and six smaller capitals
were found, and many steps, the heavier of which
were similar to the two I mentioned outside the
building. From the same place two marble slabs
2·76 metres (9 ft.) long, 1·07 metres (3 ft. 5 in.)
broad, and 0·23 metre (9 in.) thick, were with much
labour recovered. Only one side was ornamented.
Among the decorations could be distinguished a
lion's and an ox's head, executed with great spirit.

Similar smaller heads appeared on other fragments.[1] As soon as I saw the lion and the ox on these fragments, and the varied ornamentation, I was convinced they were relics of the Palace of the Boukoleon, celebrated by native and foreign writers, which anciently stood here.[2] The situation of the building shows that it was not a church.[3]

The vaults, which were shortly after demolished, were prisons, and communicated with the great vault on the shore. The Continuation of Theophanes[4] says " But Theophilos setting these oaths at naught, places Theophobos in a certain prison beneath the Boukoleon, and orders him to be guarded." Skylitses writes " A prison below the Boukoleon." George the Monk,[5] gives the following account of Theophilos. "Before his death, this Emperor accursed of God, having held a secret Senate of men likeminded with himself about Theophobos the Persian, . . . brought him into the Palace, and kept him beside him. And when the Persians

---

[1] All these marble ornaments were conveyed to the Imperial Museum of Constantinople, where they are now preserved.

[2] Ἔτυχεν ἄνωθεν ἑστὼς τῶν βασιλείων οἴκων
ἔνθα γλυφεῖσα δεξιῶς μάρμαρος χιονόχρους
βοῦν μεγαλόπλευρον τυποῖ, καὶ λέοντα μορφάζει
ἐπιπηδῶντα τῇ βοΐ, καὶ πίνοντα τοῦ φόνου·
καὶ γέγονε τὰ γλύμματα ταῦτα τῷ τόπῳ κλῆσις.

C. Manasses, v. 4862.

[3] This palace, so often mentioned by the Crusaders, whose leaders lived there, was at that time the most magnificent of the palaces. "Ville-Hardouin etend parler du *Grand Palais*, qui estoit assis sur la rive de la Propontide, et estoit de son temps nommé le *Palais de Bucoléon.*" Du Cange, *Hist.*, part i., p. 152.

[4] P. 136 ; Bυ̕. Μελ., p. 105.

[5] Theophanes Con., p. 810.

sought to know what had happened to him, the Emperor sent Petrona the Augusta's brother, and a logothetes, and cut off the head of Theophobos. Then they persuaded the Persians that he was in the Palace with the Emperor. When the Emperor miserably died of dysentery, his wretched body was borne to the Church of the Holy Apostles, and the body of Theophobos they secretly conveyed through the Boukoleon to the neighbourhood of the house of Narses, in the place now called the Theophobeia,[1] and deposited it there."[2] Other writers of the Continuation say "He sent Theophobos to the recesses of the Boukoleon and confined him." "He places Theophobos in a very gloomy dungeon beneath the Boukoleon."[3]

The name Boukoleon is corrupted from the Latin *Bucca leonis,*[4] and in the later period, the Byzantines took it as if from βοῦς and λέων, and hence the heads of these animals sculptured on the fragments found.

From the study of these ruins, especially the steps and capitals, the architect K. Demades has reconstructed the palace. From this sketch, a very faithful representation of the whole building, we get some idea of the appearance of the Imperial palaces. Further on we shall give some account

---

[1] Byzantios (Vol. I., p. 139) places the monastery of the Theophobeia on the Asiatic shore of the Bosphoros, in a village now called *Kusghuntzik.*

[2] Theophanes Con., p. 809.

[3] Genesios, p. 60; G. Kedrenos, Vol. II., p. 139.

[4] It is sometimes called *Os Leonis* by the Latin writers. Riant, *Exuviae Sacrae,* Vol. II., p. 235.

of its erection, and of the many places where it appears in the history of the Empire.

Near this palace, to the South, was the harbour of the Boukoleon. Here the Emperors took their departure by the galleys called chelandia or dromoi, either to the church of the Studium or of Our Lady at Blachernai at public displays.[1] At the festival which took place in the Sigma, and in the mystic fountain of the Triconchos. "All those invited go to their own abodes through the calidarium, and the rowers of the Imperial barge go down to the harbour of the Boukoleon, and take their stand where the vessel is."[2] I think this is the harbour which Pachymeres means when he writes, "some too inside the harbour at the Pharos,"[3] because there was no other harbour near here, to the East of the Pharos.

The palace of the Boukoleon was adorned by Constantine VII. Porphyrogennetos with representations of animals collected from various places.[4]

THE PAPIAS.

In the former chapter, I spoke of the Palace gates. The chief janitor of the Palace was called the

---

[1] Καὶ ὁ βασιλεὺς εἰσέρχεται ἀπὸ τὸ παλάτιον εἰς τὸν βασίλειον δρόμωνα μετὰ τῆς οἰκείας αὐτοῦ θεραπείας. Cons. P., Vol. I., p. 560. [Δρόμωνες et] δρομάδες autem sunt quas Sidonius cursorias appellat. G. Kodinos, (annot.) p. 249. See my Βυζαντιναὶ Μελέται, pp. 112, 117, where I have described the harbour of the Boukoleon.

[2] Cons. P., Vol. I., p. 601. προς τὸ τοῦ παλατίου νεώριον ἐν τῷ Βουκολέοντι. G. Kedrenos, Vol. II., p. 292.

[3] Vol. I., p. 391.

[4] Theophanes Con., p. 447.

Papias,[1] sometimes the Great Domestic Papias.[2] The name comes from the Arabic *Bab*, a gate, *Babi*, janitor.[3] Towards the end of the Empire, according to Kodinos Kouropalates, the office was a sinecure.

The Palace was not opened early, and was shut at evening. At some festivals the courtiers entered at night.[4] At other times "he opened the Palace very soon," and at others in the evening. "On the evening of the Sabbath of Lazarus, the Palace was opened, and the whole senate entered."[5] On certain occasions, the courtiers entered through the night (παννύχιοι), and the Palace was opened very early. In the reign of Constantine VII. it was securely closed all night.[6] Hence in his writings we continually meet with the phrase "when the palace opens."[7] By this he does not mean the whole Palace, but the palace of the Chrysotriklinos, the more private residence of the Emperor. On

---

[1] Προέρχονται πάντες ἐν τῷ παλατίῳ, καὶ ἀνοίξαντος τοῦ Παπίου. Cons. P., Vol. I., p. 171. Cf. pp. 519, 525, 550, 566, 601. G. Kedrenos, Vol. II., p. 18, ὁ παπίας τοῦ παλατίου εἰσεκόμισεν αὐτάς. C. Manasses, 4696—

   Πρὸς τὸν τῶν οἴκων φύλακα τὸν ἐν τοῖς ἀνακτόροις
   Παπίαν λέγομεν αὐτὸν κατὰ Ρωμαίων γλῶσσαν.

[2] Cons. P., Vol. I., p. 6.

[3] Sometimes also written Παππίας. Kodinos Kour., pp. 12, 28, 35, 188; Theophanes Con., p. 37; Byzantios Κπολις., Vol. III., p. 83. His wife was called Παπίαινα. Acta et Diplomata, Vol. I., p. 18. Some derive the name from πάπας or πάππας. Kodinos Kour, p. 188.

[4] Cons. P., Vol. I., pp. 108, 143, 161, 162.

[5] Ibid., p. 170; Theophanes Con., p. 619. [The Sabbath of the Resurrection of Lazarus is the Saturday before Palm Sunday. Tr.]

[6] Cf. Cons. P., Vol. I., p. 601. Luitprand has some remarks on the hour of the opening of the Palace. Hist., lib. v., 21.

[7] Vol. I., pp. 72, 99, 170.

Easter Monday, the officers of the Palace met "very early" in the chambers of the Triconchos, and proceeding to the Chrysotriklinos opened the palace. The palace so often mentioned in the accounts of processions is the Chrysotriklinos.

The Papias of the Great Palace bore as a badge of office a bunch of keys, which on state occasions he waved in front of the guest. "The Papias comes out waving his keys, and the silentiarius says Κελεύσατε."[1] Again "The Papias at once lifts his keys from the bench, and goes out shaking them so that they clash, from which all know that the Papias has come out of the Chrysotriklinos, and is ordering the courses."[2] At some festivals he had other functions. At the promotion of a proconsul, when the Emperor is sitting in the throne in the Chrysotriklinos, "the Papias takes a censer, and burns incense as at the promotion of a patrician, and retires."[3] The Papias accompanied the Holy Cross, when it was taken out in the month of August, and carried round through every quarter of the city. He then collected the offerings of the people, a portion of which was given to the second Papias.[4] If through

---

[1] Cons. P., p. 525; Kodinos Kour., p. 188. The silentiaries are defined by Agathias as "those who command silence in the Emperor's presence." Meursii, *Glossarium.*

[2] Cons. P., Vol. I., p. 521. Ὁ δὲ Ἀρδάβασδος δραμὼν πρὸς τὸν παπίαν, καὶ ἄρας ἀπ' αὐτοῦ τὰς κλεῖς βιαίως, ἤνοιξεν. Theophanes Con., p. 685; Leo Grammaticus, p. 252.

[3] Cons. P., Vol. I., p. 255.

[4] Τῷ παπίᾳ τῷ δευτέρῳ. Cons. P., Vol. I., pp. 709, 721, 723, 725; αὐτοῦ δηλονότι τοῦ παπίου καὶ τοῦ δευτέρου, ἱσταμένων εἰς τὸ πρὸς δύσιν δεξιὸν βῆλον. *Ibid.*, p. 520.

illness or any other cause he was unable to go out, the second Papias accompanied it, and they divided the offerings equally. Constantine Porphyrogennetos mentions still further duties of the Papias. In the time of Kantakouzenos, the Papias is mentioned as a military officer. The left wing of eunuchs was under the command of the great Papias.[1] Besides the Papias of the great Palace, the Papias of the Manaura and of the Palace of the Daphne are also mentioned,[2] as well as the doorkeepers of the Palace and the Secreta, who were subordinates of the great Papias.[3]

The Palace of the Byzantine Emperors was not a single building like those of modern European rulers; but consisted of a number of different structures originally founded by Constantine the Great. Others were subsequently added by successive Emperors, or built on the foundations of palaces which had either fallen in ruins, or been pulled down to build larger. Hence the many passages or galleries which connected the various parts of the Palace. Luitprand praises not only

---

[1] J. Kantakouzenos, Vol. I., pp. 262, 436, 465.

[2] Cons. P., Vol. I., p. 725.

[3] *Ibid.*, Vol. I., p. 738. The duties of the Papias, according to Kodinos Kouropalates, p. 35, were "anciently indefinite, now nothing." This writer, who ascribes to Constantine the greater part of the buildings of the subsequent Emperors Justinian, Justin, Theophilos and Basil, described the antiquities of Constantinople when her power was on the wane, at a time when most of her buildings had fallen in ruins, and only their names lingered in the mouths of the people. The student of these writers must bear in mind the density of their ignorance. In the course of this work I shall often allude to the incoherent and astonishing statements of Kodinos to shew how ignorant were the historians of the last age.

the splendour, but also the number of the palaces.[1] Within the Palace precincts, the Emperors also built many churches and chapels, where the majority of the ceremonies detailed by Constantine Porphyrogennetos were performed. These palaces are often referred to collectively as τὸ παλάτιον.[2] For a clearer understanding of them I shall divide the palaces into two classes :—

1.—Those which were connected together, and
2.—Those which were detached.

The first class I subdivide as follows :—

1. The Palace of the Chrysotriklinos.
2. The Palace of the Triconchos.
3. The Palace of the Daphne.

Thus, I think, we shall be better able to understand the much confused account of the Byzantine writers.

I may remark that the plan given in this work differs greatly from those given by Labarte, and in consequence my classification of the palace buildings is not the same as his.

The Palace of the Chrysotriklinos.

THE CHRYSOTRIKLINOS.

This, the most magnificent of the Imperial buildings, lay to the West of, *i.e.* above, the Pharos, which is still standing, and was anciently the most

---

[1] *Hist.*, v., 21.

[2] Πολλάκις δε συνεστιῶνται τοῖς ἄρχουσιν ἐν τῷ παλατίῳ τῶν Βλαχερνῶν, καὶ δείλης εἰσέρχονται εἰς τὸ πάλατιον. Cons. P., Vol. I, p. 580. καὶ τῶν μὲν ἀνακτόρων, ἃ τὸ μέγα παλάτιον λέγεται, κυριεύουσιν ἐξ ἐφόδου στρατιῶται ἐκ τοῦ Βοτανειάτου. M. Attaliates, p. 270.

easterly of the Palace buildings within the precincts. We find no record of any other building to the East of it or the Pharos. Constantine Porphyrogennetos mentions this hall more frequently than any other of the Imperial buildings, and, as I have said above, often refers to it as "the palace."[1] It was built from the foundation by Justin II. nephew of Justinian (d. 578). It had eight chambers communicating with a central hall,[2] which was domed, and lighted by sixteen windows.[3] Here stood the throne of the Emperor,[4] and in front of it, as would appear from Constantine Porphyrogennetos, were brazen rails.[5] On either side of the Emperor sat any princes who might be present.[6] The north side of the Chrysotriklinos was called the left, and the south the right, because at ceremonies and banquets the Emperor always stood or sat facing the East.

At the east end of the left hand side of the Chrysotriklinos was the Chamber or Chapel of S. Theodore,[7] where the Emperors robed on the

---

[1] Ἅπαντες . . . προερχόμενοι ἐν τῷ ἡμικυκλίῳ τῆς ἀψίδος . . . καὶ ἀνοίξαντος τοῦ παλατίου κτλ. Cons. P., Vol. I., p. 143 ; cf. p. 157. ὁ δὲ βασιλεὺς διέρχεται διὰ τοῦ αὐγουστέως, καὶ εἰσέρχεται ἐν τῷ παλατίῳ, p. 159.

[2] Εἰς δὲ τὰς ὀκτὼ καμάρας τοῦ χρυσοτρικλίνου. Cons. P., Vol. I., p. 580 ; G. Kedrenos, Vol. II., p. 48.

[3] Ἄνωθεν δὲ εἰς τὰς ις΄ φωταγωγοὺς καμάρας τοῦ τρούλλου τοῦ αὐτοῦ χρυσοτρικλίνου. Cons. P., Vol. I., pp. 582, 586.

[4] Ἐκάθισεν ἐπὶ τοῦ σέντζου ἐν τῷ χρυσοτρικλίνῳ. Cons. P. ἐν τῷ τοῦ χρυσοτρικλίνου βασιλείῳ θρόνῳ καθιδρύσαντες αὐτόν. M. Attaliates, p. 169. Σέντζος from the Latin *sessus* ; Cons. P., Vol. II., p. 224. This name was given only to the Emperor's throne.

[5] *Ibid.*, Vol. I., p. 283.   [6] *Ibid.*, Vol. I., p. 632.

[7] Ἀπέρχεται ἐν τῷ ναῷ τοῦ Ἁγίου Θεοδώρου ἐν αὐτῷ τῷ χρυσοτρικλίνῳ. Cons. P., Vol. I., p. 440 ; cf. pp. 622, 623.

occasion of a reception.[1]   A curtain was hung
before this chamber.   Here the Emperor's crown
was kept, and Moses' rod was preserved[2] along
with many vessels of gold and other precious
materials, which Constantine Porphyrogennetos
enumerates.[3]   The Emperor's mantle, and all the
rest of his imperial robes were kept in the Chrysotriklinos.[4]

On the right hand side of the Chrysotriklinos
were the silver doors[5] of the Long Room.   It led
into the ἱερὸς κοιτὼν, or Imperial bed-chamber;[6]
from which the Emperor came out through the
Long Room into the hall to meet the nobles, who
on the occasion of ceremonies stood opposite the
chamber waiting to escort him.[7]   In this room he
was guarded by the Chrysotriklinitai and armed
guards.[8]

Another chamber called the Pantheon is mentioned.[9]   One of the eight chambers was the
Phylax or Treasury,[10] where the many golden
vessels, etc. belonging to the hall were probably
kept.   "They go through the Horologion and the

---

1 Cons. P., Vol. I., pp. 115, 119, 244.

2 Cons. P., Vol. I., p. 6.   3 *Ibid.*, Vol. I., pp. 640, 92.

4 *Ibid.*, Vol. I., p. 7.   The attendants were called Chrysotriklinitai.
Ibid., pp. 30, 546.

5 *Ibid.*, Vol. I., p. 124.

6 Cons. P., Vol. I., pp. 22, 585 ; M. Attaliates, pp. 142, 169.

7 Cons. P., Vol. I., p. 175.

8 The editor of Kodinos Kouropalates (p. 186), quotes from Theophanes :
διϋπνισθεὶς [ὁ βασιλεὺς] ἐκάλεσε τὸν παρακοιμώμενον αὐτοῦ.

9 Ἐν τῇ καμάρᾳ τοῦ χρυσοτρικλίνου τῇ οὔσῃ πρὸς τὸ Πάνθεον.   Cons. P.,
Vol. I., pp. 116, 122.   There was also a body of soldiers called the
Pantheon by Kedrenos.   Vol. II., p. 876.

10 Cons. P., Vol. I., pp. 580, 582.

Chrysotriklinos and the Phylax." Thence they
proceeded to the gallery of the Forty Martyrs.[1] At
the promotion of the Zosta Patricia we read:—"The
Præpositus receives the patrician lady, who is to be
promoted, from the guards, where the bright folding
doors are."[2] It is probable that the costly vessels
of the Chrysotriklinos were protected by similar
doors. Possibly this is the Treasury in which Basil
the Macedonian, is said to have left 900 centenaria.[3] In the opinion of Reiske, this Treasury
was identical with the Church of our Lady of the
Pharos.[4] The many gold vessels preserved here
are enumerated in the Continuation of Theophanes
(p. 173).

To the East of the Chrysotriklinos was a ἡλιακὸς
or *solarium*, an open terrace, by which the church of
Our Lady of the Pharos could be approached without going through the Chrysotriklinos. At the promotion of the Zosta Patricia,[5] after the Liturgy in S.
Sophia, the patrician lady "enters the Palace through
the Eros and the Colonnade of the Forty Martyrs,
crosses the Terrace of the Chrysotriklinos, and enters
into the Pharos,"[6] "The Magistri and Patricians,
and the rest of the Senate, with the Officers of the

---

[1] I think that the Phylax beside the chamber of the Pantheon was a
door leading to the Chrysotriklinos.

[2] Cons. P., Vol. I., p. 257.

[3] Theophanes Con., p. 253. Constantine Porphyrogennetos wrote the
life of Basil.   [4] Cons. P., Vol. II., p. 618.

[5] Cons. P., Vol. I., pp. 257, 711.   οὕτω βαρβάρως ὠνομάζετο εἰς τὴν
Βυζαντινὴν αὐλὴν, ἀντι τοῦ Ζώστρια ἢ Ζώστειρα, Γαλλ. Dame d'Autour
Koraes, Posthumous Writings, Vol. I., p. 26. The Augusta had only one
Zosta.   Meursii, *Gloss s.v.*; Le Beau, *Hist. du Bas Empire*, Vol. XIV.,
p. 421.   [6] Cons. P., Vol. I., p. 261.

Bedchamber,[1] take their place on the Terrace of the Chrysotriklinos if it is fine weather, if not, they stand inside the Chrysotriklinos."[2] The door leading to this Terrace was called Monothyros or Monothyron.[3] Over the door was the picture of God in human form sitting on a throne.[4] On either side of this door was another also leading out to the Terrace.[5] These Porphyrogennetos calls the eastern doors.[6] Another set of three doors led to the Tripeton, a piece of ground lying to the west of the Chrysotriklinos. These doors which were covered with silver,[7] along with the silver table in the neighbouring Aristeterion were made by Constantine VII.[8]

The great golden table in the Chrysotriklinos was oblong. The Emperor and Patriarch had their places at the upper end of the table looking to the East, at the other end the guests gathered in a body[9] as for instance, at the banquet on Easter Monday. The Patriarch usually waited for the Emperor in the chamber next to the Pantheon.[10]

When the courtiers banquetted with the Emperor in the Chrysotriklinos, they sat at separate tables, while the Emperor sat at the golden table.[11] In

---

1 Οἱ τοῦ κουβουκλείου were the eunuchs and their chief, the praepositus. Meursii, *Glossarium.* The term κουβούκλειον denoted all the courtiers. The word is the Latin *Cubiculum.*

2 Cons. P., Vol. I., p. 137.   3 *Ibid.*, p. 289.

4 *Ibid.*, p. 519.   5 *Ibid.*, p. 290.

6 *Ibid.*, p. 592.   7 *Ibid.*, pp. 90, 92, 95. 581.

8 Theophanes Con., p. 450.

9 Cons. P., Vol. I., pp. 94, 580.   10 *Ibid.*, p. 122.

11 Ἐπὶ δὲ ταῖς κατὰ τῶν καμαρῶν τραπέζαις—ἐπὶ δὲ τῶν κάτω τραπεζῶν. *Ibid.*, pp. 768, 769, 770, 771, 772.

the Tripeton there were additional or side-tables, which were used when a great many guests were invited.[1] "In the chamber of the Chrysotriklinos which leads to the Tripeton, two side-tables stand, and another is brought in if the Emperor orders it. The one is placed on the right, the other on the left of the chamber."[2]

Only five dignitaries had the right of dining with the Emperor at his own table in the Chrysotriklinos—the Patriarch, the Cæsar, the Nobilissimus, the Kouropalates and the Zosta Patricia.[3] The seat of honour was on the Emperor's left.[4] The same order was observed in the Hall of Justinian. The Patriarch, however, sat with the Emperor at his table on all occasions.[5]

Theophilos made a silver table, which C. Porphyrogennetos often mentions, "for the accomodation of the guests and the adornment of the Palace," in which so many foreigners and courtiers feasted with the Emperor.[6] A great chandelier hung from the centre of the Hall over the table.[7] The famous golden tree so often mentioned in accounts of the Palace was constructed by Theophilos. "Birds sitting on the branches sung by some mechanism,

---

[1] Cons. P., Vol. I., p. 95.   [2] *Ibid.*, p. 70.

[3] *Ibid.*, pp. 726, 773, 775.   [4] *Ibid.*, pp. 92, 726, 739.

[5] Καὶ τοῦ πατριάρχου ὡς ἔθος καθεσθέντος παρ αὐτῷ ἐπὶ δίφρου. J. Kantakouzenos, Vol. I., pp. 64-65 ; ἐν τῷ ὑπερλάμπρῳ χρυσοτρικλίνῳ, Theophanes Con., p. 246.

[6] Εἰσερχόμενοι καθέζονται ἐπὶ τοῦ χρυσοτρικλίνου κάθως εἴθισται αὐτοῖς, καὶ μετὰ μακρὸν δίδονται μίνσαι. Cons. P., Vol. I., p. 124.

[7] *Ibid.*, p. 93 ; ἐν τῷ μέσῳ τοῦ χρυσοτρικλίνου κατέναντι τοῦ μεσαιτάτου πολυκανδήλου, p. 624 ; τὸ δὲ ἔλαιον τοῦ πολυκανδήλου τοῦ κατὰ τὸ μέσον κρεμαμένου τοῦ χρυσοτρικλίνου, p. 724.

the air being supplied by concealed passages."[1]
The walls were ornamented with mirrors and
coloured tiles "affording the more pleasure to the
guests owing to the delicious nature of the viands."
Besides making the silver doors, Constantine VII.
ornamented the walls and ceiling of the Chrysotriklinos with flowers and leaves framed in silver
circles.[2] In the great Tiring-room (κοσμήτης) of this
palace, tablets and great screens of graven silver
were hung on the windows.[3]

In the time of Andronikos the elder, when
ceremonies were performed in the Chrysotriklinos,
it could not contain all that were present.[4]

Luitprand calls it the most magnificent part of
the Palace of Constantinople.[5]

After this account of the Chrysotriklinos, it will
be easy to understand the daily life of the inmates
of the Palace, which Constantine Porphyrogennetos
has described with so much minuteness. Early in
the morning, the attendants for the week bear the
Emperor's skaramangion from the wardrobe, and

---

[1] Theophanes Con., p. 627 ; C. Manasses, vv. 5265-72.

[2] Luitprand writes as follows of Constantine Porphyrogennetos (*Hist.*,
iii., 37) : Sane τὴν ζωγραφίαν zographiam, id est picturam, perpulchre
exercebat.—τὴν δε τῆς ζωγραφίας τέχνην τοσοῦτον ἀκριβῶς ὁ ἀνὴρ ἠπίστατο
ὡς οὐκ οἶμαι τῶν πρὸ αὐτοῦ ἢ τῶν μετ' αὐτόν. Theophanes Con., p. 450.

[3] Cons. P., Vol. I., p. 582.

[4] Theophanes Con., p. 456 ; Pachymeres, Vol. II., p. 366.

[5] Chrysotriclinon id est aureum triclinium quae praestantior pars est.
Hist., v. 21. In hoc igitur Romanus aureo triclino . . . potentis-
sime degens caeteras partes palatii genero Constantino filiisque suis
Stephano et Constantino distribuerat. *Legatio ad Nic. Ph.*, cap. 9 ; G.
Kedrenos, Vol. I., p. 690. C. Porphyrogennetos mentions a χρυσοστόριον
or χρυσοιστόριον (Vol. I., pp. 710, 748). Reiske conjectures that it was
sala plena statuis aliisque imaginibus aureis. *Ibid.*, Vol. II., p. 831.

place it on the bench outside the silver doors. After the first hour, the chief of the servants comes, and with the key knocks thrice on the silver door. The Emperor answers, and the chamberlains bring in the skaramangion and other garments.[1]

CHAPTER VII.

THE PENTAPYRGION.

This was probably part of the gilded furniture of the Chrysotriklinos. The Emperor usually sat on the golden throne in front of it.[2] At his marriage, the officers of the Bedchamber "hung wreaths in the Pentapyrgion, where the Emperor's couch stands."[3] In the account of the reception of the Ambassadors from Amerimne, Constantine Porphyrogennetos gives a most minute description of the decoration of the Chrysotriklinos.[4] Elsewhere he writes, " at the golden table, which stands in the magnificent Chrysotriklinos, where too, the splendid possession of the Pentapyrgion is set forth for honour."[5] "The Chrysotriklinos was arrayed as it usually is, namely with the Pentapyrgion and the Imperial thrones and couches, the golden table, and other things."

The Pentapyrgion was a magnificent structure of wood covered over with gold. It is mentioned also

---

[1] Concerning the attendants of the Chrysotriklinos, the Chrysotriklinitai, see Cons. P., Vol. I., pp. 31, 692 ; Kodinos Kour., p. 202, ὁ προκαθήμενος τοῦ κοιτῶνος. They are very often mentioned by the former writer. The νιψιστιάριος was the attendant on the Emperor at his bath. Cons. P., Vol. I., p. 293.

[2] Cons. P., Vol. I., p. 92.   [3] *Ibid.*, p. 200.

[4] *Ibid.*, p. 580.   [5] *Ibid.*, p. 767.

in connection with the Magnaura.[1] Within and without it was hung a great variety of decorations, golden ornaments, and the Imperial robes. Unfortunately, no one has described its size and construction.[2]

It was originally made by the Emperor Theophilos, as also were the two great golden organs adorned with different coloured stones.[3] On great festivals, a small golden table was placed in the Pentapyrgion. At Easter, if any of the ambassadors of great nations were present, they were specially invited to the table of the Emperor, who sat above them at this small table in the Pentapyrgion, while they sat at the great golden table. On the left of the Pentapyrgion stood a platform with steps on which the Emperor's attendant and his cupbearer stood.[4] On Easter Thursday, the Emperor, when receiving the Patriarch, "sits on the golden throne before the Pentapyrgion."[5]

---

[1] ἐξέθετο δόγμα . . . βασιλικῆς τιμῆς μετασχόντας τῆς οἰασοῦν κατὰ τὴν Μαγναύραν ἤτοι τὸ Πενταπύργιον συναθροισθῆναι. G. Kedrenos, Vol. II., p. 100.

[2] Reiske writes (Cons. P., Vol. II., p. 683): Quid *Pentapyrgium* fuerit, cuius non infrequens Nostro et aliis mentio fit, non constat. [See also p. 171, where he defines it as "Armarium cum quinque turriculis, in quo stabant pendebantve iocalia pretiosissima."—Tr.] Du Cange (*Cpolis. Christ.*, p. 128) thinks that it was a building with five towers belonging only to the Magnaura. It is clear that it could be conveyed from the Chrysotriklinos to the Magnaura.

[3] Theophanes Con., pp. 627. 793.

[4] Cons. P., Vol. I., p. 70. Μιχαὴλ ὁ οἰνοχόος ὃν καὶ τιγκέρνην συνήθως οἱ τῆς βασιλικῆς αὐλῆς ὀνομάζουσιν. Anna Komnena, Vol. I., p. 421.

[5] *Ibid.*, p. 92.

THE TRIPETON.

West of the Chrysotriklinos was the Tripeton,[1] a place very often mentioned by C. Porphyrogennetos. It was connected with the Chrysotriklinos and the Hall of Lausos, down from which latter a flight of steps led—"when the Patriarch is about to descend the stairs of the Lausiakon."[2] It was the approach, or forecourt of the Chrysotriklinos. In his account of the feast of Pentecost, Porphyrogennetos writes, " This too must be noticed, that there stand in the chamber of the Chrysotriklinos, which leads to the Tripeton, two side-tables, and if the Emperor orders, two more extra tables are set down. One stands in the chamber on the right, the other in that on the left."[3] Again " the Emperor enters the Chrysotriklinos through the Tripeton."—"He stands in the bay leading out into the Tripeton,"—"He stands on the threshold of the door leading from the Tripeton to the Lausiakon."[4] From these words it is evident that the Tripeton was an open court between the Hall of Lausos and the Chrysotriklinos, with an entrance to the former, and three doors to the Chrysotriklinos. There is no mention of buildings or other erections in the Tripeton, except the golden organs of which Constantine Porphyrogennetos writes. " At once the organ which stands in the Tripeton begins to sound." Lower down he. again mentions it, and

---

1 I cannot explain the etymology of this word.
2 Cons. P., Vol. 1., p. 91.   3 *Ibid.*, p. 70.
    Ibid., pp. 89, 90, 286.

describes it as "golden."[1] The Tripeton is sometimes also called the Horologion, or the Portico of the Chrysotriklinos.[2] This is the place mentioned in another writer. "The emperor (Romanus Laka-penos), having struck the Patrician Kosmas in the Horologion of the Palace, caused another to be elected in his place."[3] The Horologion was probably similar to that in the Church of S. Sophia. That it stood in the Tripeton is proved beyond doubt by the following passage : "As Bardas Cæsar was going with the procession clad in a purple skaramangion, Damianos a patrician, who guarded the Emperor in his bedchamber, was sitting there [at the Horologion] and did not rise to do him honour. Seeing this the Cæsar was very wroth, and when he entered into the Chrysotriklinos, and sat beside the Emperor, weeping with rage and passion, the latter asked him the cause."[4] Constantine Porphyrogennetos writes, "Up to the portico of the Chrysotriklinos, where the Horologion stands."[5] From this it would appear that the Horologion was above the door leading from the Tripeton to the Chrysotriklinos. As regards the entrance to the Tripeton, the following words of this same author

---

[1] Vol. I., pp. 184, 202. Probably he also refers to this organ on p. 765 : μετὰ τὴν ἐκφώνησιν τοῦ μυστικοῦ ὀργάνου ἐκδιδύσκονται πάντες τὰς ἑαυτῶν στολάς. [2] Cons. P., Vol. I., p. 526.

[3] Theophanes Con., p. 441 ; G. Kedrenos, Vol. II., p. 307.

[4] *Ibid.*, p. 827.

[5] Cons. P., Vol. I., p. 622. This is probably what Manasses alludes to, *v.* 5277—

ἐξαίσιον εἰργάσατο σκεῦος ὡρονομίου,
δι' οὗ παρεῖχε καθορᾶν τῷ βασιλεῖ καθ' ὥραν,
ἐν μέσοις διατρίβοντι τοῖς βασιλείοις οἴκοις.

are unmistakeable; "All having entered into the Hall of Lausos, the praepositus came out, and placed them before the door of the Hall which leads to the portico of the Chrysotriklinos, that is, the Horologion."[1]

ARISTERION OF THE CHRYSOTRIKLINOS.

I mentioned above what Constantine Porphyrogennetos calls the Aristeterion in the great Hall of Justinian, of which we still have a relic in the Turkish name *Arista Sokaghi.* There was also a private Aristeterion of the Emperor beside the Chrysotriklinos, where certain guests feasted with the Emperor. This room lay to the right of the Tripeton, from which a door led to it. C. Porphyrogennetos says in his account of the promotion of a rector:[2] "After this, the praepositi take him to the curtain hanging before the Aristeterion, that is before the bed-chamber, and put his proper robes on him." All this was done in the Aristerion. After this ceremony, "the rector having kissed the feet and knees of the Emperor, the praepositi lead him out through the Horologion into the Lausiakon."

This banquetting hall, too, is the one mentioned in the account of the reception of Elga of Russia. After the banquet in the Chrysotriklinos, dessert was served in the Aristerion.[3] The room had its

---

[1] Vol. I., p. 605. [2] *Ibid.*, pp. 529, 530.
[3] Cons. P., Vol. I., p. 596. καὶ ἡ τοῦ κατὰ 'Ρωμαίων ἐκπλεύσαντος ἄρχοντος τοῦ 'Ρὼς γαμετὴ "Ελγα τοὔνομα . . . παρεγένετο ἐν Κωνσταν-

walls adorned with Bathyinian marble, and all the floor covered with variegated mosaic work." [1]

THE NEW CHAMBER.

In his description of the reception of Elga, Porphyrogennetos also writes: [2] "Her majesty, rising up from the throne, crossed through the Lausiakon and the Tripeton, into the New Chamber, and through it to her own chamber," and rested there. A little after this, her majesty was summoned forth, and ate with the Emperor and his household. After the meal, dessert was served in the Aristerion, when the small golden table was set in the Pentapyrgion. A private door led from the Tripeton into the New Chamber. The ladies of the court entered "in their order from the New Hall to the chamber of the Augusta"; then the courtiers "came in through the Horologion and the Chrysotriklinos." [3]

This bedchamber, which was frequently called the καινούργιον, was built from the foundation by Basil the Macedonian. [4] It had a domed roof supported on a series of sixteen marble pillars. Eight were of green Thessalian marble, six of onychite, which the sculptor had ornamented with vines and animals; the other two were decorated with monograms.

τινουπόλει . . . καὶ βαπτισθεῖσα ἐπ' οἴκου ἀνέδραμε. G. Kedrenos, Vol. II., p. 329 ; C. Porphyrogennetos in his accounts of the reception of Olga, always calls her Elga.

[1] Theophanes Con., p. 145 ; Cons. P., Vol. I., pp. 602, 603, 604.
[2] Vol. I., pp. 596, 597.
[3] *Ibid.*, p. 618.   [4] Theophanes Con., pp. 146, 332.

The walls above the pillars, and the eastern semi-dome were enriched with gold mosaics, representing the builder Basil the Macedonian sitting on a throne "surrounded by his generals, offering him as gifts, the cities which he had taken." On the roof were depicted the labours of Basil, his efforts on behalf of his subjects, and the hardships of his military expeditions. In the middle of the floor was a brilliantly coloured mosaic representing a peacock, framed in Carian marble. In the four corners of the room, which was square, there were four eagles formed of small stones of various colours. These are described as wonderful works of art, which looked as if they were alive and about to fly away. In addition to so much ornament the walls, bore a representation of Basil and his consort Eudokia in their Imperial robes. Beside them were their children, holding books. " By this the artist meant to signify that not only their sons, but also their daughters, were versed in the mysteries of the Holy Scriptures, and were not without a share of the Divine Wisdom." Such were the adornments of this most magnificent bedchamber as far as the ceiling. On this were inscribed the thanks of the parents for their children, and the children's prayers for their father and mother. The Continuation of Theophanes has fortunately preserved them.[3] That of the parents was, " We thank Thee most gracious God, King of kings, that Thou hast surrounded us with children, who thank

---

Thee for the glory of Thy wondrous works. Oh, keep them in Thy will, that none of them transgress Thy commands, that for this too we may bless Thy goodness." The children's ran: "We bless Thee, Word of God, that Thou hast raised our father from the lowly estate of David, and hast anointed him with the oil of Thy Holy Spirit. Keep him with Thy hand, together with her who bare us, granting unto them and us a portion in Thy Heavenly Kingdom."

THE LONG CHAMBER.

This room lay to the right, or the south of the Chrysotriklinos. "They enter privately with him through the Long Chamber to the Church of Our Lady of the Pharos." On the first of January, "their Majesties go privately through the Long Chamber to the narthex of Our Lady of the Pharos."[1]

The principal doors of the Long Chamber were of silver.[2] It had also three other doors, one opposite the narthex of Our Lady of the Pharos, another leading to the sacred bedchamber of the Emperor, and another to that of the Augusta. It was in fact the ante-room of the Emperor's bed-chamber. Here the accubitor kept guard, and with him, the servants, commonly called κοιτωνῖται and χρυσοτρικλινῖται.[3] I am inclined to think that there

---

[1] Cons. P., Vol. I., pp. 119, 137.

[2] Ἐξερχόμενοι τὰς ἀργυρᾶς τοῦ μάκρωνος πύλας, ibid., p. 124.

[3] Paracoemomenos, accubitor. Const. Manass.: παράκοιτον καὶ φύλακα τῆι βασιλείου κλίνης. G. Kedrenos (annot.), Vol. II., p. 925; Cons. P., Vol. I., p. 519; Leo Gramm., p. 250; Byzantios, Krolis., Vol. III., p. 80.

were apartments in this chamber for these guards. The gentlemen in waiting who attended for a week at a time in the Emperor's bed-chamber were called ἐβδομαδάριοι.

THE SACRED BED-CHAMBER OF THE EMPEROR.

In front of the bed-chamber just mentioned, Constantine VII. (Porphyrogennetos) erected a fountain supported on marble pillars. The water flowed from the mouth of a silver eagle, which did not face straight forward, but looked to one side, and held a serpent twined about its feet. He placed artistically executed pictures of many colours in the entrance to this richly adorned bed-chamber.

We find but little about it in the various writings of its builder.

After a procession to S. Sophia, the Emperor went through the whole Palace, then entered the Chrysotriklinos attended by all the courtiers " offering up prayers, and into the bay of the same Chrysotriklinos where the likeness of our Lord and God is depicted . . . and thus into the sacred bed-chamber."[1] This apartment was separated from the New Chamber by that of the Augusta.

In his account of the ceremonies to be observed when a prince is born, he says—" The ladies in waiting, the wives of the magistrates, proconsuls, and patricians . . . and of the rest of the

---

[1] Cons. P., Vol. I., p. 22.

senators enter from the New Hall and advance to greet the Augusta, each bringing what gift[1] she chooses to make. After the audience of the ladies, all the Senate enter from the Lausiakon, by way of the Horologion and the Chrysotriklinos."[2] We also read that the Emperor entered the Triconchon, and passing through there entered into his bed-chamber.[3]

From this it is apparent that there was a way to the Imperial Bed-chamber from the New Hall, as well as from the Long Chamber.

THE BED-CHAMBER OF THE AUGUSTA

Is mentioned as standing beside the New Chamber, and next the sacred Bed-chamber of the Emperor. At the reception of Elga of Russia, Constantine Porphyrogennetos writes—" Her Majesty, rising up from the throne, crossed through the Lausiakon and the Tripeton into the New Chamber, and through it into her own bed-chamber," and rested there.[4] Subsequently, describing the ceremonies to be observed when a prince is born, he says that on the eighth day, the chamber of the Augusta is decorated with cloth of gold curtains from the Chrysotriklinos. After the congratulations of the ladies, all the Senate and courtiers enter from the Lausiakon through the Horologion and the · Chrysotriklinos, and congratulate the Augusta.

---

1 Ξένιον was the term applied to the offering which those invited to the Court brought to the Augusta.
2 *Ibid.*, pp. 615, 618.   3 *Ibid.*, p. 633.   4 *Ibid.*, p. 596.

From these words it is evident that those going to the Bed-chamber of the Augusta passed through the Chrysotriklinos and the Long Chamber. There were accordingly three doors to this apartment, communicating with the Emperor's chamber, the New Hall, and the Long Chamber.

At the promotion of a Lady of the Bedchamber, (Cubicularia), "the Praepositi go away through the eastern curtain on the right hand side of the Chrysotriklinos, to the Chamber of the Augusta, and escort the candidate through the Chrysotriklinos to the oratory of the Holy Archmartyr Theodore."[1]

THE CHURCH OF OUR LADY OF THE PHAROS.

No one of the churches in the Palace is mentioned so much in the writings of the Byzantine historians as this.[2] It lay near the Pharos, to the south of it, and was, I should think, lower than the Pharos, so as not to obscure the beacons which were lighted there. No remains of this church are preserved. Perhaps, however, the strong foundations which are still to be seen to the south of the Pharos, had some connection with it. In the later ages of the Empire, according to Constantine Porphyrogennetos, the Emperors were

---

[1] *Ibid.*, p. 623.

[2] This church was a wonder to the Crusaders. Utcunque res se habeat, videtur fuisse ædes illa, quam magnificam Palatii Capellam vocat Villharduinus noster ubi de Balduini Flandrensis Comitis Electoribus agit. *Et furent mis en une mult riche chapelle qui dedans le Palais ere.* Opolis. *Christ.*, lib. iii. But it is not clear what chapel the writer means. I think he refers to the chapel in the then famous Palace of the Boukoleon.

married in this church.[1] Formerly this ceremony took place in the Manaura. Here was
treasured the "new" cross of the Emperor
Constantine VII.[2] In this church too, Leo the
Armenian first began the war against images.[3]
Many pieces of the True Cross and various
valuable chandeliers and candlesticks were preserved. They are enumerated by Constantine
Porphyrogennetos in his account of the reception of
the ambassadors from the Emir, on which occasion
the Chrysotriklinos was decorated with them.[4]
The Emperors attended service here more frequently
than at any other church.[5] The terrace in front of
the church is mentioned in the account of the
ceremonies on the day of S. Elias.[6] "The Emperor
supported by the Patriarch goes out of the
church, and crossing through the church of the
Pharos, and going out by the door which leads to
the · Terrace, their Majesties receive processional
candles from the praepositi,[7] and go in procession

---

1 Cons. P., Vol. I., p. 201.   2 *Ibid.*, p. 640.

3 Theophanes Con., p. 32. In this church Leo the Isaurian was murdered by the followers of Michael Amorrhaios. Kodinos Kour., pp. 345,
346. τῷ θ᾽ ἔτει ἤρξατο ὁ δυσσεβὴς Λέων τὸν κατὰ τῆς τῶν ἁγίων εἰκόνων
καθαιρέσεως λόγον ποιεῖσθαι. G. Kedrenos, Vol. I., p. 794.

4 Vol. I., pp. 570, 581.

5 Cons. P., Vol. L, pp. 71, 94, 114, 117, 137, 161, 162. Μιχαὴλ ὁ
βασιλεὺς καὶ ἡ σύνευνος Προκοπία σὺν τοῖς σφετέροις παισὶν εἰς τὸν τῆς Θεοτόκου
ναὸν ὃς Φάρος κατονομάζεται, προσφυγόντες ἱκέται γίνονται. G. Kedrenos,
Vol. II., p. 48 ; Genesios, pp. 7, 19.

6 Cons. P., Vol. I., p. 114 ; II., p. 214 ; ἡλιακὸς, Latin *Solarium*, is a
common word in Byzantine Greek. The name was given not only to the
piazza on the top of a building or in front of it, but also to any open piece
of ground without houses.

7 Καὶ δῆτα εὐνοῦχον τῶν εἰς τὴν βασιλικὴν δοροφορίαν συντεταγμένον αὐτῷ
τὸν κορυφαιότατον, ὃν πραιπόσιτον εἴθισται Ῥωμαίοις ἀποκαλεῖν. Theophylak-

along the Terrace, and through the narrow entrance of the Monothyros," etc. It was also called the Terrace of the Chrysotriklinos. In it was the Porphry Stone.[1]

This Terrace was a spacious place, and is such to the present day. In his account of the festival of S. Basil, Constantine Porphyrogennetos writes, " Their majesties, the patricians, and the rest of the Senate, together with the officers of the Bed-chamber, stand in the Terrace of the Chrysotrik-linos if it is fine weather." [2] The courtiers of the the Byzantine Palace were a numerous body.

THE CHURCH OF S. DEMETRIOS.

This church was near that of Our Lady of the Pharos. On the Saint's day (Oct. 26th), when the procession entered the Chrysotriklinos, the Emperor passed down the middle of the Hall, and entered the Eastern doors with the procession. The magistrates, proconsuls, patricians, and officials, stood opposite the Church of S. Demetrios, and their Majesties with the Patriarch in the fore-court of the church. Then they entered and took their proper seats. [3]

From the words used by Constantine Porphyro-gennetos in his account of the observances on the

---

tos Sim., p. 194 ; Kodinos Kour., pp. 91, 361 ; Meursii, *Glossarium* ; διὰ τῶν θαλαμηπόλων εὐνούχων. M. Attaliates, p. 51.

1 Cons. P., Vol. I., pp. 63, 290. The church is sometimes called Pharos—εἰσέρχεται ὁ βασιλεὺς πρὸς τὸ ἐκτελέσαι τὴν θείαν μυσταγωγίαν ἐν τῷ φάρῳ. *Ibid.*, p. 183. No chapel in the Pharos itself is mentioned.

2 Cons. P., Vol. I., p. 137.   3 *Ibid.*, p. 124.

eve of Palm Sunday—"and through the other door of S. Demetrios they enter the church of Our Lady of the Pharos," I conjecture that this church was beside that of Our Lady of the Pharos, and that both communicated by a common door.[1]

These are all the Imperial and ecclesiastical buildings connected with the celebrated Chrysotriklinos. All the courtiers who were summoned, entered the Hall by the Tripeton, or as it was also called, the Horologion. Thence they proceeded by a passage on the right to the Aristerion, and thence to the New Bed-chamber. Here another door led to the adjacent bed-chamber of the Augusta, through which the wives of the courtiers and others of rank went to visit the Emperor. Through the Chrysotriklinos they entered into the Long Chamber, and thence to the Sacred Bed-chamber of the Emperor, which communicated with that of the Augusta. Through the eastern door of the Long Chamber they came out to the forecourt of the churches of Our Lady of the Pharos, and S. Demetrios.

These two churches, and also that of the Pana-chrantos, which still exists under the Turkish designation of *Feneré Jesâ Medjedî*,[2] were south of the Imperial Bed-chamber. The forecourts and west porches of these churches are continually mentioned. The way to the church of the Pana-chrantos was through the Long Chamber opposite

---

1 *Ibid.*, p. 171.   Du Cange nowhere mentions this church.
2 Βυζαντιναί Μελέται, p. 322.

to the Sacred Bed-chamber, and the Terrace of the Pharos. Another church, or rather small oratory, was that of S. Theodore in the north-east corner of the Chrysotriklinos. The Terrace of the Pharos so often mentioned in the history of the Palace is the platform still preserved on the roof of the building which I mentioned above. From the Chrysotriklinos they regularly went on to the Terrace by the door Monothyros. No steps here, either at the entrance or exit of the Pharos, are mentioned. I gather that the floor of the Chryso-triklinos, which was raised on arches, was on the same level as the Terrace. At the present day, however, the Pharos is very high, and not connected with any other buildings. Accordingly, to raise the floor of the Chrysotriklinos to the same level in this hilly ground, they built the colossal foundations and walls which may still be seen, and under which the public road now runs, as I mentioned in my account of the ruins of the Pharos. The appearance of the south side of these buildings with which others—the Long Chamber, and the Aristerion— were evidently connected, plainly shews that the buildings have been removed by violent means.

The house above, through which I went to reach the Terrace of the Pharos, now occupies the entire site of the Chrysotriklinos. From its windows a full view of the houses and gardens of the Turks can be had; but I saw no sign of Byzantine buildings.

From the long list which Constantine Porphyro-gennetos gives of the golden vessels and ornaments of all kinds belonging to the Chrysotriklinos, I am led to suppose—as I said above—that the majority of them were kept in the vaults of the Pharos, and that probably the Phylax of the Chrysotriklinos was the way down to these vaults.

It is probable that the dietarii or guards of the Pharos lived in the upper chambers of the still extant building. The strong vaults below were, in my opinion, the Treasury, to which doors beside the chamber of the Chrysotriklinos called the Pantheon led through the Phylax. At the procession of the Holy Cross in August, writes Constantine Porphyrogennetos, "the Holy Cross must be brought from the Treasury of the Great Palace. After the procession, it is restored to the keeper of the Treasury, and laid past in the Sacred Treasury." According to him it was in the Great Palace, that is in the palace of the Chrysotriklinos. He mentions no other place in the Palace suitable for guarding such valuable objects.[1]

The Palace of the Triconchon.

THE HALL OF LAUSOS, OR THE LAUSIAKON.

The palace of the Triconchon was separated from the higher palace of the Chrysotriklinos by the passage or gallery called the Lausiakon.[2] The

---

[1] Cons. P., pp. 538, 547, 550. Nothing definite is known of the συστεμάτια and ἀβάκια of the Pharos mentioned on p. 645.

[2] Why this Hall was so called, I do not know. A place called Lausos, beside the Copper-market, is mentioned. See Cons. P., Vol. I., p. 169; Gyllius, *De Topographia*, lib. ii., cap. 25. Byzantios (Vol. I., p. 439) is of opinion that this Hall was called after the Palace of Lausos erected beside the *Bit Bazár*.

south end of it was connected with the Hall of Justinian, and the north with the Gallery of the Forty Saints. On Easter Tuesday, the Emperor proceeded to the Church of SS. Sergius and Bacchus, through the Hippodrome and the Asecreta.[1] The courtiers assembled in the Hall of Justinian and the Lausiakon to wait until the Emperor came out from the Chrysotriklinos. As he went through the Tripeton into the Lausiakon, the patricians and generals stood on either side of the passage, as far as the door from the Lausiakon into the Hall of Justinian. This door is continually mentioned. The bench of the Kouropalates stood beside it.[2] Proceeding thence they went to the Skyla. The Vault (τροπικὴ)[3] of the Lausiakon, was the name given to the passage between the Lausiakon and the Palace of the Triconchon. The Zosta Patricia, at her installation, went from the Tripeton to the Lausiakon, "and ascends to the Vault of the Lausiakon."[4] From the Lausiakon a bronze door opened to the kitchens, where the dishes for the Emperor and the guests in the Chrysotriklinos were cooked. "The Hetairiarch," writes Constantine Porphyrogennetos,

---

[1] Cons. P., Vol. I., p. 85.

[2] Byzantios, Κτολις., Vol. III., p. 79. Cons. P. Vol. I., p. 288. τὴν μετὰ βασιλέα πρώτην ἀρχὴν κεκτημένον (κουροπαλάτην δὲ αὐτὸν οἱ περὶ τὰ βασίλεια καλεῖν εἰώθασιν). Nikephoros Patr., p. 7. τὴν φυλακὴν τῆς αὐλῆς ἐμπεπιστευμένος, ὃν κουροπαλάτην ἡ Ῥωμαίων λέγει φωνή. Kodinos Kour., p. 184. A Gallis olim dicebatur major domus. Meursii, *Glossarium;* G. Kedrenos, Vol. II., p. 913; M. Attaliates, p. 250.

[3] Ut Latini curvam et curvulam, sic Græci τροπικὴν appellabant a τρέπω, verto, curvo, volvo, volutam, une voûte. Cons. P., Vol. II., p. 650.

[4] Cons. P., Vol. I., p. 260.

" sits in the Lausiakon before the door opening into the kitchens.¹ I have placed the kitchens to the west of the Lausiakon.

According to Kodinos, the Lausiakon and the Chrysotriklinos were built by Justinian.² Both the Lausiakon and the Hall of Justinian were long corridors, roofed over in parts.

In my opinion, the portion of the Lausiakon next the door of the Tripeton was roofed in, to protect the dishes as they were carried through it from the kitchens to the Chrysotriklinos. It is probable that the remaining portion was uncovered. Mention is made of the lamplighters of the Lausiakon and the Hall of Justinian,³ a proof that parts at least of them were roofed, in and lighted with lamps or candles.

In time of storms and heavy wind some festivals were celebrated in the Triconchon instead of in these Halls. The courtiers went to it through these corridors.⁴ Once during the reign of Michael son of Theophilos, a violent storm sprang up; and as the courtiers summoned could not stand in the open court of the Secret Fountain, they were called into the Lausiakon, at the Horologion or gate of the Tripeton, where they received the usual gifts.⁵ "Leo the Armenian gave many judgments himself, sitting in the Lausiakon."³ It was here that Theophilos the Iconoclast

---

1 *Ibid.*, p. 519.   2 G. Kodinos, p. 100.
3 Cons. P., Vol. I., p. 605.   4 *Ibid.*, p. 296.   5 *Ibid.*, p, 605.
3 Theophanes Con., p. 30. ἐχρημάτισε δὲ τὰ πλείω καὶ ἐν τῷ Λαυσιακῷ καθήμενος τρικλίνῳ. G. Kedrenos, Vol. II., p. 60 ; τὰ πλείω δὲ τῶν διοικη-μάτων ἐν τῷ Λαυσιακῷ χρηματίζειν διήνυεν. Genesios. pp. 18, 87, 88.

summoned the brothers Theophanes and Theodoros, that he might speak with them concerning images and doctrine. Finally, after fruitless arguments and questions, he ordered both to be beaten with rods in the Mesokepion of the Lausiakon.[1] This same Emperor ornamented both the Lausiakon and the Hall of Justinian with gold mosaics. He also transferred capitals to it from the palace of the tyrant Basiliskos.[2]

THE CHURCH OF S. BASIL.

In the Lausiakon a church was built, dedicated to S. Basil. Constantine Porphyrogennetos makes its site clear. In certain processions during Lent " the Cross . . . is brought out, and offered to the adoration of the whole senate in the Lausiakon, on the left [east] side, before the chapel of S. Basil." " A procession is formed before the church of S. Basil."[3] On the strength of these passages I have placed the church on the eastern side of the Lausiakon.[4] The " left " side in the first quotation is taken relatively to the path of the Emperor and his courtiers from the Lausiakon to the church. The Emperor and his train visited this church on the 1st of January [the Saint's day] and

---

[1] Theophanes Con., pp. 104, 105. The Mesokepion lay to the east of the Lausiakon.

[2] *Ibid.*, p. 147.

[3] Cons. P., Vol. I., pp. 550, 559.

[4] I think that the words of this writer, Vol. I., p. 523—καὶ μετὰ τὸ ἀπολῦσαι τὴν θείαν λειτουργίαν ἐν τῷ Λαυσιακῷ—refer to this church of S. Basil. No other church in this Hall is ever mentioned.

" remained until after the reading of the Holy Gospel."[1]

THE TRICONCHON.

North of the Lausiakon stood a building called the Triconchon and several other buildings connected with it, all bounded on the south side by the Hall of Justinian, which was connected with the Lausiakon. Among this pile of buildings, which was larger than the Chrysotriklinos, the Triconchon was the most prominent, and I have thought it well to call them collectively the Palace of the Triconchon.

The ascent to it from the Lausiakon was through the covered way of the Vault ($\tau\rho\omega\pi\iota\kappa\eta$), by a staircase.[2] The Triconchon had three "conchs" or bays, sometimes also termed apses. At Christmas the patricians and other officers " receive the Emperor in the semicircle of the apse, that is the Triconchon."[3] On the festival of S. Demetrios [Oct. 26th], Constantine Porphyrogennetos writes that the Patriarch on entering, comes in by the galleries of the Triconchon, and takes his seat in the chamber of the Chrysotriklinos which is next the Pantheon,[4] showing that there was a direct passage from the Triconchon to the palace of the Chrysotriklinos. The Triconchon derived its name from its shape.[5]

---

[1] *Ibid.*, p. 137.   [2] Cons. P., Vol. I,, p. 260 ; II., p. 649.

[3] Cons. P., Vol. I., pp. 128, 72,   [4] *Ibid.*, p. 121.

[5] Theophanes Con., p. 140. ὁ δὲ Θεοδώρητος ἰδίᾳ ἐν τῷ λεγομένῳ Τρικόγχῳ τοῦ παλατίου τυφθεὶς καὶ αὐτὸς ἐξωρίσθη. *Ibid.*, p. 892 ; *cf.* 400. On page 438 it is called Τρικύμβαλος, and the Vault beside it is mentioned.

It had three apses, the eastern, or middle apse, which faced the sea and rested on four pillars of Roman marble, and two at the sides, one on the north, and the other on the south. In the western or higher side,[1] which rested on two columns, there were three doors. The middle door was of silver; those on either side of it were of burnished bronze. From a passage in Constantine Porphyrogennetos it would appear that the two ends of the Triconchon were called Bathmidia—the Steps. " The officers of the Bedchamber stand . . . some in the apse above on the Bathmidion, and some on the left side, they also on the Bathmidion."[2]

THE SIGMA.

Through the three doors in the higher side of the Triconchon we pass into another covered building called from its shape [C] the Sigma. Like the Triconchon, its walls were covered with marbles of various colours.[3] The roof, which was solidly built and brilliantly coloured, rested on fifteen pillars of Dokimaian marble. Descending by a spiral staircase[4] to the vaults below, we find a chamber of the

---

1 [The author is here referring to the configuration of the Palace site, which slopes steeply upwards to the west.—Tr.]

2 Cons. P., Vol. I., p. 298.

3 Theophanes Con., p. 140, where the historian has a great deal to say about the Triconchon.

4 Στύραξ and στυράκιον, a name for a spiral stair. Porphyrogennetos mentions one in the church at Blachernai, Vol. I., p. 151. στουράκιον Pampinus, Corimbus. ἕλιξ, ὄνομα κύριον τὸ κατὰ κύκλον στρεφόμενον. Meursii *Glossarium*; A. Koraës, *Posthumous Writings* by A. Z. Mamoukas, Athens, 1881; p. 279, *s.v.* pressoir.

same shape, which had seventeen pillars. The floor was paved with stone from Piperai. Lower down, on its eastern side, and under the Triconchon adjoining, the architect built a "Tetraseron,"[1] similar in shape to the Triconchon above, with an apse on the eastern side and two at the north and south sides. The northern bay, which was built by Theophilos, was supported on two pillars, and was called the Mysterion, because if any one standing near the eastern or western apse said anything to himself in a low voice, another person standing on the axis of the ellipse opposite to him, with his ear against the wall, could hear what he said.

Theophilos built the Triconchon and the Sigma in the eleventh year of his reign.[2] I think that he restored them, and did not build them from the foundation. According to Kodinos this building was founded by the Emperor Constantine.[3]

I mentioned the vault under the Sigma called the Mysterion. It appears that there was also a Secret Chamber (εἰδικὸν) or Treasury in this vault.[4] We saw that Theophilos is said to have left 97 centenaria of gold, which had belonged to his father Michael, in the Imperial Treasury. This treasury of course was in the Chrysotriklinos. Basil the Mace-

---

1 Videtur idem cum τετραθύρῳ vel τετραπόρτῳ fuisse. Cons. P., Vol. II., p. 217.

2 Theophanes Con., pp. 640, 645, 806 ; Leo Gramm., p. 225.

3 P. 19. According to Leo Grammatikos, the Triconchon, the Sigma, and the Fountain, were built by Theophilos. P. 225.

4 Ὁ δὲ φιλοφρονούμενος ὑπ' αὐτοῦ κουφότητι γνώμης ὑπέδειξεν αὐτῷ τὸν ἐν τῷ ἡμικυκλίῳ, ὃ νῦν λέγεται σίγμα, θησαυρὸν ἀνακτισθέντα διὰ ὀρθομαρμαρώσεως. G. Kedrenos, Vol. II., p. 31.

donian at this proclamation " at once summoned all the leaders of the Senate, and also those of distinguished rank, and opened the Strong-room of the Imperial treasures in their presence."[1] A little further on the same writer calls it "the Store-room and Imperial Treasury."[2] C. Porphyrogennetos writes, "and at once the Protovestiarius descends from the Sigma by the wooden spiral stair-case, bringing with him the Emperor's largess" which he distributed among the guests.[3]

A great crowd gathered in the Sigma on the eve of the day on which the Emperor was to enter the city.[4] From this may be judged the size of the building where so many could dance.

THE SECRET FOUNTAIN OF THE SIGMA.

This was a building connected with, and communicating with the Sigma, on the western side of which it was situated. It was called sometimes the Apse of the Secret Fountain of the Triconchon, sometimes the Secret Fountain of the Triconchon. Constantine Porphyrogennetos gives a minute description of the procession of the Emperor and his court on Palm Sunday. " All go through the single door which leads to the treasury in the Secret Fountain, carrying candles. . . . The Emperor proceeds to the Chrysotriklinos, and the priests come out from the church of the Pharos, carrying

---

1 Theophanes Con., pp. 253, 255.
2 Ταμεῖον καὶ βασιλικὸν θησαυροφυλάκιον.
3 Cons. P., Vol. I., p. 601.   4 *Ibid.*, p. 278.

the cross of the church. . . . ." After the procession, the Emperor went out to the "semicircle of the fountain of the Triconchon, . . . he goes through [the Hall of] the Augusteus, and the apse of the Triconchon, while the courtiers stand in the same apse of the Triconchon, and greet the Emperor."[1]

This apse is continually mentioned. It was the vaulted doorway by which the Secret Fountain communicated with the gallery of the Daphne, or, as it was sometimes called, of the Augustaion. At the great festival of the Dedication of Constantinople, which was celebrated in the Hippodrome on the 11th of May, when the Emperor went to view the races, " he comes out from his God-protected chamber, and escorted as usual, passes through the gallery of the Triconchon, the apse, and the Daphne, and ascends to the windows of the Imperial Stand by the private spiral stair."[2] On Easter Eve the prefects went into the semi-circle of the Mystic Fountain of the Triconchon.[3] In another place he says, " They receive the Emperor in the semicircle of the Secret Fountain of the Triconchon " (p. 128.) The burnished single door (monothyros) of the Triconchon, probably the door which led into the gallery of the Augusteus,[4] is also mentioned.

In this Fountain of the Triconchon were three doors, and three marble platforms, on which

[1] Cons. P., Vol. I., p. 174 ; *cf.* pp. 128, 143, 297.

[2] Vol. I., pp. 341, 360.

[3] *Ibid.*, pp. 180, 600 ; Theophanes Con., p. 892.

[4] Cons. P., Vol. I., pp. 72, 298, 310.

some of the courtiers stood at public receptions.[1] It was not roofed over, and hence was sometimes termed the Exaëron.[2] In the time of Michael son of Theophilos, a great storm sprang up, and this Fountain became impassable on account of the violent wind and deep snow. The courtiers therefore went to the Lausiakon and performed the Brumalia there. In stormy weather the great receptions of the Emperor were not held at this Fountain, but under cover, in the neighbouring Triconchon. So Constantine Porphyrogennetos informs us.[3]

In the middle of this secret court stood the fountain from which it took its name. Here there were steps of white Prokonnessian marble, and in the centre of them a marble arch springing from two slender marble pillars. By the eastern side of the adjoining Sigma were two bronze lions from whose gaping mouths water continually poured, flooding the whole Sigma and refreshing the invited courtiers. On the occasion of a reception, the fountain was filled with pistachios, almonds, and pine-apples. The factions stood at the foot of the steps, the Senate opposite, with the Emperor sitting on a throne of gold and marble.[4] The Emperor Theophilos was

[1] *Ibid.*, pp. 144, 303, 349. Πούλπιτον, from the Latin *pulpitum*, was any elevated platform. Another in the Chrysotriklinos is mentioned; p. 243.

[2] Theophanes Con., p. 141. 'Εξάερον, locus aeri expositus. Area domus. τὰ αλλότρια ἐδάφη, ἐν οἷς οὐκ εἰσιν οἰκίαι καὶ τὰ τῶν γειτόνων ἐξάερα. Meursii *Glossarium*.

[3] Cons. P., Vol. I., pp. 296, 600, 605.

[4] Theophanes Con., p. 142.

so fond of this place, that he caused the routine of business and the daily processions to be performed in the Triconchon.[1] He brought the ascetic Methodios to this fountain, where he remained till his death.[2] This court of the fountain must have been of considerable size, for the festival of the torches,[3] at which a great many people gathered together and danced with torches in their hands, was celebrated here.

THE DOOR OF THE SPATHARIKION.[4]

This door was on the left side of the Secret Fountain. The patriarch went out of the Chryso-triklinos by it, and passed into the Hall of the Augusteus. By it too, all the courtiers entered who awaited the Emperor at the elevation of the Holy Cross. When he came out of the Chrysotriklinos the door was opened. Their majesties went out through it, and crossed to the Manaura, and through the galleries above it to S. Sophia. Near here, as I think, the Delphax anciently stood—

---

[1] *Ibid.*

[2] Theophanes Con., p. 645. Fountain—φιάλη—was the name generally given in Byzantine churches to a tank filled with water in front or inside of the narthex, in which the worshippers bathed their feet, hands and faces, before entering the church. The Catholics observed the same custom. G. Pachymeres, Vol. II., pp. 22, 722.

[3] Cons. P., Vol. I., p. 349. Φακλαρέα, saltatio, chorea cum facibus, Vol. II., p. 295.

[4] Πύλη τοῦ Σπαθαρικίου. Cons. P., Vol. I., pp. 96, 125, 157. Byzantios (Vol. III., p. 91, n.) says that there was a Spatharikion, i.e., a place where the Spatharioi stayed. A place of this name is merely men-tioned by C. Porphyrogennetos (p. 125); what purpose the building served I do not know.

or rather this part of the Palace was once called the Delphax. No writer except Constantine Porphyrogennetos mentions it, and we can unfortunately learn nothing from him. Subsequently the Delphax was beside the Onopodium.

THE GALLERY OF THE FORTY SAINTS.

This, which is sometimes called simply the Forty Saints, was a gallery, north of the Chrysotriklinos and the Triconchon, by which the Emperor often went to the former. " And going out of the Chrysotriklinos he passes through the gallery of the Forty Saints." [1] I do not know whether or not this gallery was named in honour of the Forty Martyrs, who are commemorated on the 9th of March. On that day the Emperor went to the church of these martyrs, "situated in the middle of the city." [2] There was a way up to the gallery from the Triconchon. The Emperor "goes into the semi-circle of the Triconchon, and passes through the gallery of the Forty Saints, and goes into the Chrysotriklinos." From these words it is clear that there was an entrance to the Triconchon from the gallery of the Forty Saints. Elsewhere he writes, "the Emperor goes into the semi-circle of the Triconchon, and passing through the gallery of the Forty Saints, enters into the Hall." This gallery extended from the side of the Secret

---

[1] Cons. P., Vol. I., pp. 85, 107, 129, 180, 348.

[2] N. Choniates, p. 431 ; N. Gregoras, Vol. I., p. 460 ; *Chron. Pasch.*, Vol. I., p. 590 ; Cons. P., Vol. I., p. 559 ; Synaxaristes, March 9th.

Fountain, to the Chrysotriklinos and the Pharos. It was thus the northern boundary of the Triconchon. Many entrances between it and the buildings along side of it are mentioned, to which I shall refer again. According to the Continuation of Theophanes, this marble-paved walk, which extended to the Pharos, was built by Basil the Macedonian.[1] From his language I think that the other galleries were also paved with marble.

THE HALL OF THE PEARL

was built by Theophilos.[2] It lay north of the gallery of the Forty Saints and parallel with it. Eight pillars of rose-coloured marble supported the roof. The walls were adorned with representations of all kinds of animals, and the floor was of mosaic work and Prokonnesian marble. The Emperor had a bedchamber either above the ground-floor of this hall, or beside it. Four pillars of Bathyinian marble upheld the " gold-starred orb of the roof." The porches on its eastern and southern sides rested on four pillars of Thessalian marble, so that there were sixteen columns in this hall. The walls and floor were gorgeously ornamented with marbles and variegated mosaics.

The chamber of this spacious hall was occu- pied by Theophilos from the spring to the autumnal equinox. At the approach of winter he went over to the Carian Hall to escape the bitter north winds,

---

and to enjoy the warmth of the mild south winds which prevail in winter. " Under one of the imperial houses, which is called the Pearl, he made this man a prisoner."[1] Near to this hall " there was a piazza facing the north, from which the old Tzykanisterion, while it existed, was seen."[2] From this I infer that the building was lofty and overlooked the ancient Mesokepion, which our author calls the old Tzykanisterion. The buildings about the Chrysotriklinos were built on lower ground, and would not obstruct the view from the upper chamber of this Hall.

After the death of Theophilos this building became the residence of the Papias. It communicated with the gallery of the Forty Saints. At the present day there is a Turkish building with a similar name[3] on the shore of the Akropolis, on the south side of the palace of the Boukoleon.

THE ERÔS.

This, like the preceding, was the work of Theophilos. " On the left side, that is to the east of the Sigma, another hall has been erected, called the Erôs, which they formerly used as an armoury."[4]

---

[1] Theophanes Con., pp. 350, 697, 698 ; G. Kedrenos, Vol. II., p. 246. The reference is to Leo, son of Basil, who was shut up in the Hall, along with his wife Theophano, for the space of three years.

[2] Theophanes Con., p. 144. Theophilos built this Hall before his marriage with Theodora. *Ibid.*, p. 790.

[3] Intzelè kiòsk, or the Hall of the Pearl.

[4] Theophanes Con., p. 143. Byzantios thinks that *Erôs* ought to be written *Arês*, because of the use to which it was put. Κπολις., Vol. I., p. 201, *note*.

" At the installation of the Zosta Patricia," Constantine Porphyrogennetos writes, " they bring her into the palace through the Erôs and the gallery of the Forty Saints, and she crosses the terrace of the Chrysotriklinos and enters [the Church of] the Pharos." Coming back " she goes out to the Erôs, and proceeds to the side of the Manaura."[1] This building is seldom mentioned, and we know but little about it.

At the promotion of a demarch, the same writer says, " The newly appointed demarch goes away, through the Lausiakon, the Erôs, and the Daphne, into the [Hall of the] Augusteus, and sits there."[2]

This building was full of all kinds of weapons, old and new. Whether it was originally built for an armoury, we have no means of determining. Constantine Porphyrogennetos says nothing about the weapons.

THE CHURCH OF S. JOHN.

This church was built by the side of the Secret Fountain of the Triconchon, and was separated from it by the gallery of the Forty Saints. There was a direct way from the fountain to the church, as may be inferred from the words of Constantine Porphyrogennetos. " They enter the apse of the Secret Fountain of the Triconchon, and while all the aforementioned are standing in front of the Church of S. John and receiving the Emperor," etc. (p. 297). Further on, describing the ceremonies at the evening

---

races, he writes, " As they stand in the semi-circle of the Triconchon in front of the Church of S. John." (pp. 307, 309.) The church must have been on the north side of the Secret Fountain, since the opposite side was occupied by other buildings.

These are all the buildings on the north side of the Gallery of the Forty Saints.

THE CARIAN VESTIARY.[1]

This building also was erected by Theophilos. It was situated to the east of the Hall Pyxites, and on the right side of the passage called the Vault (τροπική). It got its name from the fact that the pavement was of Carian Marble, " like some broad river." It was the wardrobe where the precious silken robes were kept. Mention is made of " the great pieces of embossed silver-work, from those stored in the Carian Vestiary," and " the embossed silver work " kept there.[2]

In this building many costly silver vessels and gold-embroidered stuffs were preserved, for use at the

---

[1] Βέστια παρὰ τοῖς 'Ρωμαίοις τὰ ἱμάτια, ἐξ οὗ καὶ βεστιάριον κυρίως ἐν ᾧ τὰ βασιλικὰ ἐνδύματα φυλάσσονται. Meursii *Glossarium.* Gold and silver vessels were preserved in the Vestiary. Cons. P., Vol. I., p. 242. The officers of the wardrobe were called βεστιάριοι, βεστιαρῖται, and βεστή- τωρες. The Chosbaïtai were vestiaries. Vestiaritae igitur erant Chosbaïtae omnes ; sed non vicissim omnes vestiaritae erant Chosbaïtae. *Ibid.,* Vol. II., p. 847. Pachymeres writes (Vol. II., p. 556) οὕτω γὰρ [βεστιάριος] ὁ τῆς δαπάνης χορηγὸς τοῖς ἐπὶ τῶν νηῶν ὀνομάζεται. Michael Attaliates calls the Vestiarius πρωτοσβέστης (p. 192). I think that the Chosbaïtai who guarded the Emperor's throne were what are now called Cherbátai (Χερβάται). Cons. P., Vol. I., pp. 269, 344, 719, 738. The learned Roiske is of a different opinion. (Cons. P., Vol. II., p. 847.)

[2] Cons. P., Vol. I., pp. 582, 592.

magnificent receptions of ambassadors.   The gold and silver utensils for the Emperor's table were also kept here.   The officer who had charge of all these was called the Vestiarius.[1]

Theophilos is often praised by many Byzantine writers for the great and magnificent buildings he erected in Constantinople and the Palace precincts.[2]

THE EIDIKON OR TREASURY.

" The Patriarch goes out through the single door of the Eidikon, . . .   the officers of the Bed-chamber receive him when he is about to descend the staircase of the Lausiakon, and they pass through the Lausiakon, . . .   and conduct him to the Tripeton, where he stands in front of the Horologion."[3]   A door led from the Treasury to the Lausiakon.   " Through the single door which is at the Eidikon," " at the door leading to the Eidikon."[4]   " And certain robes of the Emperor and Augusta . . .   some of cloth of gold and some gold embroidered which were in the Eidikon."[5] Many ships were equipped from this private Treasury.[6]   The Government stores were called Genikon.[7]   Here probably were what Choniates

---

1 *Ibid.*, pp. 582, 592, 594.

2 Theophanes Con., p. 139.   He paid great attention to the wall of the harbour, where his name appears on many towers.

3 Cons. P., Vol. I., pp. 91, 174.

4 *Ibid.*, pp. 169, 174, 180, 263, 297, 519.

5 *Ibid.*, pp. 671, 673.

6 Theophanes Con., p. 173.   At p. 257 the accumulations of Michael, the father of Theophilos, are enumerated.

7 *Ibid.*, p. 260 ; I. Meursii *Glossarium*, s.v. Γενικόν.

terms the Chrysoplousia, mentioned in the account of the insurrection against Andronikos. "They plundered, not only what money they found stored up in the Chrysoplousia (and that was, exclusive of the ingots not cut into money, twelve centenaria of gold, thirty of silver, and two hundred of bronze coinage), but everything else besides."[1]

This private storehouse for the Emperor's property was, according to Kodinos, built by Constantine the Great.[2] Near it were the Asekreteia—probably the offices of the overseers of the business of the treasury. So I infer from the words of Constantine Porphyrogennetos, "They open the Asekreteia, and the door leading to the Eidikon."[3]

Here too were the σκρίνια τῶν βαρβάρων, or offices for business with such nations as the Saracens and Persians. "An account of the Persian ambassador's expenses is kept in the Scrinia." The clerks who worked in these offices were called the Chartularies of the Barbarians.[4]

Descending from the Triconchon through the Vault, this Treasury was on the left hand, the Vestiary and the kitchens on the right. "The Hetairiarch sits down in the Lausiakon, before the bronze door which opens into the kitchens." This was done by the servants of the Palace daily.

THE BATHS OF THEOKTISTOS.

These baths, along with several other buildings,

---

[1] P. 453   [2] P. 19.   [3] Vol. 1., pp. 519, 520.
[4] Cons. P., Vol. I., pp. 400, 404.

were built by the all powerful Theoktistos, who had charge of affairs in the time of Theodora, mother of Michael the Drunkard. " This same Theoktistos, being joint ruler with Theodora, made houses and baths, and a garden in the place now called the Apse, that he might be near the Palace ; and for safety, and his own protection, he placed an iron gate at the Daphne, and appointed a janitor to guard it."[1]   The apse mentioned was in the higher or western side of the Secret Fountain in the Triconchon.   Constantine Porphyrogennetos, who mentions everything in the Palace grounds, says nothing about the baths.   Probably they were destroyed after the death of Theoktistos.[2]

THE HALL PYXITES.

South of the Sigma, and near its staircase, Theophilos built some halls. " Pyxites was the name of one, and there was another higher up which had no name."[3]   Along the walls there were inscribed lines addressed by one Stephen of the Capitol. The other hall was built between the Pyxites and the Bath of Theoktistos, as a residence for the Court clergy, who are often mentioned in the history of the Palace.

---

[1] Theophanes Con., p. 815.   Labarte (p. 143) has misunderstood this passage.   He translates πρὸς τὸ πλήσιον αὐτὸν εἶναι τοῦ παλατίου, by "qui est près du palais," instead of "afin qu'il soit près du palais."

[2] Bardas Cæsar put him to death in the Palace.   Theophanes Con., pp. 657, 822 ; G. Kedrenos, Vol. II., p. 157 ; Leo Grammaticus, p. 235.

Theophanes Con., p. 143.

CHAPTER VIII.

THE KAMELAS.

The Emperor Theophilos, who built and ornamented so many edifices, after the erection of the above-mentioned Triconchon, the Carian Vestiary, the Pyxites, the Eros and the Hall of the Pearl, erected some further buildings.[1] On the open ground south of the Triconchon, he built the Hall called Kamêlas, and the sleeping chambers adjoining called the second and third. He thus built a series of three bedchambers. The Kamêlas, the most brilliant of all, had six pillars of Thessalian marble supporting the ceiling, which was spangled with gold. The lower part of the walls was lined with slabs of the same marble, and the upper was ornamented with sculptures of figures gathering fruit. The floor was paved with Prokonnesian marble. Built in connection with these chambers was a chapel containing two sanctuaries, one in honour of Our Lady, the other dedicated to Michael, the leader of the heavenly hosts.

THE MESOPATOS.

South of the Kamêlas was the Mesopatos, which faced the Chrysotriklinos. Constantine VII.

---

[1] Theophanes Con., p. 144.

Porphyrogennetos set this building apart for the Palace library. "The oracle was a Sybilline one, recorded in some book in the Imperial Library."[1] "And the place below this, which is called Meso-patos, is the dwelling of the eunuchs[2] entrusted with the women's quarters." These words lead me to believe that the eunuchs of the Palace occupied a portion of the library ; or that after the death of the bibliophile Constantine, the library was transferred to other quarters, and the whole building occupied by them. According to Zosimos, this library was built by Julian.[3] "He also built the library in the Emperor's Porch, and placed there all the books he possessed." The historians, unfortunately, do not indicate the situation of the public library of Constantinople. That mentioned by Manasses[4] lay "near the church of the Wisdom of God," outside the Palace. The building which contained so many MSS., and was the abode of so many scholars, is never mentioned in the writings of Constantine Porphyrogennetos, although he mentions parts of the Palace about which all other writers are silent.

THE VESTIARY OF THE AUGUSTA.

The third bedchamber connected with the Meso-

---

[1] Theophanes Con., p. 36. Καὶ τὸ βιβλίον βασιλικῇ βιβλιοθήκῃ ἐνθεῖναι διὰ Θεοφάνους, ibid., p. 689 ; Περὶ πρέσβεων Ῥωμαίων πρὸς ἐθνικούς, p. 4 ; Gyllius, lib. ii., cap. 20.

[2] [Καρτζιμάδων] Theophanes Con., p. 145. Carzimasium autem Græci vocant amputatis virilibus et virga puerum eunuchum. Luitprand, *Hist.*, lib. vi., sec. 6.

[3] P. 140.   [4] *Vv.* 4257-4303.

patos, to the south of which it stood, was that of the Augusta. It was originally built expressly for a vestiary by Theophilos, and was so used in the time of the Continuation of Theophanes. " He also built the Kamêlas, and the second bedchamber adjoining it, and the one next it again in order, the third, which is now the Vestiary of the Augusta."[1] This chamber had a roof similar to that of the Kamêlas, and a floor of Prokonnesian marble.[2] The walls were magnificently adorned, not, however, by Theophilos, but by his son, Michael. These three bedchambers were all adorned with marbles, gilding, and many coloured mosaics.

THE MOUSIKOS.

Under this third bedchamber, to the south of the Kamêlas and Mesopatos, there was an underground apartment, the roof of which rested on seven pillars of Parian marble, five on the south, and two on the eastern side.[3] Slabs of Pegannousian, Carian, and green Thessalian marble were laid on two of its walls. It was called the Mousikos from the artistic effect of the marbles, and the skilful polishing of the stones of the roof. " If you saw it you would say it was a meadow, teeming with different coloured flowers."[4]

On the west side of this there was another building rivalling it in beauty. Its roof rested on

---

[1] Theophanes Con., p. 144.   [2] *Ibid.*, p. 145.
[3] *Ibid.*, p. 146.   [4] *Ibid.*, p. 146.

five columns of Carian marble, three on the
south, and two on the west side. Nothing is said
by the historians as to what purpose it served.

THE CHAPEL OF S. ANN.

Near the Vestiary of the Augusta—"at the foot
of it"—was another building divided into two
rooms.[1] Here the Emperor Leo built a chapel, dedicated to S. Ann. The roof was supported by four
pillars of Bathyinian marble, and the floor was laid
with Prokonnesian stone. Beside the chapel was
the bedchamber of the Augusta, communicating
with the Mousikos under it by a steep stair. "It
lies to the west of the Mousikos. The descent to
the above-mentioned bedchamber is by a stair, and
the entrance likewise."

THE TETRAKOUBOUKLON.

This other hall is mentioned in the Continuation
of Theophanes, as a building of Theophilos, near to,
and on the east side of the above mentioned
buildings. It had four magnificent bedchambers.
Two of them looked to the Mesopatos. Of these
"one has its golden ceiling contained under four
apses." The other two looked in the direction of
the Lausiakon. The floor of this hall was paved

---

[1] *Ibid.* On p. 98 it is said that Theophilos built "beneath the
bed-chamber" a church dedicated to Our Lady, the triapsidal church
to the name of the Heavenly Captain, "and on either side of it to the
names of Holy Women-martyrs." He probably renewed the Church of
Our Lady of the Pharos, and that of S. Ann. No other church near the
bed-chamber is mentioned, except that of the Pharos.

with Prokonnesian marble and coloured, though not with mosaic. A fire subsequently destroyed these adornments.

These were the principal buildings erected by the Emperors in the neighbourhood of the Triconchon. No others in this vicinity are mentioned. North of the buildings constructed by Theophilos, there was a garden extending as far as the Hall of Justinian, which was the southern boundary of these palaces. The northern boundary was the gallery of the Forty Saints, the eastern the Lausiakon, the south the Hall of Justinian which I shall presently describe, and the western the gallery of the Augusteus.

The Palace of the Daphne.

We proceed now to describe the many and varied palace buildings of the Daphne, which were connected with the wall separating the Palace from the Augustaion. In my own opinion, it is the most intricate and obscure portion of all the Palace to describe.

The palace of the Daphne was separated from that of the Triconchon by a passage called the gallery of the Augusteus, or sometimes of the Daphne. West of this was a building called the Daphne. " The Daphne was so called because here stood a pillar which was once the most prophetic Daphne of Apollo." [1] Constantine Porphyrogen-

---

[1] G. Kodinos, pp. 100, 271.

netos calls it. the Daphne of S. Stephen the first Martyr.[1]

THE OCTAGON.

The Octagon, or Octagonal Chamber, was so called, because it had eight porches, in which, according·to Kodinos, there were teachers of every branch of knowledge.[2] A passage led from the Bedchamber of the Daphne into the Octagon. "Their Majesties go out of the bedchamber of the Daphne . . . into the Octagonal Chamber, and there they put on their robes."[3] This building stood in the palace of the Daphne, in front· of the Church of S. Stephen, and lay to the east of it. "After this their Majesties enter with the Officers of the Bedchamber into the Octagon which is in front of S. Stephen's . . . and go into the Bedchamber of the Daphne." "Their Majesties put off their 'pagan' robes in the Bedchamber of the Daphne, and go out to the Octagonal Chamber." "The Augusta enters the Octagon, which is outside S. Stephen's."[4]

---

[1] Vol. 1., p. 550. Λέγουσι δὲ καὶ τοῦτο περὶ τῆς δάφνης, ὅτι ὑγιείας ἐργαστηριόν ἐστιν· ὅθεν καὶ φύλλα αὐτῆς ἐπεδίδοντο τοῖς ἄρχουσι παρὰ τοῦ δήμου, τῇ πρώτῃ τοῦ Ἰανουαρίου μηνός. Geoponicorum auctor, ii., 2, quoted in notes on G. Kodinos, p. 271. To this day many in Constantinople burn bay leaves and drink a decoction of the ashes as a remedy for intermittent fevers.—Δαφνίνην φορῶ βακτηρίαν, τοῦτο λέγειν εἰώθασιν οἱ ὑπό τινων ἐπιβουλευόμενοι, παρόσον ἀλεξιφάρμακον ἡ δάφνη. Souidas.

[2] G. Kodinos, p. 83. Gyllius, lib. ii., cap. 20.

[3] Cons. P., Vol. I., p. 26.

[4] Cons. P., Vol. 1., pp. 21, 33, 212. The Octagon mentioned in the *Chronicon Paschale*, Vol, I.. p. 623, lay in τὰ πέριξ τοῦ Ἁγίου Θεοδώρου τοῦ Σφωρακίου, the place now called *Vefá meîdáni*, north of the gate *Oun cabán*.

These passages show that the Octagon, the Church of S. Stephen, and the Bedchamber of the Daphne, were all close together.

In his account of the Nika Riot, Kedrenos writes, "Then indeed both the Octagon, and the baths of Severus called the Zeuxippos were burnt."[1] No other writer mentions the burning of the building. It was not far from the Senate-House, and probably the flames reached it.

The Council of Constantinople, which is commonly known as the Quinisextan, met in this palace in a building called the Dome. One hundred and seventy bishops were present. No one, however, mentions the site, or the vulgar name of the building where they met. Phrantzes has the following remarks on the Council. "The nuns in the convent of the Ever Blessed he ordered to depart to the Church of the Holy Prophet John the Forerunner in the Dome, where in the reign of Justinian Rhinotmetos the Quinisextan Holy Synod assembled, for at that time it was a magnificent palace near the Ever Blessed, on the north side."[2] The words shew how little Phrantzes knew of these once famous palaces.

This little Church of S. John the Forerunner, which Phrantzes alone has mentioned, was at one time a Mussulman school, and is now a mosque called *Achmet Pasha Medjedi.*[3] It stands near

---

[1] Vol. I., p. 647. [2] P. 307.

[3] Βυζαντιναὶ Μελέται, p. 303, where there is also a representation of this church. The Patriarch Constantius' Κτολις, p. 67. and Byzantios, Κτολις, Vol. I., p. 576.

the Church of the Most Blessed, and barely holds a hundred worshippers. All the historians of the Councils of Constantinople say that the Quini-sextan[1] Council met in the Dome of the Palace, an apartment called the Great *par excellence*. The Council did not meet in the Five Chambers, for they were built by a later Emperor, Basil the Macedonian;[2] and it was out of the question to hold a Council which lasted for many months in the Chrysotriklinos, on account of the many ceremonies which took place there. I think that a building suitable both for its size, and its proximity to the celebrated Church of S. Stephen, is found in this Octagon. No one of the historians, however, calls it the Dome, and no building of that name is mentioned by Constantine Porphyrogennetos.

I remarked above that in all his account of the Palace, this writer never speaks of a library. All the chief monasteries of Constantinople had libraries for the use of the monks. One of them has fortunately been preserved, that of the once famous monastery of Christ Almighty,[3] to the west of the mosque *Zeïrék djamii*. It is an octagonal building of stone, now used as a mosque. According to the Turkish priests it was formerly a library, or as they called it *Kitâb hané*. This Octagon of the Palace of the Daphne, or, as Kodinos calls it, the

---

1 Πενθέκτη, Quinisexta. Le Concile se tint dans une salle du palais Impérial, en Latin trullus, c'est à dire dôme. *Histoire chronologique et dogmatique des Conciles de la Chrétienté*, par M. Roisselet de Sanctières, Paris, 1846. Vol. III., pp. 102, 131.

2 Theophanes Con., p. 335.   3 Βυζαντιναί Μελέται, p. 352.

Octagon with four porches (τετραδίσιον ὀκτάγωνον),[1] was near the Bronze Gate, and was most likely a school where "teachers of every branch of knowledge" taught, until the reign of Leo Syrogenes. Possibly it was the Palace library. But in the most exhaustive account of the Palace, this Octagon is mentioned as a part of the Palace where the Imperial ceremonies were performed, and nothing is said of books or scholars.

THE CHURCH OF S. STEPHEN IN THE DAPHNE.

Close to the Palace of the Daphne was the Church of S. Stephen. As to the site of this Church which is often mentioned, the words of Constantine Porphyrogennetos are clear. "The usual ecclesiastical ceremony having been performed in the Church of the first martyr Stephen in the Daphne." "Passing through the Hall of the Augusteus he enters S. Stephen's . . . and goes to his own Bedchamber."[2] On the eve of the Feast of Lights [Epiphany] when the Emperor and Patriarch attended service here together, the Emperor went into the Bedchamber of the Daphne near the Church of S. Stephen.[3] This church lay to the east of the Octagon and the Bedchamber,[4] as is evident from the account of the coronation of the Augusta. "The Patriarch comes through the Daphne, and enters the Church of S. Stephen,

---

[1] P. 88.
[2] Cons. P., Vol. I., pp. 71, 129, 196, 628.   [3] *Ibid.*, p. 140.
[4] Labarte (p. 66) places it in the Hippodrome beside the Imperial Stand.

and receives their Majesties." After a little he " goes out by the Octagonal Bedchamber."[1] Still more explicit are the words in the description of the coronation and nuptials of the Augusta. " The Augusta goes out to the Octagon, which is outside the church of S. Stephen, and the Emperor and the Augusta go into S. Stephen's and the betrothal takes place."[2] This church was built by Pulcheria sister of Theodosios.[3]

Near this church, to the south of it, was the hippodrome of the Palace which is the one meant by Constantine Porphyrogennetos when he describes the creation of a patrician. "He goes into the church of the hippodrome, to S. Stephen's." This passage does not refer to the chapel of S. Stephen in the Imperial Stand of the Great Hippodrome, for he continues "and escorted by the officers, he goes to the Consistory, and lights candles."[4] The vessels preserved in this church are enumerated by Constantine Porphyrogennetos.[5] The Proto-pappas of the Daphne is also mentioned.[6] The marriages of the Emperors were sometimes performed here. "He is married in the church of S. Stephen which is in the Daphne."[7]

---

[1] Cons. P., pp. 202, 203 ; G. Kedrenos, Vol. I., p. 713 ; II., p. 17. According to this writer, Zeno deposited in this church the Gospel according to St. Matthew, written by the hand of the Apostle Barnabas, Vol. II., p. 619. This church was repaired by Basil the Macedonian. *Ibid.*, Vol. II., p. 239.

[2] Cons. P., Vol. I., p. 212.   [3] G. Kedrenos, Vol. I., p. 592.

[4] Cons. P., Vol. I., p. 251.   [5] Vol. I., p. 640.

[6] Cons. P., Vol. I., pp. 539, 540, 549.

[7] Καὶ στέφονται ἀμφότεροι ἐν τῷ εὐκτηρίῳ τοῦ Ἁγίου Στεφάνου· Theophanes Con., pp. 625, 655, 816 ; Kodinos Kour., p. 351.

"They marry to him [the Emperor Michael] Eudokia daughter of Dekapolites, with whom he is crowned in the church of S. Stephen which is in the Daphne. The nuptial chamber was in the Manaura, and the Senate banquetted in the Hall of the Nineteen Couches." This church was originally built by Constantine the Great who "used it as a winter bedchamber."[1] "The damsel Epiphania, who is also called Eudokia was married in S. Stephen's in the Palace."[2]

THE BEDCHAMBER OF THE DAPHNE.

When a triumph was celebrated in honour of a victory, "The Emperor escorted by the courtiers goes into the Bedchamber of the Daphne." "The Emperor goes into the Bedchamber of the Augusteus which is there." On the festival of the Nativity, "The Emperor passing through the Augusteus enters S. Stephen's . . . he comes out, and goes into his bedchamber to wait the time."[3] There was a door leading from the Octagon into this chamber.[4] We learn very little about its site from the historians. As I said before, it was near the church of S. Stephen. This apartment was sometimes also called the Bedchamber of the Augusteus.[5]

THE GALLERY OF S. STEPHEN.

This was the name given to the passage leading from the Bedchamber of the Daphne to the Gallery

---

1 G. Kodinos, p. 18.   2 *Chron. Pasch.*, Vol. I., p. 703.
3 Cons. P., Vol. I., pp. 71, 72, 129, 608.   4 *Ibid*, p. 136.
5 *Ibid.*, pp. 71, 72, 180.

of the Augusteus, which separated the Palaces of
the Daphne and the Triconchon.   At the coronation of the Augusta, Constantine Porphyrogennetos
writes, "the Emperor signs to the praepositus . . .
and he brings in the Augusta . . . through
the Gallery of S. Stephen into the Augusteus,
from the Bedchamber in the Octagon" (p. 208).
This was done that the Augusta might not have to
pass through the midst of the people who were
gathered in the Hall of the Augusteus.[1]   This
gallery divided the Octagon, the Church of
S. Stephen, and the Hall of the Augusteus from
the [Palace] hippodrome which lay to the south of
them.   I do not know whether there was a door in
the Hall of the Augusteus leading to the gallery.
The only entrance was through the Bedchamber
above the Octagon, by which the Augusta went to
the gallery of the Daphne.

THE HALL OF THE AUGUSTEUS

extended from the Octagon and the church of
the Daphne to the gallery of the same name.
It is continually mentioned in connection with the
ceremonies of the Palace.   The Emperor went
through it to reach the Octagon.[2]   From it he

---

[1] From some words of C. Porphyrogennetos, it appears that the
Augusta appeared with her face veiled.   καὶ ἐπισκεπάζονται ἥ τε Αὐγούστα
καὶ τὸ παιδίον ἐφαπλώματα χρυσούφαντα, Vol. I., p. 618.   On this Reiske
remarks, Vol. II., p. 729 : Videtur ex his verbis colligi posse, Augustam
suum vultum nudum proceribus conspiciendum non dedisse, sed aut
pone velum, aut indutam calyptram cum iis egisse, more a Persis trans-
sumto et in aulam Turcicam propagato.
[2] Cons. P., Vol. I., p. 72.

passed through the narrow entrance and porch of the Augusteus called the Golden Hand,[1] entered the brazen gate of the Onopous and so went to the Consistory. On the Sunday of the Antipascha (Low Sunday), "a procession (μεταστάσιμον) is formed in the Consistory, and their Majesties go up to the Augusteus." That this hall, which was often called simply the Augusteus, lay north of the Octagon is evident from the language of Constantine Porphyrogennetos. "Their Majesties change their 'pagan' robes in the bedchamber of the Daphne, and going out to the octagonal bedchamber, proceed through the Augusteus."[2]

What is called the portico of the Augusteus was a doorway leading to the gallery of the Daphne or Augusteus.[3] This door is mentioned in the account of the ceremonies to be observed at Christmas. "The officers of the Bedchamber come into the Augusteus and stand in lines in the form of a II ; and when the Emperor enters, the great doors of the Augusteus are at once made fast."[4]

At the promotion of a demarch, "He proceeds through the Lausiakon, the Erôs, and the

---

1 *Ibid.*, pp. 9, 129, 136.

2 Vol. I., p. 33. Ἔνδοθεν γὰρ τῆς μεγάλης πύλης τοῦ Αὐγουστέως ἵστανται οἱ νηψηστιάριοι, βαστάζοντες τὰ χρυσᾶ καὶ ἐκ λίθων τιμίων κατεσκευασμένα χερνιβόξεστα. *Ibid.*, p. 9. The "pagan" robes were those worn on days when there was no festival. Διβητήσιον τὸ παγανὸν was a robe without ornamentation (p. 181). The "pagan" races were those held when the Emperor was not present (p. 334). "It must be observed that [no promotion] takes place on a feast day, but only on a pagan Sunday" (pp. 261, 367.)

3 *Ibid.*, p. 209.   4 *Ibid.*, p. 136.

Daphne to the Augusteus." [1]   By Daphne I think the writer means the gallery of that name, which was also known as the gallery of the Augusteus.

" Be it known that the gallery from the Augustaion to the Apse was garnished with various embroidered hangings." [2]   The Augusteus must have been a place of considerable size, for in it the Emperor sometimes received all the officers, his kinsmen, and the Patriarch. [3]   The coronation of the Augusta was often celebrated in this Hall. [4] From this I infer that part of it was roofed over.

THE CHURCH OF OUR LADY IN THE DAPHNE.

" And their Majesties proceed to the first built (πρωτοκτίστῳ) church of our Most Holy Lady." [5] What the writer means by calling it " first built " I do not know.   Probably it had, like the two following chapels, been built shortly before by Basil the Macedonian, the father of Constantine Porphyrogennetos.

THE CHURCH OF THE HOLY TRINITY.

Near the above, and probably connected with it, was the church, or rather chapel, of the Holy Trinity.   Our historians record but little about

---

[1] Cons. P., Vol. I., p. 270.   [2] *Ibid.*, pp. 573, 574.   [3] *Ibid.*, p. 630.
[4] *Ibid.*, p. 205.   Τῇ δὲ κέ τοῦ 'Οκτωβρίου μηνὸς ἐστέφθη Μαρία ἡ γυνὴ Λέοντος ἐν τῷ τρικλίνῳ τοῦ Αὐγουστέως.   G. Kedrenos, Vol. I., p. 792; II., p. 822.   The commentator on Kodinos Kouropalates (p. 355) is quite mistaken when he remarks on the passage: ἐστέφθη ἐν τῷ τρικλίνῳ τοῦ Αὐγουστέως ἡ βασίλισσα Εἰρήνη, idemque est quod dicitur χρυσοῦν τρίκλινον a Justiniano 2 exstructum.   This and similar mistakes arise from insufficient study of the Palace.   [5] Cons. P., Vol. I., p. 7.

these two small churches: Both of them lay to the south of the palace of the Daphne, possibly near the Hall of Justinian. When a procession was made to the Great Church, the Emperor went to the church of Our Lady and lit candles, thence he proceeded to the adjoining church of the Trinity.[1] Constantine Porphyrogennetos mentions a recess (στενάκιον) in this church, where sacred relics were preserved.[2] On the 25th of March, "the procession goes chanting a processional hymn from the church of Our Lady of the Pharos to the church of the Holy Trinity in the Daphne, and when it returns their Majesties give a banquet in the splendid Hall of Justinian."[3]

THE BAPTISTERY.

After worshipping in these two churches, the Emperor proceeded to the Baptistery "where the three large and beautiful crosses stand." In the procession at Christmas, the Emperor and the courtiers "pass through the Daphne into the church of the Holy Trinity ; and having lit candles there . . . he goes out, and likewise lights candles in the Baptistery at the crosses."[4] This Baptistery is sometimes called simply the Crosses. " Having lit candles and prayed, . . . he goes to the Crosses."[5] These three buildings, which are mentioned together, were all near each other.

---

1 Cons. P., Vol. I , p. 8.
2 Cons. P., Vol. I,, p. 8.
4 *Ibid.*, pp. 129, 532.

Ibid., p. 763.
Ibid., p. 174.

The Baptistery was farthest south. Their site is evident from the route followed by the Emperor. He went first to the church of Our Lady, then to the Trinity, and lastly to the. Baptistery. Constantine Porphyrogennetos calls these three churches " the chapels of the Daphne." [1]

THE THERMASTRA.

To get to the Consistory, one had to go through the Palace hippodrome, and the Thermastra. That the latter was near the hippodrome, is evident from the following words of Constantine Porphyrogennetos. " The domesticus of the schools and the domesticus of the excubita . . . went down to the Thermastra; for the captain of the watch was at his own post in the hippodrome."—" They entered through the Thermastra to the secret fountain of the Sigma."—" Within the gate leading from the Thermastra to the Lausiakon." [2]

In this part of the Palace it is difficult to distinguish the different doors and passages of the Thermastra, by which the people went to the Consistory. It was an underground chamber and is seldom mentioned.

The roof of the great underground chamber which

---

[1] Vol. I., p. 176.

[2] Cons. P., Vol. L, pp. 272, 340, 602, 605. He mentions a place in this neighbourhood called the Kastrêsiakòn. Possibly the Thermastra bore this name. μεθίστανται αἱ γυναῖκες καὶ ἀπέρχονται ἐπὶ τοὺς ἐλεφαντίνους πυλῶνας τοῦ καστρησιάκου. Vol. I., p. 211. The καστρήσιος of the Emperor's table is also ·mentioned : λαμβάνει ἀπὸ τῶν χειρῶν τοῦ καστρησίου ὁ πατριάρχης τὸν θυμιατόν. Ibid., pp. 542, 744, 748, 750, 755.

I mentioned in speaking of the Hall of Justinian, is supported by eight marble pillars. The height of the pillars to the capitals is 3·75 m. [12 ft. 2 in.]. The capitals are of the ordinary Byzantine form and workmanship. The length of the vault is 30 m. [97 ft. 6 in.], the height 5·25 m. [17 ft. 6 in.], and the walls are 2·25 m. [7 ft. 4 in.] thick. This gives some idea of the solidity of the building, and enables us to understand how it has remained so long intact. Through this vault people went from the Hall of Justinian and the covered hippodrome to the most northerly buildings of the Palace.

This vault lies in a street now called *Giúno Giorméz*, or the Dark Alley.

THE IVORY GATE.

This gate, which led into the Thermastra, was on the east side of the great covered hippodrome, or promenade of the Palace. It is mentioned by Porphyrogennetos, "And they open the Ivory Gate"—"They go up through the Ivory Gate"—"They rise from the table, and going out by the Ivory Gate, each one goes to his own place."[1] From the following words of the historian Kinnamos it would appear that this gate was also a prison. "Thomas . . . being taken into the prison in the Palace which is usually called the Ivory, there ended his life."[2] He was of course imprisoned in the gatehouse. Other writers are silent on this point. It was at this gate that the assassins of Michael, son

---

[1] Pp. 171, 518, 600, 602.   [2] P. 297.

of Theophilos came in the early morning, and concealed themselves.[1]   The priests of the Palace, the Imperial Clergy as they were called, passed the night outside the Palace.   " For an ancient custom prevailed, that the priests should remain outside the Palace at night, until the time appointed for them to enter at dawn."[2]   On the eve of Palm Sunday, after vespers in the church of S. Demetrios, all the courtiers went away by the Ivory Gate.[3]

THE GOLDEN HAND.

From the Hall of the Augusteus, one entered another called the Onopous or Onopodium.   The passage by which the two were connected was called the Passage ($\sigma\tau\epsilon\nu\grave{o}\nu$, $\sigma\tau\epsilon\nu\acute{a}\kappa\iota\nu$), the Porch of the Augusteus, and the Golden Hand.   Constantine Porphyrogennetos usually terms it the $\sigma\tau\epsilon\nu\acute{o}\nu$.[4]   It was a narrow passage roofed over.   "The Emperor goes through the narrow passage of the Golden Hand, and comes into the Onopous."—"Through the narrow passage of the Golden Hand he enters the bronze gate of the Onopous."   From this we learn that the door which closed the Golden Hand was called the Bronze Gate.   "He goes through the Augusteus and the passage, and the Onopous."—"And they escort him as far as the passage of the Onopous."—"And going through

[1] G. Kedrenos, Vol. II., p. 66.   [2] J. Genesios, p. 24.

[3] Cons. P., Vol. I., p. 171.

[4] Cons. P., Vol. I., p. 136.   Reiske does not in the least understand its situation.   Vol. II., p. 168.

the narrow passage, that is, the Golden Hand, he ascends to the Onopous."—"The porch of the Augusteus or the Golden Hand."[1]

From these passages it is evident that beside the Hall of the Augusteus there was another called the Onopous or Onopodium; into which one entered through the Golden Hand. The door here is continually mentioned in connection with the various ceremonies, and its situation is quite plain from the words of Constantine Porphyrogennetos. This portico was vaulted and rested on two marble pillars.

THE ONOPOUS OR ONOPODIUM.

The majority of the Palace buildings bear Greek or Latin names. It should be kept in mind that at the time when the Palace was founded, Latin was understood by all, owing to the emigration of so many persons from Rome. Hence we find Cubiculum, Consistory, Numera, Candidati, the Hall of the Nineteen Accubita, Boukoleon (Bucca leonis), and a great many more foreign names current in the months of the Byzantines until the final capture.

I think that the Onopodium, and its neighbour the Delphax which I mentioned before, bear names which were used by the ancient Byzantines, or were current among the populace before the Palace buildings were erected. Anciently there must have

---

[1] *Ibid.*, Vol. I., pp. 72, 147, 163, 176, 232, 573, 578.

been in this spot, stalls or stables where asses and swine were kept; and the Palace buildings inherited these incongruous names.

On Low Sunday, "A procession is formed in the Consistory, and their Majesties go to the Hall of the Augusteus, and change their robes, . . . The first reception, of the patricians, takes place at the Onopodium. . . . They proceed to the Great Consistory where the prefects stand."[1] From these words it is evident that the Onopodium was near the Consistory, in fact was connected with it. On Orthodoxy Sunday (the First Sunday in Lent) the Emperor went into the Consistory where the senate congratulated him, while the Master of Ceremonies and the silentiarii remained in the Onopodium.[2] At the feast of the Annunciation "The Emperor, escorted by the officers of the Bedchamber, goes through the passage of the Golden Hand, and proceeds to the Onopous. As he stands at the Bronze Gate, the patricians and generals receive him . . . Then these same . . . together with the whole Senate, go to the Consistory."[3] At another festival, that of the Exaltation of the Holy Crosses, after the ceremony in S. Sophia, the Emperor entered the Palace by the Bronze Gate.[4] He then went through the Schools and the Excubita to the Consistory, where the Senate was waiting, and the Master of Cere-

---

[1] Cons. P., Vol. I., p. 97.   [2] *Ibid.*, p. 159.   [3] *Ibid.*, p. 163.

[4] *Ibid.*, p. 128. [This Bronze Gate is the Palace gate opening into the Augustaion. It should not be confounded with the Bronze Gate mentioned in the preceding quotation, which was at the end of the Golden Hand.—Tr]

monies and the silentiarii received him. On the eve of the Feast of Lights (Epiphany), the Emperor and the Patriarch went out of the Palace to the Hall of the Augusteus, and there embraced each other. The Patriarch went to the Great Church accompanied by some officers of the Bedchamber and Consistory, while the Emperor returned to the Palace. From the account which Constantine Porphyrogennetos gives, it appears that the Hall of the Augusteus was near the Onopodium and the Consistory.[1]

At the coronation of the Emperor, he went out from the Augusteus and proceeded to the Onopodium, where the first reception of the patricians took place, after which they went down to the Great Consistory.[2]

These passages do not inform us whether the Onopodium was roofed over, or not.

At the promotion of a magister, "the triple door of the Onopodium is also guarded."[3] He probably means the doors leading to the Exaëron of the Nineteen Couches. From the foregoing passages we know that one door leading from the Hall of the Augusteus to the Onopodium was called the Golden Hand, or the Bronze Gate. Another door is mentioned called

THE DOOR OF THE PLATFORM.

Constantine Porphyrogennetos writes, "as the Emperor comes out from the door of the Platform that is

---

[1] Cons. P., Vol. I., p. 142. [2] *Ibid.*, p. 192. [3] Cons. P., Vol. I., p. 234.

to the Onopodium."[1] It appears from other passages that it was a marble balcony leading from the Nineteen Couches to the Onopodium. "The praepositus signs to the ostiarius who holds the curtain of the marble platform which leads out to the Onopodium."[2] This writer therefore mentions the following doors in the Onopodium : the Golden Hand leading from the Hall of the Augusteus, this door of the Platform on the west side, and the three doors leading from the Onopodium to the Consistory. I have discovered no door from it to the gallery of the Augusteus. A καμελαύκιον or baldaquin is mentioned in connection with this platform.[3]

THE CONSISTORY.

This was a spacious building situated to the north of the Onopodium. It communicated with it by three doors of ivory, termed the left hand, middle, and right hand, doors.[4] Mention is made of the Winter Consistory, the great Summer Consistory, and the Ante-consistory, where ambassadors sat before they were admitted to the presence of the Emperor. From the language of Constantine, I infer that there were three chambers, two of them on the east side of the Great Chamber with the porphyry stone and the Throne upon it.[5] The

---

[1] 'Η πύλη τοῦ τουλπίτου. *Ibid.*, p. 130.
[2] Cons. P., Vol. I., pp. 11, 143. Platforms are mentioned in S. Sophia and the entrance to the Chrysotriklinos. *Ibid.*, pp. 134, 243.
[3] *Ibid.*, p. 11.
[4] *Ibid.*, pp. 73, 84, 107, 168, 234.
[5] Cons. P., Vol. I., pp. 398, 404, 407.

building was called the Consistory because the chief officers of state often sat together there with the Emperor. On this account the meeting itself was called a Consistory.[1]

At the reception of the Persian ambassadors, we are told, " the usher (ἀδμισσιονάλιος) must conduct the ambassador, and place him beside the wall within the curtain of the great Summer Consistory. The doors of the Consistory are also opened if he has horses among his presents. . . . The Decurion goes into the lesser Consistory."

All the ambassadors were received in the Consistory without weapons. " They [the Western ambassadors] do not come armed into the presence of the Emperor because they are not barbarian ambassadors."[2]

The Crucifix of S. Constantine and Moses' rod[3] were also kept in the Consistory. Here too there was a baldaquin, covering the Porphyry Stone, on which the Emperor's throne stood. Porphyry steps led up to it.[4] From the Onopodium they descended into the Consistory by steps through the three doors which we have mentioned. "The Spatharioi descend the steps of the Consis-

---

1 Κονσιστώριον, θεῖον συνέδριον, Hesychios ; Κονσιστώριον, παρὰ 'Ρωμαίοις οὕτω λέγεται τὸ συνέδριον καὶ τὸ σύστημα ἔνθα περὶ τῶν ἐπειγόντων βουλεύονται, Souidas ; ἔνθα ἵστανται ὕπατοι, κονσιστώριον καὶ οἱ λοιποὶ συγκλητικοί. Cons. P., Vol. I., pp. 97, 257. Κωνσιστωριανὸς, Consistorianus. Meursii *Glossarium.*

2 Cons. P., Vol. I., pp. 405, 394, 396. It is probable that this custom has descended to the Turks from the Byzantine Court.

3 Cons. P., Vol. I., p. 10. This rod is also mentioned as being in the Chapel of S. Theodore in the Chrysotriklinos. See ch. vi. of this work.

4 *Ibid.*, pp. 63, 69, 73, 98, 130, 163, 181, 232, 233.

tory,"—"The three doors of the Consistory are opened,"—The Emperor "sits down in the Great Consistory and the magistrates enter."[1]

When the precious throne was set in the Consistory it was guarded by silentiarii and chosbaïtai.[2] As long as it was there, no one remained in the Consistory at night. All the doors of the buildings around were securely shut, and not even the patricians were admitted. "They change their robes in the Indoi as they have not permission to enter while the throne stands there."[8]

THE CHURCH OF OUR LORD.

This church is often mentioned. In the procession to the tomb of S. Mokios,[4] the Emperor received the magistrates in the Church of Our Lord, whence all proceeded together to the shrine of the saint. The gate of the narthex was of bronze. "As the Emperor enters the bronze gate of Our Lord's."[5] The Emperor, at the feast of the Annunciation, passed through the Gallery of Our Lord, and entered the Apse of the Triconchos. From it he went through the Gallery of the Forty Saints to the Chrysotriklinos.[6] Treasures of great

---

1 *Ibid.*, pp. 63, 405.

2 The Chosbaltai were vestiaries who had charge of the Emperor's sandals. Cons. P., Vol. II., pp. 42, 847. [See note on p. 219.—Tr.]

8 Cons. P., Vol. I., p. 234. I think that Labarte is mistaken in saying that there was a banquetting-hall beside the Consistory. See "Les Salles à manger " in his work.

4 Cons. P., Vol. I., p. 98.

5 *Ibid.*, pp. 84, 107, 230.

6 *Ibid.*, p. 169.

value were preserved in the church.[1] The Emperors were sometimes crowned outside it. "He himself [the Emperor] sat outside the Church of Our Lord, in the place where the Emperors were wont to be crowned . . . before going on horseback to the Church of the Holy Apostles." On the way back they put off their crowns, in the porch of this church.[2] From it they ascended into the Augusteus by the porticos.[3] The passage from the gate of the Spatharikion to this church was called the Gallery of the Lord. The Emperor on coming out of the Palace, passed through the Gallery of the Forty Saints, the gate of the Spatharikion, and this gallery, and thus arrived at the Church of Our Lord.[4]

According to Kodinos, this church which stood at the north side of the Consistory, was built by the Emperor Constantine the Great.

THE OVAL.

This building was so called from its shape. It stood on the left side [south] of the church of Our Lord which again was to the south of the Manaura.

On the second day of the first week, "the courtiers go through the Gallery of the Forty Saints, the Sigma, and the Church of Our Lord, and thence proceed through the Sakella, the Oval, and the passage leading to the terrace of the Manaura, and enter the Great Hall."[5] Constantine Porphyro-

---

[1] *Ibid.*, pp. 591, 641. [2] *Ibid.*, pp. 32, 128, 593-4.
[3] *Ibid.*, p. 270. [4] *Ibid.*, pp. 169, 635. [5] *Ibid.*, pp. 545, 567.

gennetos states that it is a mistake to call the Hall of the Manaura the Oval, "for the charter room of the Treasury is called the Oval."[1] A similar chamber in the Palace of Blachernai is mentioned. The Emperor "took the air (ἐναιθρίαζε) sitting in the middle of the Oval."[2] Kodinos states that this building was erected by Constantine the Great.

According to some authorities, it was in this building that the Quinisextan Council of 691 A.D. met.[3] No one has left any account of the dimensions of the building, and the apartments it contained.

So far we have been considering the chief buildings on either side of the gallery of the Daphne

---

[1] *Ibid.*, p. 593. Σακέλλα ὅπου τὸ χρυσίον τίθεται. Σακέλλιον ὁμοίως. Hesychios. Βαλάντιον, μαρσύπιον, ἐξ οὗ καὶ σακελλάριος. Souidas.

[2] Καὶ ἀστραπτῶν περὶ τὸ παλάτιον εἰλουμένων, καὶ τοῦ βασιλέως φεύγοντος ἀπὸ τόπου εἰς τόπον, ἐν ἑνὶ τῶν κοιτωνίσκων τῷ λεγομένῳ ᾠάτῳ κατέλαβεν αὐτὸν ἡ ὀργή, ὥστε αἰφνίδιον εὑρεθῆναι νεκρόν. G. Pachymeres, Vol. I., pp. 405, 621. G. Kodinos, p. 227. An Oval in Nikaia is also mentioned, *Acta et Diplomata*, Vol. III., p. 65.

[3] Byzantios, Κπολις, Vol. I., p. 206, note. Βυζαντιναὶ Μελέται, p. 303. Cons. P., Vol. II., p. 263. Ὥρισε ἡ ἐν τῷ τρούλλῳ τοῦ μεγάλου παλατίου συστᾶσα θεία καὶ οἰκουμενικὴ ἁγία σύνοδος, ἡ καὶ πενθέκτη λεγομένη. Meursii *Glossarium.* Καὶ ὁ τῆς ἐν τῷ Τρούλλῳ τέταρτος τῆς οἰκουμενικῆς ἕκτης συνόδου. N. Gregoras, Vol. I., p. 407. No one, however, notices the building in which this Synod met. The language of Du Cange on the subject is equally vague. "Le triclinium *Tholotum* qu' *Anastasius Dicorus* fit batir, qui est cette partie du palais nommé *Trullus*, où fut tenu le Concile *in Trullo. Hist. de l'Empire*, etc. Pt. i., p. 152. Banduri says the same. Vol. II., p. 355. Willelmus Tyrius, lib. xxii., cap. 4. The Synaxaristes, who has valuable information on all matters Byzantine collected from the writings of Simeon Metaphrastes, says in his account of this Synod, celebrated on the 14th of September: αὐτὴ ἡ ἁγία καὶ οἰκουμενικὴ Σύνοδος, συνηθροίσθη ἐν τῷ τρούλλῳ τοῦ παλατίου τῷ λεγομένῳ ᾠάτῳ, ἐπὶ τῆς βασιλείας Κωνσταντίνου τοῦ Πωγωνάτου. Ed. Zakynthos, 1808, Vol. I., p. 52. [See also p. 230, note, of this work.—Tr.]

and those above the Hall of the Augusteus. Other galleries and buildings, mentioned even more frequently than these await our attention. In the study of such questions as this we have to proceed with great caution, and begin with the buildings which stood near those still in existence, that we may not go astray.

THE EXAËRON OR AREA.

North of the Octagon and of the church of S. Stephen, lay the gallery or Hall of the Nineteen Couches famous in Byzantine history. The northern portion of it was the Area or Exaëron.[1] The courtiers descended to it from the Hall of the Candidati, by doors.[2] Descending from the Exaëron they entered the Onopodium, and some stood there and others at the Golden Hand, the entrance to the Hall of the Augusteus.[3] They descended into the Exaëron by steps on account of the steepness of the ground.

THE HALL OF THE NINETEEN COUCHES.

No spot in the Palace precincts is mentioned so

---

[1] 'Εξάερον, Locus aeri expositus, τὰ ἀλλότρια ἐδάφη, ἐν οἷς οὐκ εἰσὶν οἰκίαι, καὶ τὰ τῶν γειτόνων ἐξέδρα. Meursii *Glossarium.* Area, αὐλή, πρασιά, ὕπαιθρον, ἅλως, ἀλώνιον, σχολάζων τόπος. Γλωσ. A. Koraês *Posthumous Works,* ed. A. Z. Mámoukas, Athens, 1881, p. 10. In the procession to the church of the Studium, they went to the spacious court (αὐλή) of the church by the gate called *Narlí kapí,* passed through the exaëron and entered the right-hand porch of the church (Cons. P., Vol. I., p. 563). This makes it plain that C. Porphyrogennetos uses *exaëron,* of an open space, and such the place is to this day.

[2] Cons. P., Vol. I., p. 20.

[3] *Ibid.,* p. 21.

often as the Hall of the Nineteen Couches, or, as it is frequently called, the Great Hall. According to Kodinos, it was built by Constantine the Great.[1] On festivals and great processions, especially on Easter Sunday, "Their Majesties go out of the Palace . . . and the customary salutation takes place in the Great Hall of the Nineteen Couches.[2] On the Feast of Lights [Epiphany] the Patriarch goes into the church of S. Stephen in the Daphne; and when the Emperor is about to recline at table in the Hall of the Nineteen Couches, he summons the Patriarch. After the usual salutations, the Patriarch again returns to S. Stephen's, and puts off his pallium.[3] In this Hall of the Couches, the courtiers and bishops who accompanied the Patriarch stood on the "right and left sides" of the apartment. Constantine Porphyrogennetos terms those who occupied the best places the first accubiti (τοὺς πρώτους ἀκκουβίτους).

At the coronation of the Augusta, the people gathered in the tribune of the Nineteen Couches, the patricians stood in the Onopodion, and the senators in the portico of the Nineteen Couches.

---

[1] P. 18.

[2] Τρίκλινος τῶν ιθ' ἀκκουβίτων, Cons. P., Vol. I., p. 187. This Hall is called both ἀκκούβιτα and ἀκούβιτα. Ibid., pp. 63, 73, 146. In the Middle Ages the Aristeria were called accubita, Joannes Lydos, p. 130. Ἐξκούβιτα, excubita, is the cohors imperatoria. J. Meursii Glossarium. For the signification of this word see Reiske's notes on Cons. P., Vol. II., p. 124. Ἡ τε λέξις τῶν ἀκουβίτων τῶν Λατίνων ἐστὶν (ἀκούμβω γὰρ παρὰ Ῥωμαίοις τὸ ἀναπίπτω), σημαίνει στρωμνὰς ἡρμένας εἰς ὕψος καὶ μαλακὰς, αὗται δὲ τρυφῆς καὶ μαλακίας εἰσίν. Kodinos Kouropalates, p. 301. μετὰ τὴν ἀπόλυσιν τῆς ἐκκλησίας, ὅτε ἀκουμβίσωσιν οἱ δεσπόται ἐπὶ τῆς τραπέζης. Cons. P., Vol. I., pp. 52, 47, 54.

[3] Cons. P., Vol. I., p. 146.

This portico leading from the Exaëron to the Great Hall is often mentioned.[1]

In the middle of this Hall, the remains of deceased Emperors and Augustae were placed on a golden couch, called the "Bed of Sorrow," before their interment in the Church of the Apostles.[2]

Outside of the Hall was the tribune of the Area, where at the election of a Caesar all the officers and military stood, congratulating the Emperor and the Caesar. "Their Majesties sit down in the Great Hall of the Nineteen Couches, and the Patriarch comes in at once and awaits them in the church of S. Stephen. . . . The patricians form a Consistory at the portico of the Nineteen Couches, and the remaining senators go out and stand on the steps of the Area on either side of the terrace." This passage shews that in front of the Nineteen Couches there was an open space, the Exaëron or Area, and round it steps for the use of those commanded to attend the Imperial festivals. "And they stood on the steps of the terrace area, on either side of the terrace."—"They stood on the steps of the area."[4]

The silver pillars of this hall, behind which the Emperor robed, are mentioned.[5]

In the Area there was a terrace, or terraces, and

[1] *Ibid.*, pp. 204, 62, 619.

[2] *Ibid.*, p. 275. καὶ ταύτην βασιλικῶς τιμήσας καὶ ἐν τῇ χρυσοκολλήτῳ καὶ διὰ μαργαριτῶν καὶ λίθων κλίνῃ τεθεῖσα . . . θάπτεται ἐν λάρνακι. Theophanes Con., p. 478.

[3] Cons. P., Vol. I., p. 218.

[4] *Ibid.*, p. 628.

[5] *Ibid.*, pp. 25, 62.

steps leading up to them. Part of the floor was called the Tribune.[1] At the election of a Caesar, their Majesties and the Patriarch went up to the tribune, and the Emperor said what he wished to the people. The people replied if they had anything to answer. Before this part of the ceremonies, Constantine Porphyrogennetos writes of their Majesties passing with the Patriarch through the great Hall of the Nineteen Couches, not having yet arrived at the terrace of the Tribune. From this it is clear that it was at the lower or eastern part of the Hall.[2] The great door of the Tribune is mentioned in the account of the coronation of the Augusta. We learn from a phrase in Constantine Porphyrogennetos that there were chambers in this Hall. He speaks of the servants in the chambers of the Nineteen Couches.[3]

Great companies of guests sat and feasted together in this spacious Hall, and used to greet the Emperor in Latin.[4] At the Imperial table the chiefs of the Blue and Green factions stood on the

---

[1] Ἐν τῷ τριβουναλίῳ λεγομένῳ δεκαεννέα ἀκκουβίτων.   G. Kedrenos, Vol. II., p. 942. τούτῳ τῷ ἔτει ἰνδικτιῶνι γ΄ τῇ ἡμέρᾳ τοῦ Πάσχα, ἐστέφθη Κωνσταντῖνος ὑπὸ Λέοντος τοῦ πατρὸς αὐτοῦ ἐν τῷ τριβουναλίῳ τῶν ἐννεακαίδεκα ἀκουβίτων. Theophanes, Vol. I., p. 616.   Nikephoros Patriarches, p. 64.

[2] Cons. P., Vol. I., pp. 218, 222, 226.   ἐκεῖθεν οὖν εὐφημούμενος κατέλαβε τὴν λεγομένην Χαλκῆν, καὶ δι᾽ αὐτῆς εἰσελθὼν ἔφθασεν ἄχρι τῶν ἐξκουβίτων. G. Kedrenos, Vol. II., p. 280.

[3] Cons. P., Vol. I., pp. 577, 589.   I think that by the words καὶ προτίθεται κλήτωριον ἐν τῷ περιβλέπτῳ τρικλίνῳ τῶν καθισμάτων (pp. 773, 781), he means the Hall of the Stand in the Hippodrome.   Cf. 778.

[4] Λέγουσι οἱ πέντε βουκάλιοι, Κονσέρβετ Δέους ἡμπέριουμ βέστρουμ, ὅ ἐστι μεθερμηνευόμενον Φυλάξει ὁ Θεὸς τὴν βασιλείαν ὑμῶν, etc., etc.

right and left respectively, along with many of the members.

On the day of S. Elias, "a banquet is set before the Emperor on a separate table in the middle of the Hall of the Nineteen pleasant Couches, and the praepositi feast with the Emperor."[1] The couches were ranged along the walls of the Hall, and in the middle there was a great clear floor. The Emperor sometimes banquetted here with certain of the distinguished courtiers, others sat at the lower or eastern couches.[2]

From other words of Constantine it is evident that this Hall was near another called the Hall of the schools.[3] The portico of the Great Hall is also mentioned, which, as I said, led into the adjoining Onopodium. From this Hall they descended into the Onopodium, and through it entered the Consistory.

As I said before, the deceased Emperors lay in state in this Hall; and here the clergy of S. Sophia and the Senate met together. All the Emperors were interred in churches or monasteries outside the Palace, with the exception of John Tzimiskes, who was buried at the Bronze Gate.[4]

The writers of the Continuation of Theophanes thus narrate the ceremonies at the interment of

---

[1] Cons. P., Vol. I., p. 778. Joannes Kantakouzenos makes the following remarks about the mode of these feasts (Vol. III., p. 28). Τῶν ἐπιφανῶν δὲ Περσῶν οἱ ἄλλοι καὶ ʻΡωμαίων ἐπὶ ταπήτων ἦσαν ἀνακεκλιμένοι πρὸς τὸ ἐσθίειν ὅσον ὁρᾶσθαι ὑπὸ βασιλέως.

[2] Cons. P., Vol. I., pp. 362, 370.

[3] Vol. I., p. 12.

[4] Cons. P., Vol. I., pp. 26, 218, 219, 226.

Constantine VII. Porphyrogennetos. "Having washed the body, they set it in the Hall of the Nineteen Couches, and honouring it with psalms, straightway bore it out, and placed it at the Bronze Gate, where the arch priest and priests, the magistrates, patricians, and the whole Senate exchanged a final embrace. Then the Master of Ceremonies, as was his wont, called out, 'Come forth, O King. The King of Kings and Lord of Lords summons thee.' Whereupon the great multitude raised shouts and shrieks and lamentations. When he had called this three times, they raised the prince, and bore him from the Imperial house to the Thoroughfare (Mesê), and so to the church of the Holy Apostles."[1]

On the ninth day of the Dekaêmeron, the so-called Gothikon was celebrated in this Hall. As the Emperor was sitting at supper, musicians entered, and two Goths, wearing masks and sheepskins, with the woolly side out, uttering good wishes to the Emperor in "Gothic," a barbarous jargon, which we now find hard to explain or to understand, and holding small shields in their left hands and staves in their right. They and a band of performers gambolled and danced, and greeted the Emperor in their unintelligible Gothic tongue without ceasing, until the end of the banquet. In his account, Constantine Porphyrogennetos mentions the "two entrances of the Great Hall." In another passage he speaks of the "great door of

---

[1] Theophanes Con., p. 467.

the Couches." So that the other was probably known as the "smaller."[1]

Subordinate to the domesticus of the Couches were the following officers, topoteretai, chartularii, scribes, protomandators, drakonarioi, skeuopohoroi, signophoroi, senatores, and mandatores.[2] The accubitores were the guards of this Hall.[3]

In the time of Alexios Komnenos, Varangi are also mentioned, who were quartered in the Nineteen Couches as guards.[4] Constantine Porphyrogennetos never mentions them.

That the space covered by this Hall was large, is evident from the account of the feast which took place on Christmas-day.[5] Besides many magistrates, proconusls, and patricians, the officers of the different ranks to the number of a hundred and sixty-eight, the twenty-four Hagarenes of the Praetorium, twelve friendly Bulgars, and twelve poor brethren were invited. The Hagarenes sat opposite the Emperor at the sixth and seventh tables, the Bulgars and poor brethren at the ninth. The Emperor sat at a separate table facing the East, so that some of his guests were behind him, and others in front. On either side of the tables were benches. On the sixth day of this feast the Patriarch and twelve abbots were invited.

---

[1] Cons. P., Vol. I., p. 381 ; II., p. 355.

[2] Cons. P., Vol. I., p. 717.

[3] Κόμης ἐξκουβιτώρων, *Chron. Pasch.*, Vol. I., p. 611 ; Nikephoros Patriarch., p. 36.

[4] J. Meursii *Glossarium*, s. v. Βαράγγοι. Kodinos Kouropalates, pp. 264, 265. [Cleasby, *Icelandic Dict.*, s.v. Væringi.]

[5] Cons. P., Vol. I., p. 741.

After them two hundred and sixteen abbots of different monasteries were entertained. On the eleventh day the feast came to an end in the Hall of Justinian, when two hundred and sixteen guests banquetted at separate tables.[1]

After the ceremony on the 20th of July (S. Elias' day) a banquet took place in this Hall, which Constantine Porphyrogennetos styles "pleasant."[2]

In the reign of Constantine VII., Porphyrogennetos, the roof of the Hall decayed and fell in. The building, or at least part of it, was therefore roofed over. The Emperor restored the old gilt ceiling, which was destroyed, and made it brilliant and new in appearance. He also formed octagonal niches, which he adorned with round windows, and a variety of carvings formed like wreaths of vines, and all kinds of leaves and branches. All these were gilded to the delight and admiration of the beholders.[3]

The many things that Luitprand relates in praise of the size and beauty of the building, while sneering at the builders and occupants, are very curious. "There is a house beside the hippodrome,[4] facing the north, of wonderful loftiness and beauty, which is called the Nineteen Couches. Here are set nineteen tables at which they recline to eat, and do not sit as in other places. All the vessels are not of silver but of gold."

---

[1] *Ibid.*, p. 753. Χωριστῶν τραπεζῶν, the ἀποκοπτῶν τραπεζῶν of C. Porphyrogennetos.

[2] *Ibid.*, p. 778.

[3] Theophanes Con., p. 449.

[4] i.e., the Palace hippodrome, *Hist.*, vi, 8.

THE DIKIONION.

Between the Hall of the Nineteen Couches and the Onopodium, there was a building called the Dikionion. At the coronation and nuptials of the Augusta, she went into the Onopodium, and thence to the Dikionion.[1] The senators and others subsequently formed a consistory in the Great Hall as far as the Dikionion and the Onopodium. From the following it appears that it was a covered passage supported on two pillars, leading from the Great Hall to the Onopodium. " When the Augusta comes from the Terrace, the patricians go to the Golden Hand escorting her, and the company of the prefects extends to the Dikionion. When the Augusta arrives at the middle of them, they exclaim, 'For many long and prosperous years.' The patricians in the Golden Hand do the same, . . . the Augusta passes through, and enters the Hall of the Augusteus." The officers followed the Augusta, and went with her into the Hall.

THE SCHOOLS, OR THE HALL OF THE SCHOOLS.

This gallery was alongside the Hall of the Nineteen Couches, or rather, was connected with, and lay to the north of it. On the second day of the Renewal (Easter Monday), the Emperor went through the Great Hall, the Schools, and the Bronze Gate to S. Sophia. At Christmas, the

---

[1] Cons. P., Vol. I., p. 211, *et sqq.*

Emperor went through the Schools, and coming to the fifth School, lit his candle before the Cross. The door of the fifth School is also spoken of. From this I should suppose that there was a fixed place for each School in this Hall. On the Feast of the Annunciation, again, the Emperor passed through the Couches and the Schools, and went out by the Bronze Gate.[1]

At the reception of the Mussulman envoys in the time of Constantine and Romanus, which took place in the Schools, sailors were posted on every side of the building, armed with leathern bucklers and swords.[2]

Mention is made of a dome with eight pillars in the first School, under which a very beautiful silver cross stood. I think this is the στρογγύλον alluded to by Constantine Porphyrogennetos. "The Emperor goes also into the Schools, within the door where the cross stands, and takes his

---

[1] *Ibid.*, pp. 73, 131-2, 163. Many Schools are mentioned in the works of the Byzantine writers. *Chronicon Paschale*, Vol. I., p. 502. The Schools were seven in number. χρὴ τὸν μάγιστρον προευτρεπῖσαι τὸν κόμητα τῆς ἕκτης ἢ ἑβδόμης Σχόλης. Cons. P., Vol. I., p. 391. The Scholares were the guards of the Palace. *Ibid.*, Vol. I., p. 60. Procopius in *Anecdotis* et Agathias *Scolares* palatii ter mille ac quingentos numero fuisse testantur. *Cpolis Christ.*, Vol. II., cap. iv. Sunt autem scholae idem atque cohortes et quidem quae hic designantur scholae . . . militum palatinorum, non tam pompaticorum, quam vere militantium et Imperatorem domi forisque comitantium et protegentium. *Ibid.*, p. 837. Agathias, p. 310. ἐν δεξιᾷ καταλιπόντες τὸ τῶν σχολῶν σύνταγμα. M. Attaliates, p. 112. Ὁ Ἰουνίωρ . . . πρῶτος ἐποίησε κανδιδάτους καὶ πρωτίκτωρας, καὶ τὸ τάγμα τῶν σχολαρίων συστησάμενος, ἐκάλεσεν αὐτὸ Ἰουνιώρων εἰς τὸ ἴδιον ὄνομα. G. Kedrenos, Vol. I., p. 451; II., p. 940. J. Meursii, *Glossarium*, *s.v.* σχολάριοι.

[2] Cons. P., Vol. I., p. 579.

place in the chamber of the στρογγύλον."[1] There was a door at the Bronze Gate leading to the Schools, "as far as the great door of the Schools which leads out to the dome of the Bronze Gate."[2]

THE LIGHTS.

East of the Hall of the Schools there was another similar Hall or passage called the Lights (λύχνοι). From the Hall of the Nineteen Couches they ascended to the Lights, where a silver cross stood.[3] A chamber in this Hall is mentioned, which was, I think, situated in the part connected with the Schools.

In some processions the foreigners who happened to be in the city at the time assembled here to greet the Emperor. "The last reception takes place at the Tribune, that is before the Lights." This Hall was near, or rather was connected with, the Great Hall. From it doors led to the Schools. "The Blue faction stands at the Lights to receive the prefect."[4] Kodinos writes as follows concerning this Hall : "The Emperor Constantine built the Lights or the dome of the seven lights which is still standing in the Schools."[5] This leads one to suppose that the latter building was roofed over.

---

[1] Vol. I., p. 131. ἀπερχόμενοι ἐν τῷ ὀκτακιόνῳ θόλῳ ἤγουν εἰς τὴν πρώτην σχόλην, ὅνπερ τὴν παλαίαν καλοῦσι χαραγήν. *Ibid.*, p. 11.

[2] *Ibid.*, Vol. I., pp. 11, 19, 27.

[3] Cons. P., Vol. I., pp. 12, 13. Reiske, *ibid.*, II., p. 83, thinks it got the name : forte quia ibi in processionibus transeunte Imperatore lychni accendebantur.

[4] Cons. P., Vol. I., pp. 13, 20, 27, 40, 265.

[5] G. Kodinos, p. 18.

THE TRIBUNE.

The Tribune was a place near the Lights and the Curtains. "The Emperor Romanus made a procession to the Tribune, and all accompanied him thither with arms."—"The Emperor Romanus made a procession to the Tribune."[1] According to Kodinos,[2] the dances of the two factions took place here in the time of Heraclius. The Tribune is continually mentioned, especially in the account of the coronation of the Augusta. "She, comes out through the middle door of the Tribune." "In the Tribune, where the sceptre and cross stand." Leo at his coronation, "having been covered with a breast-plate by the Candidati in the Tribunal, and having put on the Imperial robes and diadem," shewed himself to the people.[3] According to Constantine Porphyrogennetos, the Lights was called the Tribune. "The first reception takes place at the Tribune, i.e., before the Lights" (εἰς τὸ τριβουνάλιον, ἤγουν εἰς τοὺς λύχνους).[4] In describing the Palace I look upon this writer as the safest guide. Some speak as if the Tribune were in the Hall of the Nineteen Couches. Constantine Porphyrogennetos says it was in the Lights. The Lights, the Nineteen Couches, and the Hall of the Candidati were close together, and

---

[1] Theophanes Con., pp. 389, 891.
[2] P. 36. Souidas, *s.v.* τριβουνάλιον.
[3] Cons. P., Vol. I., pp. 210, 411. Kodinos Kouropalates, p. 859. Tribunalium enim palatium erat augustissimum. G. Kedrenos, Vol. II., p. 823.
[4] Vol. I., pp. 35, 40. Describing the Hippodrome (p. 312), he mentions a tribune on which the urn stood.

the buildings are often confused. In my opinion, a part of the Lights was called the Tribune. In his account of the procession of the Emperor to S. Sophia, the writer above-mentioned says that the drapers and the silversmiths decorated the Tribune with silken hangings and rugs (p. 572).

THE HALL OF THE CANDIDATI.

The Hall or Long Room (Μάκρων) of the Candidati was close to the Consistory, for there was a direct passage from one to the other. " The three ivory doors of the Consistory and those leading to the Long Room of the Candidati are made safe, . . . and the officials stand in the Long Room of the Candidati, and the same patricians go to the Bronze Gates of the Curtains." [1]

At the promotion of a prefect, " the Master of Ceremonies raises him up, and conducts him to the winter consistory, . . . and he comes to the Long Room of the Candidati." [2] Once Constantine Porphyrogennetos mentions a room called the Indoi. I think it must have been in this Hall. " In the morning the senate change their robes in the Long Room of the Candidati, and the patricians in the Indoi, as they are not allowed to enter the Hall of the Nineteen Couches while the throne stands there." [3] Near this Hall was the *secretum* of the prefects, but it is difficult to determine its exact site. [4] According to the *Chronicon Paschale,* [5]

---

[1] *Ibid.,* pp. 234, 239.   [2] *Ibid.,* p. 265.   [3] *Ibid.,* pp. 234, 236.
[4] *Ibid.,* p. 197, 577.   [5] Vol. I., p. 501.

the Candidati were chosen from the Scholars. These were of the sixth school. In the account of the Hall of the Schools I mentioned the first and fifth Schools. Probably there were places for each of the Schools. At the reception of Olga of Russia " she went out through the Anadendrarion, the Hall of the Candidati, and the Hall where the Kamelaukion stands, and the magistri are created." This Hall lay to the south side of the Manaura. "And the factions stand in the Hall of the Candidati, on either side near the steps of the Manaura.[1]

THE CURTAINS.

This building was north of the Halls of the Schools, the Lights, and the Candidati. The historians do not state whether the place was open or roofed in. On the feast of the Annunciation, after the ceremony in S. Sophia, the Emperor passed through the Schools and the Curtains.[2] A bronze gate stood between the Curtains and the Hall of the Schools. "Accompanied by them as far as the bronze gate of the Curtains." The Emperor was " accompanied by all the dignitaries of the Praetorium' as far as the bronze gate of the Curtains."[3] He went from the Curtains to the Bronze Gate [leading into the Forum] through the Hall of the Schools. Gates led from the Curtains to the Schools, the Lights, and the Hall of the Candidati.

---

[1] Cons. P., Vol. I., pp. 595, 197, 213. This Hall had a bronze door opening to the Manaura, *ibid.*, p. 578.
[2] *Ibid.*, p. 168.   [3] *Ibid.*, pp. 239, 252, 265.

CHAPTER IX.

THE CHURCH OF THE HOLY APOSTLES.

THIS church was near the Schools, on their south side, and consequently between them and the Bronze Gate. " The fourth reception takes place at the entrance of the Holy Apostles, that is at the Schools."—" The fourth reception is at the Holy Apostles, or the Schools."—" The Green faction stands at the Holy Apostles, at the Schools."[1] From these passages it is evident that this church was either within or very close to the Schools. It is seldom mentioned, but, according to George Kodinos,[2] it was founded by the Emperor Constantine.

THE BRONZE GATE.

After the study of the many galleries and halls of the Palace I come now to a building which is mentioned more frequently than any other, not by Constantine Porphyrogennetos alone, but by all the Byzantine historians. It was called the Bronze Gate (ἡ Χαλκῆ), on account of its roof of gilded bronze.[3] By this building the Emperor and his

---

[1] Cons. P., Vol. I., pp. 13, 19, 40, 252.   [2] P. 18.

[3] The Patriarch Constantius is wrong in calling the Senate-house Chalké. Ἐλάσσονες Συγγραφαὶ, ἐν Κπόλει, 1866, p. 380—καὶ λοιπὸν ἐνττ-

courtiers went in and out of the Palace, to which it was the principal entrance, like the Gyrolimne at Blachernai. It was the great Imperial Gate of the Palace, and no one but the Emperor might enter it on horseback.

The Bronze Gate, or rather gatehouse, was built by Justinian after the Nika Riot, and was beautified by many of the succeeding Emperors. Prokopios[1] gives us the best description of the erection of the building by Justinian. " The outwork, which they call Chalkê, is of this sort; four upright walls, very lofty, stand in the form of a square. In all respects they are similar to one another, except that those facing the north and south are somewhat shorter than the others." Eight arches supported the domes, four the lofty dome in the middle; and two others north and south of it were each supported by a pair of arches. "All the ceiling is decorated with pictures, not such as are formed with wax melted and laid on to harden, but made of small stones fitted together, gay with various colours, which represent men and other objects. . . On one side is represented war and battle, and many cities are being taken— some in Italy, some in Libya—and the Emperor

---

ρησαν τὴν εἴσοδον τοῦ παλατίου τὴν χαλκόστεγον, καὶ ἐκαύθη μετὰ τοῦ πορτήκου τῶν σχολαρίων. *Chron. Pasch.*, Vol. I. p. 621 ; Theophanes, Vol. I., p. 283 ; G. Kedrenos, Vol. I., p. 647 ; ὁ δὲ περὶ αὐτὸν τὸν κίονα χαλκὸς ἅπας κέραμος ἦν διάχρυσος, τὴν εἴσοδον τοῦ παλατίου Κωνσταντίνου τοῦ μεγάλου βασιλέως ἐπικαλύπτων, ἥτις καὶ μέχρι τοῦ νῦν Χαλκῆ προσαγορεύεται. *Ibid.*. pp. 656-7 ; Aedificium id erat aeneis tegulis tectum, per quod in magnum palatium aditus patebat. Cons. P., Vol. II., p. 91.

[1] Vol. III., p. 203,

Justinian is conquering by his general Belisarius.
. . . In the middle stand the Emperor and the
Empress Theodora as if rejoicing and celebrating a
victory, and ruling over the Vandals and Goths.
They are attended by prisoners of war and captives,
and the Roman Senate surrounds them, all in
festal array. . . As far as the mosaics above,
all the interior is covered with magnificent marbles,
not the walls only, but also all the floor." According to Kedrenos [1] this splendid house of the Bronze
Gate was built by the architect Aitherios, and
Anastasios the Counsellor.

The magnificence and splendour of the famous
Bronze Gate are evident from these words of Prokopios. But what is of more importance to us is
its site, and the doors leading from the Augustaion
to the Palace. Little is said by later writers of the
exterior of the building so extolled by Prokopios.
Within or close to it, John Tzimiskes built entirely anew the chapel of Christ the Saviour, in
which he was buried. Leo the Deacon writes thus
of it [2] : "Going out from the Palace he proceeds
to the chapel dedicated to Christ the Saviour at
the Bronze Gate, to propitiate the Deity ; having
viewed this narrow chapel, which can scarcely contain fifteen persons, and has a crooked and difficult
approach . . . he is urged by her to build this
one, larger and more comely, from the foundation."
"And passing through the chapel of the Saviour

Christ in the Bronze Gate, he continues on his way." [1]

Constantine Porphyrogennetos, describing the procession of the Emperor and the court to S. Sophia, says that the fourth reception took place outside the Bar of the Bronze Gate. "Thereafter the fifth reception takes place before the great door leading into the Augustaion." From this we learn that outside of the Bronze Gate there was a door leading from the Palace into the Augustaion. From the Augustaion they entered the Imperial buildings by the same gate "at the Bar leading into the Bronze Gate." [2]

What was called the Bar or Bars (κάγκελλον, κάγκελλα) was in the Palace wall, and had an extensive court behind it. Here there were two doors, the great gate and a smaller one, leading from the Augustaion into the Gatehouse. The fourth reception took place at the smaller gate. " The Emperor passes through the Excubita and the Schools, and goes out to the great door, and, proceeding through the Milion and the Augustaion, enters the Horologion door of the Great Church." [3] When the Emperor came out from S. Sophia he " entered the great door of the Bronze Gate." [4]

Describing the return of the Emperor to the Palace on the feast of the Holy Cross, Constantine

---

[1] N. Choniates, p. 353—καὶ τὸν ἐν τῇ Χαλκῇ καταλαβόντος ναὸν τοῦ Σωτῆρος. G. Kedrenos, Vol. II., pp. 240, 556.

[2] Cons. P., Vol. I., pp. 14, 32, 57, 63. In many other places he calls this the Great Gate.

[3] *Ibid.*, p. 63 ; *cf.* p. 163.   [4] *Ibid.*, pp. 69, 146.

Porphyrogennetos writes : " The Emperor with the procession enters the little door of the Bronze Gate ;" and in another place, " through the little door of the Bronze Gate he goes to the Holy Well."[1]

There were thus two doors, both of iron, in the exit of the Bronze Gate. They are mentioned very frequently in the accounts of the processions to S. Sophia. " Thence amid acclamations he came to the Bronze Gate, and, having entered through the iron door of the same Bronze Gate, he proceeded to the Excubita."[2] At the coronation of Leo the Armenian, as he went from S. Sophia to the Palace, " he arrived before the doors of the Bronze Gate." From these passages I conclude that the Bronze Gate should be placed between the Patriarcheion and the Senate House, where I have marked it on the map. Then the Emperor, when he came out from the Bar of the Bronze Gate, would have to turn to the right, and proceed as Constantine describes.

At the Imperial door of the Bronze Gate, Zeno erected a statue of himself and his first wife Ariadne. On the left side of the gate there were four columns from the temple of Artemis in

[1] *Ibid.*, pp. 127, 155, 183—καὶ δὴ εἰσιὼν καὶ πρὸ τῶν χαλκηλάτων ἐπιστὰς πυλῶν. Genesios, p. 6.

[2] Theophanes Con., pp. 383, 719; Cons. P., Vol. I., p. 19—οἵτινες ἐλθόντες ἐν τῇ Χαλκῇ ὥρᾳ τετάρτῃ τῆς νυκτὸς, καὶ τοὺς φύλακας ἐξαπατήσαντες.— ἐκεῖθεν οὖν εὐφημούμενος κατέλαβε τὴν λεγομένην Χαλκῆν, καὶ δι' αὐτῆς εἰσελθὼν, ἔφθασεν ἄχρι τῶν ἐξκουβίτων, G. Kedrenos, Vol. II., pp. 29, 280 ; Leo Gram., p. 289.

Ephesus.[1]   Probably these columns stood in the Bar.

From the Hall of the Schools a door led into the great dome of the Bronze Gate.[2]   " Thus the third reception takes place within the Bronze Gate, that is, at the door of the Schools leading to the dome of the Bronze Gate."—" He passes through the Schools, and goes out by the great door of the Bronze Gate."   According to the same writer, there was a vaulted forecourt behind the two iron doors opening to the Augustaion, where the receptions took place on great festivals.   " The notary of the Green faction stands outside the iron door of the same passage in which the vault is."[3]   Elsewhere he calls this vault "the Bar" and "the passage" ($\sigma\tau\epsilon\nu\acute{a}\kappa\iota o\nu$).

When the Emperor passed through the galleries of the Schools, the Excubita, and the Bronze Gate, and the Bar outside, he "turns to the right with the procession and goes to the Holy Well."[4]   If the door of the Bronze Gate was north of the church of Our Lady in the Coppermarket, which lay east of the still extant eastern door of S. Sophia, then the Emperor would have to turn to the right, as he went to the Holy Well by the usual way—"and as he was approaching the Imperial buildings, and indeed was in front of the divine likeness of the Word of God who was made flesh for us, at the place called the Bronze Gate."

[1] G. Kodinos, pp. 33, 34. $\tau\hat{\eta}s$ 'Αρτέμιδος θεᾶς, ἐκ τοῦ ναοῦ τοῦ 'Εφεσίου ἥκασι, p. 176.   [2] Cons. P., Vol. I., p. 13.
[3] *Ibid.*, p. 27.   [4] *Ibid.*, Vol. I., p. 608.

The monk Lazarus, who lived in the time of Theophilos son of Michael, placed this picture there—"The picture of the God-man in the Bronze Gate this man set up with his own hands."[1] "The Bronze Gate, the most magnificent and wonderful house, which was falling into decay through time and the negligence of those in power, Basil, the Macedonian, restored and made the common court of justice."[2] The Emperor Constantine built the palace of the Bronze Gate and the Hall of the Nineteen Couches."[3] According to Leo the Deacon, Nikephoros Phokas built, or rather repaired, them.[4] Romanus repaired this gate.[5] "The Emperor Romanus . . . burnt the bills (ὁμολογίας) at the porphyry omphalion of the Bronze Gate, amid the acclamation of all."[6] This omphalion was probably under the great dome mentioned by Prokopios.

In the days of Niketas Choniates the Bronze Gate was converted into a gaol. "He also transferred thither the bronze gates, which formerly closed the entrance to the Great Palace. They were broad and exceeding high, and to our day enclose the prison which is called from them the Bronze Gate."[6]

---

[1] Theophanes Con., pp. 18, 103 ; G. Kedrenos, Vol. I., p. 704. Balsamon says, "to the holy shrine of this church [every one] entered unhindered." Byzantios, Κπολις., Vol. I.. p. 194.

[2] Theophanes Con., p. 259 ; G. Kedrenos, Vol. II., p. 204.

[3] G. Kodinos, p. 18.   [4] *Ibid.*, p. 128.   [5] *Ibid.*, p. 127.

[6] Theophanes Con., p. 429 ; G. Kedrenos, Vol. II., p. 318. Omphalia were the ornaments of many splendid buildings. They are mentioned in connection with the Bronze Gate, the Hall of Justinian, etc.

[6] P. 582. τὴν τοῦ παλατίου χαλκόστεγον, ἥτις ἦν ἡ νῦν καλουμένη Χαλκῆ καὶ εἰς εἰρκτὴν χρηματίζουσα. Zonaras; G. Kodinos, p. 226; G. Kedrenos,

THE CHYTOS.

This was the name of a passage between the Hall of the Schools and the Bronze Gate. "And he goes out by the little door of the Bronze Gate, the Chytos, and proceeds to the Holy Well." "And he enters by the Chytos of the Bronze Gate to the Holy Well." "Entering by the Chytos of the lesser door of the Bronze Gate."[1]

From all the above passages it is evident that the Bronze Gate lay beside the Palace wall, and that by it people went in and out of the Palace on the great festivals. In front of it were iron bars, with two doors, a great and a little, and two others behind them, also of iron. I think that these doors of the Bronze Gate which led into the Augustaion, were between the Senate House, on the south, and the Patriarcheion on the north.[2] In my opinion the iron rails were in the Palace wall, because in front of them were the Passages of Achilles, open and accessible to all the people. Behind them, and extending to the two inner doors, was a chamber or covered forecourt, where the officers and courtiers waited for the Emperor on great festivals. I say it was roofed in, because at the reception of the Persian ambas-

---

Vol. II., p. 613. We have already seen that Basil the Macedonian turned it into a court-house.

[1] Cons. P., Vol. I., pp. 159, 181, 231, 240 ; Vol. II., p. 123.

[2] No one but the Emperor entered the Palace on horseback. ἐν δὲ τῷ παριέναι μεθ' ἵππου Ἄραβος ἐριαύχενος τὰ ἀνάκτορα, καὶ μέλλειν εἰσιέναι διὰ τῆς πύλης μεθ' ἣν ἡ ἐκ τῆς ἕδρας ἀπόβασις ἐφεῖται μόνοις τοῖς αὐτοκράτορσιν. N. Choniates, p. 69.

sadors they hung in the forecourt, which Constantine Porphyrogennetos here calls the Bar, a chain with the silver chandelier belonging to the church of Blachernai.[1]

THE PORTA REGIA.

This gate was probably known as the Porta Regia in earlier times, and afterwards received another designation. The learned Reiske thinks that the Bronze Gate anciently bore this name.[2] Identical in meaning are the names of the lake Rhegion, now called *Kioutzouk tzekmetze*,[3] and the modern fortified land gate opposite the Greek hospital, with the seven towers, which was formerly called the Gate of the Rhegion.[4] Constantine the Great "built also two rostra, and called the place of the rostra Regia.[5]

With regard to the site of the Porta Regia, we learn nothing clearer from Constantine Porphyrogennetos. At the creation of an Augustalis or proconsul, "When he has gone out with the prefects as far as the Porta Regia, . . . he takes his seat in his chariot with the prefect of the Prætorian guard, and proceeds to the Prætorium,"

---

[1] Cons. P., Vol. I., p. 570.

[2] *Ibid.*, Vol. II., p. 367. Reiske, through his ignorance of the ground, has fallen into some mistakes, which he himself frequently acknowledges.

[3] Κέφαλος τρισπίθαμος αὐγάτος ἐκ τοῦ ῥύγιν. Koraës, Ἄτακτα, Vol. I., p. 21, l. 169.

[4] Βυζαντιναὶ Μελέται, pp. 77, 78.

[5] Theophanes Con., p. 523. The first descriptions of Byzantion are for the most part vague.

a building in front of the church of S. Anastasia.[1] At the promotion of the Kouropalates, the patricians accompanied him to the church of our Lord, and thence to the Regia.[2]   The Kouropalates was attended by the courtiers as far as the Regia, and others through the Schools, and to the Bronze Gate.   Leo at his coronation came "to the Palace, and all the senators met him inside the Porta Regia."[3]   The Persian ambassador entered the Palace by the Porta Regia, and rested in the School of the Magister near the Regia.[4] From all these passages it is evident that the Regia was a gate leading out of the Palace.   Perhaps it was the gate elsewhere called the Gate of Meletios.

THE GATE OF MELETIOS OR MELETE.

"The fifth reception is at the place called Achilles near the great gate of Meletios,"—"They hold a reception then opposite the Achilles, at the Gate of Melete."[5]   This gate, which Constantine Porphyrogennetos calls the great gate, and mentions along with the Baths of Achilles beside S. Sophia and the Bronze Gate,[6] seems to me to

---

[1] Cons. P., Vol. I., p. 388.   [2] *Ibid.*, p. 230.

[3] *Ibid.*, p. 415.   [4] *Ibid.*, p. 404.

[5] *Ibid.*, pp. 37, 56.

[6] *Ibid.*, Vol. II., p. 143. 'Αχιλλεὺς erat nomen thermarum, haud procul Chalcen et St. Sophiam.   Sic dictæ illæ thermæ a celebri statua Achillis ibi conspicua.   In the consulship of Theodosios Augustus [the younger] and Maximus, ἐκδησαν τὰ ὅρια καὶ τὸ δημόσιον ὁ 'Αχιλλεὺς.   *Chron. Pasch.*, Vol. I., p. 582.   Byzantios, Κπολις., Vol. I., p. 526.

have been east of S. Sophia, and north of the Church of our Lady in the Coppermarket. The peristyle which surrounded the Augustaion probably took its name of the Gallery of Achilles, from this Bath. Unfortunately, it is hard to determine from the above indications, the site of the Achilles and the Gate of Meletios, though so frequently mentioned by Constantine. As I said before, it is probable that the name was sometimes given to the Porta Regia. I have placed it north of the church of Our Lady in the Coppermarket.[1] These considerations lead me to place the Baths of Achilles here also, and between the two this Gate of Meletios.

THE GATE MONOTHYROS.

In the description of the Numera, I mentioned the Gate Monothyros, which may still be seen in the Palace wall. I suppose it is to this door one of the writers of the Continuation of Theophanes[2] alludes, when he says, "underneath which at the very entrance of the gate called Monothyros, is the most beautiful chapel of S. John the Divine [the Düippion], which the Emperor Basil himself built."

Two other gates of this name in the Palace are mentioned, one leading from the Chrysotriklinos to

---

[1] In Theophanes Con., p. 449, we read : ὅπισθεν γὰρ καὶ πλησίον τῆς πανθαυμάστου ἐκκλησίας τῆς μεγάλης στάβλος ἦν τῶν ἱππαρίων τοῦ πατριάρχου · καὶ τοῦτον ἰδὼν ὁ ἀγαθός, [Constantine VII. Porphyrogennetos] οὐ δίκαιον κρίνας οἰκητήριον μετεποιήσατο καὶ γηροκομεῖον τοῦτο κατεσκεύασεν. It lay to the north of the Porta Regia.

[2] P. 336.

the Terrace of the Pharos, the other to the vaulted ascent between the Lausiakon and the Triconchon.

There is no mention of buildings beside the Palace wall north from the Numera to the Bronze Gate. At the great entrance of the Bronze Gate there were, no doubt, quarters for the guards and janitors. In all likelihood the Numera were originally barracks for the soldiers of the Palace. These however kept guard mainly in the galleries. From the description which we have already given, it is clear that the Emperors built their palaces at a distance from the walls of the Augustaion, that they might be more easily defended against the citizens in a riot.

From the Bronze Gate to the south end of the Numera, there was a space unoccupied by buildings. This space, which extended from north to south parallel with the Numera, and communicated by doors with the Hall of Justinian, was the hippodrome, or rather hippodromes, of the Palace, which some occasionally confuse with the Great Hippodrome.

THE HIPPODROME OF THE PALACE, OR THE OPEN HIPPODROME.

The Emperor Theophilos, "rising from his throne, mounted his horse, and went through the Gallery of Achilles, and by the side of the Baths of Zeuxippos, and came into the open hippodrome. Going in under the Stand, he went through the Daphne, into the covered hippodrome below. Then he dismounted, and went into the Skyla in the Palace."[1] From this it is clear that beside the open hippodrome, on the east side of it, there was another which was covered over. In this latter the Emperor and the courtiers took exercise in stormy and rainy weather. The historians, however, record extremely little about either. The uncovered hippodrome was for the use of the Emperor and his children. "The hippodrome in the Palace was so called, because it was the custom of the Emperors when they took exercise in private, to ride on horseback there."[2] "In the morning the janitors open the Hall of Justinian, and the Skyla, and the door leading into the Hippodrome."[3] This shews that there must have been an entrance to the hippodrome from the Hall of Justinian. From the account of the creation of a patrician, I infer that there was a chapel in the stand of this hippodrome. The dedication of it is unknown. "They go out in procession to the church of the hippodrome, and there light candles, . . . and return to the consistory."[4] The same writer mentions a church of Our Lady in the first bay of the Mangana of the Great Hippodrome.

On the feast of the Adoration of the Cross, after service in the church of the Pharos, the courtiers went out, and sat in the hippodrome.[5] The following passages : "He passes through the hippodrome and the thermastra, and arrives at the consistory— "The præpositi and the officers of the Bedchamber

[1] Cons. P., Vol. I., p. 507.
[2] Cons. P., Vol. I., p. 518.
[4] *Ibid.*, p. 239.

[3] G. Kodinos, p. 101.

[5] *Ibid.*, p. 161.

enter from the Caballarius, or from the church of
Our Lord, or from the hippodrome, or the Tzykanisterion, or the Daphne"—" It should be known
that the hippodrome was decorated by the prefect
with purple hangings ; "[1] together with those
already quoted, all prove that there was a hippodrome inside the Palace, and that it had a stand
for the Emperor.   Naturally too, there would be
raised seats from which spectators could get an un-
interrupted view of the competitors. I have placed
the stand at the end of the hippodrome, alongside
the gallery of S. Stephen in the Daphne.

Theophanes says in his account of the Nika Riot,
" When the Emperor heard of the effrontery of
the populace and Hypatios, he entered the Palace,
and ascended what is called the Pulpita, behind the
stand of the hippodrome."[2]   In this horrible disturbance Justinian could not possibly have been in
the stand of the Great Hippodrome.

THE PROMENADE OF THE PALACE, OR THE COVERED HIPPODROME.

" Because in the higher ground near the Bronze
Gate, opposite the promenade of the Palace, a
monument to the famous Pulcheria was erected,
and in the same place the statue of Ariadne and
Zeno stands."[3]   This promenade was on the east
side of the upper hippodrome.   Constantine Porphyrogennetos calls the hippodrome of the Palace

---

[1] *Ibid.*, pp. 250, 557, 573.   [2] Vol. I., p. 284.
[3] G. Kodinos, p. 34.

the open (ἀσκέπαστος), and the promenade the covered (σκεπαστός) hippodrome. The northernmost, the open Palace hippodrome, is frequently mentioned. It, as well as the covered one below, served as the promenade of the Emperor and his court. The lower was smaller than the upper. To this day the site of the Palace hippodromes remains more level than the rest of the ground.

Both of these hippodromes, which lay on the east side of the Numera beside the Hall of Justinian, communicated with the galleries in the Palace of the Daphne. The entrance from the Augustaion was by the Gate of the Skyla, and the Monothyros beside the Numera.

I think their length must have been about three hundred paces. They were divided from the Numera by the wall in front, which is still preserved, and on which, as I said, traces of arches are yet to be seen.

From the Imperial stand in the north end of the open hippodrome, one entered the gallery of the Daphne and of the Forty Saints. East of the covered hippodrome there were built three small chapels, probably connected with one another, which the Emperor entered on great festivals. They were divided from the covered hippodrome by a wall.

In the later writers, these hippodromes are frequently confounded with the Great Hippodrome. Owing to this their statements are often hard to understand. It is unfortunate that Constantine Porphyrogennetos has given us no account of any of the equestrian or other games celebrated in them.   Such an account would have been of great value.

THE HALL OF JUSTINIAN.

This hall,[1] frequently called simply the Justinian, is very often mentioned in the descriptions of the state ceremonies given by Constantine Porphyrogennetos.   It is the place a portion of which is now called *Arista Sokaghi*.   The rising ground above it which led to the Augustaion was anciently called the Skyla.   Porphyrogennetos calls it a "most seemly and noble hall."[2]   So too, Pachymeres, describing its fall in the reign of Andronikos Palaiologos, says that it was "magnificent as to the walls, magnificent as to the ceiling, and of exceeding beauty."[3]

On Easter Tuesday, "the magistrates go into the Hall of Justinian before following the Emperor to

---

[1] [The word which we have throughout translated " hall " is τρίκλινος in the original. The author has the following note.] The word belongs to the inhabitants of the East. Anciently every apartment, except the vestibule, had couches along three sides which were used for sitting on in the day, and for sleeping on at night. Thus any room came to be called τρίκλινος or τρικλίνιον [triclinium]. In Byzantine history, especially in descriptions of the Palace, the name was applied not only to the great apartments where the guards and soldiers were quartered, but to the many galleries and passages which connected the different groups of the Palace buildings. Sleeping rooms were specially termed κοιτῶνες. Rooms were called πεντάκλινοι, ἑπτάκλινοι, ἐννεάκλινοι, etc., according to the number of couches they contained. See Banduri, *Imp. Orient.*, Vol. II., p. 601 ; *Triclinium,* ou lit triangulaire des Anciens, que les sophas couverts d'une toile blanche représentent exactement. *Voyage littéraire de la Grèce,* par M. Guys ; Paris, 1776 ; Vol. I., p. 431.

[2] Vol. I., pp. 293, 592, 775.

[3] Vol. II., p. 145,

the Church of SS. Sergius and Bacchus." [1] On their return, they again passed through the same hall. At the same festival the Emperor went out from the Chrysotriklinos, passed through the Tripeton into the Lausiakon, and thence to the upper end of the Hall of Justinian, "to the first omphalion." From other words of Constantine Porphyrogennetos it appears that there was more than one omphalion in this hall. "When he (the drungarios) comes into the great Hall of Justinian, he makes obeisance at each one of the great omphalia to the master of ceremonies and to the silentiaries."[2] From this hall the Emperor went westward up to the Skyla. Thence he proceeded to the Great Hippodrome, where the courtiers and the populace were waiting to welcome him. [3] The Saracen ambassadors "sat in the Hall of Justinian at the East end next the Mesokepion." [4]

At the reception of Olga of Russia, a platform was erected in the Hall of Justinian, and on it the great throne of Theophilos was set.[5]

On the 25th of March a banquet was given, and all the courtiers and officers in Imperial posts feasted with the Emperor in the very magnificent Hall of Justinian.[6] In this hall the foreigners and distinguished courtiers supped with the Emperor, who sat at a separate table at the upper or Western end of the hall. Because this and other great

---

[1] Cons. P., Vol. I., pp. 86, 90, 91.
[2] Vol. I., p. 524.   [3] *Ibid.*, p. 86.   [4] *Ibid*, p. 585.
[5] *Ibid.*, p. 595. The throne was always elevated on a base, which was often called τοὐλπιτον.   [6] *Ibid.*, p. 762.

banquets were held here, Constantine Porphyrogennetos, and Anna Komnenê after him, call this hall the Aristeterion *par excellence.* This name remained current among succeeding generations of Greeks, from whom the Turks borrowed the word, and so we were able to identify this part of the site of the ancient Palace.[1]

This hall faced the East, and was connected with the Lausiakon, which extended to the Chrysotriklinos. It was the most spacious and splendid of all the halls and galleries of the Palace.[2]

On Palm Sunday the ceremonies took place in the Chrysotriklinos. Those invited went from the church of Our Lady in the Pharos to the church of the Holy Trinity in the Daphne, and thence to the Hall of Justinian, where the Emperor sat at his separate table. On Maundy Thursday the banquet[3] was held in the same hall, and all the

---

[1] Regarding the Imperial table in this hall and elsewhere, see Kodinos Kouropalates, pp. 57, 62, 63, 298. Byzantios says of this Aristeterion, (Κπολις., Vol. I., p. 204) μετὰ δὲ ταῦτα ἦτον τὸ Ἀριστητήριον, τὸ ἄλλως καλούμενον Δελφικὸν καὶ Δελφική, ὅπου ἡρίστων συνήθως οἱ αὐτοκράτορες, ἄλλο παρὰ τὸ Ἑστιατόριον τῶν ιθ' Ἀκκουβίτων. C. Porphyrogennetos in his account of the ceremonies in the Chrysotriklinos indicates that the kitchen of the Aristeterion lay beside the Tripeton. There is no mention of a kitchen in this hall, where so many courtiers and ambassadors feasted.

[2] Basil the Macedonian, having returned from "Tephrike and Germany," made "a very great banquet in the hall Justinian." Cons. P., Vol. I., p. 502. In the Anthology, Vol. II., p. 265, there is the following epigram which mentions this hall—

Φαιδρὸν Ἰουστινιανὸς ἄναξ ἐμὲ χῶρον ἐγείρει
'Ηελίῳ παρέχων θάμβος ἀνερχομένῳ.
Οὔποτε γὰρ τοιοῦτον ἐπὶ χθονὸς ἔδρακε κάλλος
'Υψόθεν οὐρανίην οἷμον ἀπερχόμενος.

[3] Κλητώριον, συμπόσιον, convivium. Cons. P., Vol. II., p. 891. κλητωρεύειν ad convivium vocare. Notat quoque κλητώριον triclinium vel salam, in qua convivia celebrantur. *Ibid.*, p. 824.

generals and courtiers were invited to feast with the Emperor, who sat as usual at a separate table.[1] On the evening of the Great and Holy Sabbath (Easter Eve) after the procession to S. Sophia, a banquet was held in the Hall of Justinian. On the morrow of New or Low Sunday the ceremonies were repeated in this hall. On Whitsunday the banquet was held in the "splendid hall of Justinian."—"An Imperial banquet having been prepared, the Emperor sits down at a separate table in the Hall of Justinian."[2] On the 20th of July (S. Elias' day), after service in the chapel of the prophet Elias in the New Church, many guests were invited to this hall. On the 6th of April (S. Eutychius, Patriarch of Constantinople), after the Divine Liturgy in S. Sophia, the Emperor returned to the Palace, and was present at a banquet in this Hall with many of his friends and courtiers.[3]

Mention is once made of the Tympaneon in this famous hall. "They, too, make obeisance below in the Tympaneon of the Hall of Justinian, and sit down on the benches."[4] Perhaps it was a place where the musicians at the dramatic festivals had their station. From the use of the word κάτω, I should infer that it was at the east end of the hall, near the Burnished Door of the Lausiakon.[5] Owing

---

[1] *Ibid.*, Vol. I., pp. 763, 764, 765, 777.

[2] *Ibid.*, Vol. I., pp. 765, 775, 777, 780, 782.

[3] Cons. P., Vol. I., p. 780.

[4] *Ibid.*, Vol. I., p. 524. Reiske translates, in tympaneo (id est in statione tympanorum) in triclinio Justiniani. A similar word is τυμπάνιον, a sort of head dress. Kodinos Kouropalates, p. 362.

[5] Καὶ κατέρχονται . . . εἰς τὴν γανωτὴν πύλην τὴν εἰσάγουσαν εἰς τὸ λαυσιακὸν, καὶ δι' αὐτῆς τῆς πύλης εἰσέρχονται εἰς τὸ λαυσιακόν. Cons. P.,

to the steep slope of the ground here, the word κάτω in Constantine signifies East, and ἄνω West.

On the 8th of September, at the feast of the Nativity of the Blessed Virgin Mary, after the Liturgy in the church of Our Lady in the Copper-market, the Emperor and all the Senate went to the Hall of Justinian. All banquetted with him in this hall. A few days later, on the 14th—the day of the Exaltation of the Holy Cross—the courtiers and generals were invited to a banquet with the Emperor in this hall. Here the dramatic festivals took place.[1]

Pachymeres, when referring to Andronikos Palaiologos, says of this hall : " At the Hall of Justinian, which was built by the younger Justinian, remarkable for its size, and wonderfully spacious to the view of those entering by the doors for the first time, reaching up to a great height, splendid as to the walls, splendid as to the ceiling, and of exceeding beauty. . . ."[2] No one has lauded it so much as he. I consider that a great part, if not all, of this hall, was roofed over. "The Hall of Justinian and the Lausiakon were not decorated, except that, as usual, holophota were hung up, with no lack of the usual chandeliers."[3]

This hall was built by Justinian II., Rhinotmetos,[4] and adorned by Theophilos with various

Vol. I., p. 518. This door is sometimes called the door of the Kouropalates.   [1] Cons. P., Vol. I., p. 592.

[2] Vol. II. p. 145.   [3] Cons. P., Vol. I., p. 580.

[4] Labarte writes (p. 218): Justinien Rhinomète, à la fin du septième siècle, dota le palais impérial d'une vaste galerie qui prit son nom ; on peut la comparer, pour l'étendue et la disposition, à la grande galerie du

mosaics.[1] It was sometimes called the Hall of Justinian Rhinotmetos in consequence of the decorations placed there by that Emperor. " And a nuptial couch was designed, and placed in the hall of Justinian Rhinotmetos."[2] The passage refers to Romanus, son of Constantine VII., and Anastasia, daughter of Kamateras. In Chapter VI. I described some remains of this hall, which are preserved in a Turkish garden.

THE SKYLA.

The Hall of Justinian formed the southern extremity of the palaces of the Daphne and the Triconchon. Its eastern end was, as I said, connected by the Burnished Door with the Lausiakon, which extended as far as the Tripeton and the Chrysotriklinos. " When the Papias opens the door, the Senate enters through the Skyla[3] and the Hall of Justinian and the Lausiakon to the

---

Musée du Louvre. Ἰουστινιανὸς δὲ εἰς τὰ τοῦ παλατίου κτίσματα ἐπεμελεῖτο. καὶ ἔστησε τὸ Ἰουστινιανοῦ τρικλίνιον λεγόμενον, καὶ τὰ τοῦ παλατίου περιτειχίσματα. Theophanes, Vol. I., p. 561.

[1] Theophanes Con., p. 147. It is probably for this that Constantine calls this the New Hall (I., 97), ἐν τῷ νέῳ τρικλίνῳ τῷ καλουμένῳ Ἰουστινιανοῦ. Manasses calls the builder the young Justinus.

Δεῖγμα λαμπρότητος αὐτοῦ καὶ μεγαλοπρεπείας.
Ὁ χρύσεός τε καὶ τερπνὸς ἐν ἀνακτόροις οἶκος,
Ὃς ἔτι τοῦ δομήτορος τὴν κλῆσιν περισώζει.
—v. 3301.

[2] Theophanes Con., p. 458. Kantakouzenos mentions the house of Justinian in the place now called *Tekfûr Serai* on the land walls. Vol. II., p. 537. This has led Byzantios into error. See Κτολις., Vol. I., p. 201.

[3] Σκῦλα τὰ ἀπὸ τῶν πολεμίων ἀνῃρημένα τὰ ἐκ τῶν νεκρῶν, λάφυρα δὲ ἐκ τῶν ζώντων. Souidas ; Cons. P., Vol. II., p. 726. Probably such spoils were anciently stored here.

Chrysotriklinos.[1] As to the northern end, Constantine Porphyrogennetos is quite explicit. In his description of the ceremonies at the feast of S. Demetrios in the Pharos, he writes : "It should be understood that the magistri and proconsuls stand in the Skyla, that is, at the end of the Justinian."[2] Genesios writes : "And about a certain part of the Palace, the name of which is Skyla, Michael defiled the edge of Leo's raiment by treading on it." "When they came to the Skyla he defiled the raiment of Leo."[3] This happened after the coronation of Leo the Armenian. Describing the murder of Theoktistos, the favourite of Theodora, Genesios also writes : "He is dragged along the ground by ten hypaspistai outside to the Skyla."[4] I think it was here the spoils taken in battle were anciently stored and not, as Byzantios thinks,[5] in the Skylomangana, which were the kennels of the hounds (σκύλοι) used in the chase.

The Skyla stood near the hippodrome of the Palace. "The patrician elect goes out through the Skyla to the hippodrome."[6] On the Emperor's birthday a banquet was held in the Hall of Justinian at two tables. From the account of the banquet, I infer that the tables were set near the Skyla, for the attendants who were present guarded the

---

[1] Cons. P., Vol. I., p. 114.
[2] *Ibid.*, pp. 123, 249, 277, 523. These passages leave no doubt about the site of the Skyla.
[3] Genesios, p. 7 ; Theophanes Con., p. 604.
[4] Genesios, p. 88.　　　　　　[5] Κπολις., Vol. I., p. 213.
[6] Cons. P., Vol. I., p. 249.

robes of the guests in the Skyla. The guests
" handed them to the attendants at the Skyla."[1]

THE APSE OF THE SKYLA.

Mention is also made of the Apse of the Skyla,
which must have been situated on its south side,
because the north was blocked up by the Numera.
" They seek the prefect in the Apse of the Skyla "
—" He seeks the quæstor in the Apse of the
Skyla."[2] On the eve, and on the day of the
festival of S. Elias, the courtiers came to the
Palace, and made their way through the Skyla to
the Hall of Justinian, and the Lausiakon, to the
Chrysotriklinos.[3] This is clear proof that there
was a door through the Skyla, leading to the
Augustaion.

At the reception of the Saracen Ambassadors,
Constantine Porphyrogennetos says, " and they
entered, and sat down in the western end of the
Hall of Justinian on the benches there ; " that is
near the so called Skyla, " the upper end of the
Hall of Justinian."[4] Describing the installation of
the president of the Senate, he says that after
the ceremony in the stand of the Hippodrome, the
president is escorted through the Skyla, and is met
in the entrance of the Hall of Justinian by the
silentiaries. . . . then he enters into the
Lausiakon."[5] The passage shews that the site of
the Skyla was at the upper end of the Hall of
Justinian.

---

[1] *Ibid.*, p. 277. [2] *Ibid.*, pp. 273, 274. [3] *Ibid.*, p. 114.
[4] *Ibid.*, p. 584. [5] *Ibid.*, p. 442.

At the reception of Olga of Russia, the Empress sat at the Skyla . . . and her daughter-in-law on the sellium.[1] From this I should suppose that the Skyla was a large and beautifully ornamented chamber.

At the promotion of the president of the Senate, after some ceremonies in the Stand of the Great Hippodrome, "he enters by the Skyla, and is met in the entrance to the Hall of Justinian by the silentiaries . . . then he enters the Lausiakon . . . and proceeds to the Emperor."[2] That there was an entrance to the Imperial apartments is evident also from the following words used of the attendants on Leo the Armenian, "when they arrived at the Skyla, for so a place at the Imperial entrances is called. . . ."[3] The murderers of Leo the Armenian dragged his body through the Skyla out to the Great Hippodrome.[4]

The courtiers waited in the Skyla for the Emperor when he returned from the Church of SS. Sergius and Bacchus, and accompanied him through the Hall of Justinian to the Chrysotriklinos. The Skyla was a large place, as appears from the fact that the patricians, who were a numerous body, waited in the Skyla to greet the Emperor on his return from the same church on Easter Tuesday.[5]

---

[1] *Ibid.*, p. 595.   [2] *Ibid.*, p. 442.   [3] Theophanes Con., p. 19.
[4] Theophanes Con., p. 40.   They murdered Leo in the Palace "where none of the Emperors had ever before been murdered ; " *ibid.*, p. 778. G. Kedrenos, Vol. II., p. 67—τὰς πρὸς τὸν Ἰουστινιανοῦ τρίκλινον φερούσας πύλας συνέπτυξεν. Genesios, p. 89.   [5] Cons. P., Vol. I., p. 89.

A Terrace beside the Skyla is also mentioned. "The Emperor proceeds escorted by them all, . . . when they are about to enter the door leading from the Justinian to the terrace."[1] Possibly the Terrace and the Apse were one and the same structure.

Every day the attendants of the Palace opened the doors of the Hall of Justinian and the Skyla, and the door to the hippodrome of the Palace.[2]

THE WOODEN STAIRCASE OF THE PALACE.

I have already had to explain the passage in the Byzantine writers relating to the wooden staircase by which the Emperor could pass unobserved from the Church of Our Lady in the Coppermarket to the catechumenia of S. Sophia. In the course of the ceremonies performed in the Palace, the ascent of the Emperor from Our Lady's to S. Sophia is not mentioned at all. Constantine Porphyrogennetos writes : "and he goes up by the wooden staircase and enters the catechumenia of the Great Church;" and again, the Emperor "passes through the Manaura and its upper gallery, and enters the catechumenia of the Great Church by the wooden staircase."[3]

---

[1] *Ibid.*, p. 286.

[2] *Ibid.*, p. 518. After the study of the whole Palace, Constantine Porphyrogennetos' writings are easy to understand. Labarte (p. 181) thinks that the Emperor addressed the populace collected in the Great Hippodrome from the terrace of the Skyla. I think that Constantine rather means the Palace hippodrome beside the Hall of Justinian. People in the Great Hippodrome could not have heard the Emperor speak 150 yards away, more especially when the lofty tiers of seats intervened.

[3] Cons. P., Vol. I., pp. 125, 157.

According to my calculation, the walls of the Palace were over a hundred feet from the walls of S. Sophia. No staircase from the Palace walls to S. Sophia is mentioned. I have no hesitation in holding that there was a gate in the Palace wall to the left of the Church of Our Lady, an Imperial gate, by which the Emperor entered the south chapel of the church, and thence went on to S. Sophia. This gate was the gate of Meletios, or the Porta Regia, which Constantine Porphyrogennetos mentions,[1] and which was beside the church of Our Lady in the Coppermarket. Thus the ascent so frequently referred to, from the Palace to S. Sophia, is more intelligible.[2]

THE CABALLARIUS.

The space known by this name lay, I think, between the Manaura and the Church of Our Lord. " The præpositi enter with the officers of the Bedchamber, either from the Caballarius, or from the Church of Our Lord, or from the hippodrome, or the Tzykanisterion, or from the Daphne."—" The remains are borne out through the Caballarius, and placed in the Nineteen Couches."[3] I suppose that it is this which Kodinos calls the Caballas.[4] He says it was built by Constantine the Great. Probably it was roofed over. How the name originated I do not know ; but it is, no doubt, of great

---

[1] *Ibid.*, p. 56 ; Vol. II., p. 143.
[2] Labarte (p. 192) holds that the Emperor went to the catechumenia of S. Sophia from the Manaura, by a staircase supported on arches.
[3] Cons. P. Vol. I., pp, 557, 275.   [4] P. 19.

antiquity, like Delphax and Onopous. The Caballarius is seldom mentioned.

These are the principal buildings and galleries of the connected palaces.

A PROCESSION TO THE CHURCH OF S. SOPHIA.

After the description of so many civil and ecclesiastical buildings, and of the galleries through which the Emperor and the courtiers accompanying him passed, it will be well to place ourselves under the guidance of Constantine Porphyrogennetos and follow him as he describes the procession at one of the great feasts. To do so will facilitate our study of this veritable maze of buildings.

He begins his work, *De Ceremoniis,* by describing " the forms to be observed when a procession is made to the Great Church, or the order and arrangement of the seemly and splendid progresses in which the Emperor goes to the Great Church."[1]

On the eve of one of the great feasts, the præpositi[2] enter the Chrysotriklinos and remind the Emperor of the festival of the morrow, and the Emperor gives orders for the procession on that day. The præpositi go out, and give the necessary orders to the servants of the officers of the Bedchamber[3] and the two demarchs. They con-

---

[1] Vol. I., p. 5.

[2] The præpositi were all eunuchs. Their introduction into the Palace was borrowed from the Persian court.

[3] Κουβούκλειον, cubiculum. C. Porphyrogennetos applies this name sometimes to the Chrysotriklinos, sometimes to all the attendants in it.

vey similar orders to the domesticus of the Numera, the count of the walls, and all the military and civil officers, that all may attend to their respective duties. They notify the prefect of the city to see after the setting in order and cleansing of the Imperial exit by which the Emperor is to pass, and to adorn all the thorough-fares leading from it with laurel, rosemary, and sweet-smelling flowers of various colours.

Very early the following morning—the morning of the festival—the præpositi and all the attendants of the Chrysotriklinos go into the Caballarius and wait there. When the Chrysotriklinos has been opened by the Great Papias, they enter and sit down at the curtain before the chamber Pantheon, on the left side of the Chrysotriklinos. Next, the vestitores, or officers of the wardrobe, enter the Chrysotriklinos, and take the rod of Moses, which is preserved in the Chapel of S. Theodore on the left side of the exit to the Terrace of the Pharos.[1] The servants of the Bedchamber and the dietarii take the chests[2] in which the

The word is sometimes used of the octagonal chamber of the Daphne, which was between the bed-chamber of that palace and the chapel of S. Stephen.

[1] In his plans Labarte places this chapel in the chamber on the right side of the way out to the Terrace of the Pharos. When speaking of the position of the chambers of the Chrysotriklinos, and of all the Palace buildings, C. Porphyrogennetos supposes he is facing the east, and consequently the right hand is south, and the left north. Moreover, owing to the eastward slope of the ground, to go east was to descend. These facts should be kept in mind while reading C. Porphyrogennetos. [In this connection see chapter v., p. 148.]

[2] Ταβλίον—θήκη, κιβώτιον ; French, layette, tiroir. Cons. P., Vol. II., p. 44.

Emperor's robes and crowns are kept. The Imperial spatharioi take armour and shields and spears. The allaximoi take the Imperial robes and place them in the octagonal chamber of the Daphne, in front of the chapel of S. Stephen the first martyr. Thence they proceed to the neighbouring Onopodium, and the spatharioi with the arms stand beside them.

After these preparations, the Emperor comes out from his sacred bedchamber, clad in a skaramangion. Having first prayed in the apse of the Chrysotriklinos, where the likeness of our Lord is depicted, he meets the præpositi, who up to this time have been waiting in the Pantheon. After the prayer before the picture, he is clad in his goldbordered sagum,[1] and goes out through the Phylax. This Phylax or Treasury in the left side of the Chrysotriklinos, so often mentioned, leads out to the gallery of the Forty Saints. From this gallery he goes into the Sigma, where many courtiers receive him. Escorted by them from the Sigma, he proceeds to the "first built" chapel of Our Most Blessed Lady on the south side of the covered hippodrome. Here he receives candles from the præpositi, and returns thanks to God with thrice repeated prostrations, and with burning of lights. He does the same in the adjoining chapel of the Holy Trinity, and at the same time venerates the holy relics in a recess in this church.[2]

---

[1] A garment reaching to the knees.

[2] Sacred relics were often preserved in some confined part of the church, especially inside the sanctuary. In the church of the Blachernai only the

After this he goes into the Baptistery, where the three great and beautiful crosses stand, and at a sign from the præpositus the officers of the Bed-chamber light the candles. After these prayers the Emperor returns through the Hall of the Augustaion, where the attendants of the Chrysotriklinos and his personal attendants await him, and receive him with acclamation. Hence the Emperor proceeds, accompanied only by the officers of the Bedchamber and the koitonitai to the octagonal chamber in front of the chapel of S. Stephen where, as we saw, the Imperial robes have already been conveyed. Here the officers of the Bedchamber salute the Emperor with the customary salutations. Hence he goes with all the præpositi to the church of S. Stephen, and adores the great cross of Constantine with thrice-repeated pro-strations and with burning of lights. After this ceremony he goes into the bedchamber of the Daphne, which lies above the octagonal chamber. Soon the referendarius[1] conveys to the courtiers the Patriarch's orders about the ecclesiastical arrangements, which the præpositi announce to the Emperor.

From the bedchamber of the Daphne the Emperor again goes to the octagonal chamber, and the præpositus calls "in a loud voice" for the vestitores to come and array the Emperor in his

Emperor viewed the pallium (omophorion) and holy raiment of Our Lady. Βυζαντιναὶ Μελέται, p. 394.

[1] An officer of the Patriarch, who conveyed his orders to the Emperor and the officers of the Palace. Cons. P., Vol. II., p. 60.

splendid robes. As soon as this is done they retire. All the officers of the Bedchamber surround the Emperor, and the præpositi crown him.[1] After this ceremony the Emperor, wearing his crown, goes out from the chamber, through the Hall of the Augusteus. Here stand the logothetes of the dromos, of the kanikleion,[2] and various other officials. Within the great gate of the Hall stand the nipsestarioi, holding gold and jewelled basins.[3] The Emperor stands at the Golden Hand, *i.e.*, at the porch of the Hall of the Augustaion, outside the great door, where all the officers of the Chrysotriklinos are awaiting him.[4] At a sign from the Emperor the præpositus, having bowed his head, goes out and introduces the magistri, proconsuls, generals, and castellans,[5] who stand in their proper places, and salute the Emperor. When all are thus standing, at a sign from the Emperor, the

---

[1] When the Emperor entered the church he took off his crown, ἀποστέφεται as C. Porphyrogennetos puts it. Ἀπὸ τῶν ἐκεῖσε, διέρχονται ἐν τῷ νάρθηκι τῆς τοῦ Κυρίου ἐκκλησίας, καὶ ἐκεῖσε ἀσφαλιζόμενοι ὑπὸ τῶν κουβικουλαρίων τῶν πυλῶν, ἀποστέφονται παρὰ τῶν πραιποσίτων οἱ δεσπόται, καὶ εἰσέρχονται ἐν τῷ ναῷ τοῦ Κυρίου. Vol. I., pp. 32, 107. Leo Grammaticus says of Michael, "When he came to the Imperial doors, he did not put off his crown as is the custom of the Emperors, but went in with it on, up to the holy doors," p. 246.

[2] Κανίκλειον, the ink-bottle containing the scarlet ink used by the Emperor to sign his name. The officer who held it was called ὁ τοῦ κανικλείου, or ὁ ἐπὶ τοῦ κανικλείου. Koraës, Ἄτακτα, Vol. I., p. 320 ; Cons. P., Vol. II., p. 58.

[3] *Ibid.*, Vol. II., p. 61.

[4] This door led from the upper end of the Hall of the Augustaion to the Onopodium.

[5] [Κλεισουράρχαι, or commanders of the frontier forts. See Cons. P., Vol. II., p. 72. Tr.]

præpositus says, "sonorously and harmoniously," κελεύσατε.[1]

From the Golden Hand the Emperor proceeds to the Onopodium, where the navarchos and all the crew of the Imperial galley are waiting, and the Imperial spatharioi bearing the Emperor's armour. At a sign from the præpositus they too wish a long and prosperous reign to the Emperor. From the Onopodium, where up to this time the Emperor has been standing with the courtiers and all the higher officers, they all go to the Great Consistory, where are the great cross of Constantine and Moses' rod, which was placed there early in the morning. Here the protasekretes and all the Imperial notaries and chartularies surround the Emperor. After the customary salutations in the Consistory, the Emperor goes to the Hall of the Candidati where the clergy of the Patriarch are waiting. Here the Emperor kisses the cross of Our Lord, which is brought from the sacristy of the neighbouring church of Our Lord. Hence he proceeds to the octagonal dome in the first School where the beautiful silver cross stands, and gives thanks to God with triple prostrations, and with lighting of candles.

From the Schools the Emperor goes to the adjoining Hall of the Nineteen Couches. Here those

---

[1] [The author translates this here by πολυχρονίσατε. Reiske, in Cons. P., Vol. II., p. 603, has a long note on the word. He translates it : placeat vobis, velitis, juvet, etc. Leiche always translates jubete, "stricte ad litteram et exemplum Latinorum medii ævi." Reiske thinks it arises from the Greeks confusing juvet with jube (which they would pronounce alike), and translates accordingly. Tr.]

who hold the Roman sceptres called βῆλα and others stand in a line right and left, ready to accompany the Emperor. In this spacious hall the many servants of the Palace, the courtiers, the dipanitai, and all the nomikoi (precentors) stand saluting the Emperor. After the customary prayers and wishes for long life, the Emperor goes up to the Lights, where the silver cross stands.

In this procession, the dealers in garments and the silversmiths [1] decorate the Tribune with purple hangings and draperies, and with all sorts of gold and silver work. On the right and left sides of the tribunal stand the foreigners who happen to be in Constantinople, the Saracens, Franks, and Bulgars, the guild-masters of the city, and the officers of the prefect. Hence the Emperor, accompanied by all who are assembled here, goes through the Hall of the Schools, and returns thanks to God with triple prostrations and with lighting of candles in the entrance of the Church of the Holy Apostles. Here the chiefs of the Blue and Green factions are received. Within the Bronze Gate, under the great dome, the physicians stand on the left, those of the palæstra on the right, and greet the Emperor, wishing that God may guide him through many prosperous seasons. Thence he goes to the bronze door where the organ-players [2] stand on either side and greet him in the wonted manner.

---

[1] From the accounts of many Imperial processions it appears that the Imperial decorations were insufficient, and they procured more from the dealers in such goods in Constantinople.

[2] Ὀργανάρια—Qui organis canunt, organa pulsant. Cons. P., Vol. II., p. 92.

From the great dome of the Bronze Gate the Emperor goes to its inner door, between the bronze door and the two outer doors, the larger and the smaller. This place Constantine Porphyrogennetos more than once calls the Bar of the Bronze Gate.[1] Here the demarch of the Blue faction stands with the White faction behind him. Another reception is held before the great door opening into the Passages of Achilles in the Augustaion, where the demarch of the Green faction is waiting with the Red faction. After the demarch come the demokratai of the Blue and Green factions. The accounts given by Constantine Porphyrogennetos make it plain that between the inner and outer doors of the Bronze Gate, there was a spacious court where all the courtiers stood greeting the Emperor.

The reader will understand the route of the Emperor from the Chrysotriklinos, through the many surrounding chapels, halls, and galleries more clearly if he consults the accompanying map, and from it too he will perceive the correctness of my disposition of all these buildings in the Palace precinct.

From the Bronze Gate, which the historians justify us in calling the Great Gate of the Palace, the Emperor proceeds through the Middle of the Augustaion to S. Sophia.

The sixth reception takes place at the Horologion of the church, where the demarch of the Blue faction with the White faction receives the Emperor.

---

[1] Τὸ κάγκελλον τῆς Χαλκῆς, Vol. I. p. 14.

From this door the Emperor, wearing his crown, goes into the entrance of the outer narthex, and then puts it off. As he stands at the door of the narthex,[1] the Patriarch with his suite receives him. The Emperor, still without his crown, approaches the Patriarch and kisses the Gospels held by the archdeacon. Then he greets and embraces the Patriarch, and both proceed together to the Imperial doors of the inner narthex. There they give thanks to God " with triple prostrations, and lighting of candles." After the prayer of the Patriarch is finished they both enter the church. As they walk to the soleas, the bearers of the sceptres and all the vessels follow them, and take their stand right and left in their appointed stations. The Roman vela and ptychia[2] are placed on either side of the soleas. The magistri, proconsuls and other senators, with the Emperor's servants, stand on the south side of the church where the Emperor passed. When the Emperor and the Patriarch arrive at the porphyry omphalion in the soleas, in front of the Beautiful doors, the Patriarch goes within the rails[3] alone, and through the Sacred door on the left-hand side.

After the customary prostration, the Emperor having returned thanks to God, enters with obeisances, through the holy door, held open by the

---

[1] Three great doors lead into the outer narthex of S. Sophia.

[2] The πτυχία, according to some εὐτύχια, were, I think, silk hangings on which designs were painted or embroidered. Cons. P., Vol. II., p. 668.

[3] From these words of C. Porphyrogennetos, it is clear that there were rails in front of the doors of the bema, that the people standing in the choir and soleas might be kept away from the doors of the sanctuary.

Patriarch, and advancing to the Holy Table he kisses the altar covering which the Patriarch lifts, and offers to him. Then they spread the two white veils (ἀέρας) on the altar, and the Emperor kisses the two holy cups offered by the Patriarch, the golden patens, and the corporal cloth. After this, the Emperor and the Patriarch kiss the holy gilded Crucifixion. The Emperor takes a censer from the hands of the Patriarch, and burns incense before it; then he takes leave of the Patriarch and goes into the chapel of the metatorion. In this chapel, which now no longer exists, the Emperor kisses the Holy Cross, and proceeds to the metatorion. When the elements are brought in, the Emperor follows[1] them, along with the Senate and the officers of the Bedchamber, while those who hold the sceptres, etc., stand in their set places. When they arrive at the Holy door, they stand with the elements on the soleas. The archdeacon censes the Emperor, then the Patriarch, and finally the Holy Altar. After the elements are brought in, the Emperor takes leave of the Patriarch, and goes into the metatorion through the right side of the bema. At the time of Communion, he comes out from the metatorion, and receives the Holy Eucharist from the Patriarch on the right side of the bema, then embraces the Patriarch again, and

---

[1] Gr. ὀψικεύειν, ὀψικάτωρ, ὀψίκιον, obsequi, obsecator, obsequium, a term applied usually to all the attendants on the Emperor, or to officers or others of rank who followed him in processions, and, in fact, on all occasions. Θεραπεία, French suite, cortège. Koraës, Ἄτακτα, Vol. I., p. 279.

returns to the metatorion, where he breakfasts with such senators as are prominent, or intimate with him. After this the præpositi enter. The Emperor puts on his mantle, and they admit the Patriarch, who has now finished the Liturgy. He embraces the Emperor, and both proceed to the chamber of the Holy Well. The Emperor stands at the door post, and gives his bounty to the arch-deacon, the doorkeepers, the singers, the poor, and the vergers.[1] Thereafter he goes through the door to the Holy Well, and the Patriarch puts his crown on again. He receives purses ($\dot{a}\pi o\kappa\acute{o}\mu\beta\iota a$) from the Patriarch, and hands them over to the præpositi. Then the Patriarch gives perfumes[2] to the Emperor, receives the usual bounty from him, and after embracing one another the Emperor goes through the porch of the Holy Well to the square of the Milion.

Here the Blue faction with their demarch receive him, and as usual wish him a long and prosperous reign. Then the Emperor, accompanied by the officers and courtiers, goes through the middle of the Augustaion to the iron door of the Bronze Gate, where the demarch of the Green with the Red faction greet him. From the Bronze Gate he

---

[1] Prosmonarii. On p. 19, C. Porphyrogennetos calls these ostiarii. They were those who guarded and cleaned the church of S. Sophia.

[2] Ἀλειπτά, the name given to the vases of myrrh commonly kept in the palaces of the Byzantine Emperors. Mention is often made of these in the public processions. Ἀλειπτά unguenta vel pyzides unguentarias odoratas. Mos est orientalium in refectionem amicis abeuntibus addere et venientibus offerre odoramenta et unguenta. Reiske in Cons. P., Vol. II p. 121.

goes through the door leading into the Schools, and there the demarch of the Blues with the White faction receives him. Another reception takes place at the entrance of the church of the Holy Apostles,[1] just at the Schools, where the Green faction again receives him. The last reception takes places at the Tribunal before the Lights.

After it the Emperor passes through the Lights and the great Hall of the Nineteen Couches. As he passes, the precentors, the dipanitai, and others of the officials of the Palace stand in their stations, and salute him. In the doorway between the Hall of the Candidati and the Exaëron of the Hall of the Nineteen Couches, two vocalii[2] stand, singing music appropriate to the festival.

From the Exaëron the Emperor enters the Consistory, where the protasecretes, and the protonotarius of the notaries of the Asecreta, the chartularies, and the rest, greet him. In the Onopodium the Emperor's attendants with their chiefs, stand waiting for him. The magistri, proconsuls, patricians, and officers in attendance enter by the narrow passage of the Golden Hand, and stand on the right, while the attendants of the Chrysotriklinos stand on the left. As the Emperor proceeds with this train, all present, both those standing by and those who follow, welcome him.

---

[1] This church was near the Schools.

[2] Certain singers were called vocalii. Those of S. Sophia were called ἁγιοσοφῖται ; those of the Holy Apostles ἀποστολῖται. The vocalii sang the βασιλικὰ, or hymns in honour of the Emperor. Cons. P., Vol. II., p. 869.

Here the Emperor enters the Hall of the Augusteus alone, and the doors are closed.

From the Hall of the Augusteus he goes into the octagonal chamber before the chapel of S. Stephen, and putting off his crown, which he has worn all the way from S. Sophia, and his mantle, he goes into the bedchamber of the Daphne, clad in a divetesion.[2] From this room he goes to the sacred palace, the Chrysotriklinos, preceded by the præpositi, the officers of the Bed-chamber, and the personal attendants of the Imperial bed-chamber. All these, before the arrival of the Emperor, stand on the east side of the Chrysotriklinos, so as to face him and welcome him, exclaiming, "May God direct your reign for many prosperous years."

When they have all withdrawn, the Emperor returns thanks to God in the apse of the Triconchon, when the image of our Lord is depicted, and then goes into his sacred bed-chamber.

In this manner the feasts of Easter, Whitsunday, the Transfiguration, Christmas, and Epiphany were celebrated.

In the progress of the Emperor through the chapels and halls of the Palace nothing is said of the Augusta. My opinion is that she went to the church of S. Sophia with her attendants without any acclamation or commotion, and witnessed the ceremony from the south catechumen's gallery. As I have already mentioned, the church of S.

---

[2] A sort of cape reaching to the waist, worn by the Emperor in time of mourning, and on common festivals. Cons. P., Vol. II., p. 244.

Sophia had a metatorion in that gallery, and in it, no doubt, the Augusta attended service. The two metatoria communicated by a staircase, now shut up, called the κλῖμαξ μητατωρική.

In the above account I have followed Constantine Porphyrogennetos, who describes very minutely the path of the Emperor from the Chrysotriklinos through so many buildings to the Bronze Gate, and S. Sophia, and thence back to his own chamber. The Emperor was attended not only by the servants of the Palace, but also by all the military and naval officers who were in Constantinople at the time. Special mention is made of the leaders of the turbulent Blue and Green factions. I have not attempted to describe the garments of those who accompanied the Emperor, with their strange and puzzling names, which throw but little light on our subject, nor have I given the many phrases used to greet the Emperor, which Constantine Porphyrogennetos has elaborately recorded for our information.

After the dry and often repellent study of so many buildings, it will be well for the reader to follow this procession with the map before him. By this means he can confirm with his own eyes all that has been written, and can satisfy himself that the numerous buildings of the connected palaces have been correctly arranged.

The esteemed writers, whose words concerning the history of the Palace of Constantinople I quoted in an earlier chapter, impress upon us the difficulty of our task. For this reason I judge it

well to use these accounts of the progress of the
Emperor and his train to confirm still farther all
that I have written.

After the description of this protracted procession through the buildings in the Palace, and of
the service in S. Sophia, Constantine Porphyrogennetos describes other ceremonies which took place
in the churches and chapels of the Palace at the
lesser festivals. Second only to the accounts of the
ceremonies in the Palace, and worthy of careful
study, are the descriptions which this invaluable
work contains of processions to the great churches
of Constantinople where the Emperor attended
service along with the Patriarch on the festivals of
the Saints to whom the churches were dedicated.
No one else has described so clearly the church of
the Holy Apostles, where the Emperors, as well as
some eminent Patriarchs and priests, were buried.
In his account of the procession on the feast of
Orthodoxy [3] he has given the best account we
possess of the church of Blachernai, so venerated by
the Byzantines on account of its far-famed sanctity,
and its proximity to the lofty palace.

The lesser festivals in the Palace, the banquets
in the Chrysotriklinos and the Hall of Justinian,
the robes, the bewildering crowd of subordinates,
and the peculiar acclamations for the Emperor and
the Augusta which they uttered on their way, he
has detailed with manifest delight. Students of

mediæval Greek life cannot but set a high value on such details.

The ceremonies held inside the Palace may be very well understood after previous study of this procession from the Palace to S. Sophia.

CHAPTER X.

To obtain a still clearer understanding of the many different buildings of the Palace of Constantinople, it will be well to describe " the ceremonies to be observed at the coronation and marriage of the Augusta."[1] From the account of these ceremonies given by Constantine Porphyrogennetos we gain much information which he alone affords; information which throws light not merely on the private life of our Emperors, but also on many details of the Palace. I recommend the study of such descriptions to all interested in the Palace, which, as I said before, has been made the subject of so many discordant accounts by native and Western writers.

At an early hour, all the senators present themselves, and put on the robes suitable to the occasion in the Consistory. At the command of the Emperor, the patricians and members of the Secretum proceed to the Golden Hand, which leads from the Onopodium to the Hall of the Augusteus. A seat is placed in the Hall, on which the Emperor sits wearing his crown. After some time, the Master of Ceremonies, attended by five silentiaries, enters behind the invited guests, who are all standing in

---

[1] Cons. P., Vol. 1., p. 207.

their proper order.   The Emperor signs to the praepositus, and he and his officers go to the church of S. Stephen in the Daphne, above the Hall of the Augusteus.   The Patriarch comes in here, and proceeds to the Augusteus, where the Emperor with his crown on is waiting, and rises to receive him. Behind the Emperor's seat is spread an ἀντιμίνσιον,[1] on which his mantle[2] is laid.

When the Patriarch takes his stand on the ἀντιμίνσιον the bishops and clergy of the Patriarch's Secreta enter, at a sign from the Emperor to the praepositus, and line the Emperor's way to the Apse.

During all this time, the Augusta has been waiting in the upper bed-chamber of the Daphne.   At the command of the Emperor, the praepositus conducts her, clad in an Imperial sticharion,[3] through the gallery of S. Stephen to the Hall of the Augusteus, and thence to the Emperor, who is standing in the Apse with his train.   The Patriarch begins the prayer over the mantle.   When it is finished, the Augusta takes candles, and gives them to the primicerius and ostiarius.   After this, the Emperor removes the Augusta's maphorion, which the cubicularii take and spread round her.[4]   The Patri-

---

[1] [*I.e.*, *antemensium*, properly a prothesis or credence table, or the cloth used in the East instead of a portable altar. Cons. P., Vol. II., p. 164. Tr.]

[2] Χλαμὺς or χλανὺς, a garment reaching to the knees worn over the others. Chlamys erat pallium Romanum super reliquas vestes gestari solita. *Ibid.*, p. 467.

[3] [A long, close-fitting inner garment. *Ibid.*, p. 477. Tr.]

[4] [Reiske explains that the maphorion probably covered her head and shoulders, and was spread out by the attendants that the company might

arch takes her mantle and hands it to the Emperor, who immediately puts it on her. The Patriarch recites a prayer over the Augusta's crown and ornaments. He then hands the crown to the Emperor, who puts it on her head, and so with the ornaments of the crown.[1]

Immediately after the ceremony, the Patriarch and all his clergy enter the church of S. Stephen in the Daphne. Another seat is placed for the Augusta, and she sits down beside the Emperor.

All those summoned to attend are introduced by the Master of Ceremonies, and prostrate themselves before the Emperor and Augusta. Then the silentiaries enter, and after the usual obeisance to their Majesties, take their stand behind them. At a sign from the Emperor, the praepositus gives the order πολυχρονίσατε, and they all go out acclaiming the Emperor and Augusta.

From the church of S. Stephen the patricians go to the Onopodium, and the prefects to the Portico of the Nineteen Couches, the door leading from the Onopodium to that Hall. The candidati, domestici and others, go to the Tribune. When the clergy depart, the senators' wives, and afterwards the other ladies of the Court, are ushered in from the Portico of the Augusteus. They are headed by an ostiarius carrying a wand; and at a sign from him,

---

not see her with her head uncovered. Cóns. P., Vol. II., p. 259; *cf.* 26. Tr.]

[1] C. Porphyrogennetos calls them τρετενδούλια. They were strings of pearls and precious stones, hanging from the crown down to the neck. They may be seen in the figures of the Emperors on coins.

they do obeisance to the Emperor and Augusta,[1] being supported meanwhile by two silentiaries. After this obeisance, all the senators' wives proceed to the Golden Hand, and there wait.

The ladies follow the Augusta as she comes from the Hall of the Augusteus. She enters the Onopodium[2] attended by all the officers of the Bedchamber, and the patricians standing here do obeisance to Her Majesty, greeting her with : " For many faithful years."

After these good wishes, the Augusta proceeds to the Dikionion, where the senators and patricians salute and acclaim her. Then they move off through the middle door of the Tribune, and take their stand on either side of the steps, while the other chief officers proceed to the Tribune, where the cross and sceptres stand.

The Augusta, conducted by the praepositus and primicerius, comes into the centre of the Tribune and takes her stand in the midst of the senate and patricians. Then all those invited exclaim, " Holy, Holy, Holy, Glory to God in the highest, and on earth peace ; " and utter the acclamations proper to a coronation. Subsequently, the Augusta goes

---

[1] Καὶ τῇ ιϛ' τοῦ Δεκεμβρίου μηνὸς [A.D. 761], ἐστέφθη ἐν τῷ τρικλίνῳ τοῦ Αὐγουστέως ἡ βασίλισσα Εἰρήνη, καὶ ἀπελθοῦσα ἐν τῷ εὐκτηρίῳ τοῦ Ἁγίου Στεφάνου ἐν τῇ Δάφνῃ, ἔλαβεν τὰ τοῦ γάμου στέφανα σὺν τῷ τοῦ Κωνσταντίνου υἱῷ Λέοντι τῷ βασιλεῖ. Theophanes, Vol. I., p. 687.

[2] Ignorance of the arrangements of the Palace has caused many errors in the MSS. The words εἰσέρχεται and ἐξέρχεται are often confused. In this case the Augusta *entered* from S. Stephen's in the Daphne to the Onopodium through the burnished entrance door called the Golden Hand ; not ἐξέρχεται εἰς τὸ 'Ονοπόδιον, as the text of C. Porphyrogennetos has it.

from the middle of the Terrace [1] to the centre of the chancel rail, and receiving candles from the hands of the ostiarius, venerates the cross, the chief officers doing the same. As soon as they have completed the acclamations proper to the proclamation, and have said, "Strengthen this kingdom, O Lord," the senate enters the Portico of the Nineteen Couches, and a consistory is formed extending to the Dikionion and Onopodium. The wives of the senators, as soon as the senate moves off, make their way to the ivory doors of the Kastresiakion to await the arrival of the Augusta at the Hall of the Augusteus. The senate waits until both sides have repeated the customary greetings. Then the Augusta bows on this side and that to the two parties. After some other greetings she goes into the Octagon. Hence the Emperor and she proceed to the neighbouring church of S. Stephen, and when the marriage ceremony is concluded, they leave the church.

The Patriarch then celebrates the Holy Liturgy in this church of S. Stephen, and after it the Emperor and Empress re-enter, and the nuptial crowning is performed. At this ceremony, the Emperor wears his Imperial diadem while he is being crowned with the nuptial wreath. With the nuptial crowns on their heads, the Emperor and Augusta go through the portico of the Golden Hand, and are received with prostrations and obeisance by the patricians. Then the prae-

---

[1] Between the Hall of the Nineteen Couches and the Onopodium.

positus signs, and all exclaim, "For many long and prosperous years;" and after some of the usual salutations, all move off and accompany them to the nuptial chamber[1] and stand on either side at the stairs of the Manaura. The singers sing songs, and the organs of the Green faction sound. When the Emperor and Augusta pass, the courtiers go to the nuptial chamber and the Emperor stands there crowned, while all utter the customary acclamations.

Their Majesties, both crowned, go to the nuptial chamber, where the Emperor's bed stands, and place their crowns on it. Then they immediately proceed through the gallery[2] to the Eros and the Nineteen Couches, where they rest. Thereafter they go with some friends to the nuptial chamber according to custom.

In this account mention is made of S. Christina, a church or chapel which is not spoken of anywhere else. When the Augusta crossed the Golden Hand, the patrician and other ladies entered, and escorted her to the bridge. Certain who were summoned went with her to the apse of S. Christina's, while the others retired. Shortly after, in describing the ceremonies on the third day, when the Empress went to the bath, the same writer says that the

---

[1] The writer, unfortunately, does not explain where it was. From his language, it is possible that it was in the Manaura and not in the Emperor's sacred bed-chamber, nor in the Augusta's. Cons. P., Vol. II., pp. 256, 590.

[2] Namely the Gallery of the Lord, through which the Emperor proceded to the Eros, a building which stood beside the Gallery of the Forty Saints.

prefects escorting her went as far as the descent of S. Christina's.

The Emperor appointed some patrician ladies to go through the Octagon to the Augusteus, and witness the coronation of the Augusta. At the marriage, he ordered that the groomsman and certain patricians should enter by the same way. At the conclusion of the ceremony these retired and took their place among the other patricians.

In this description, the following words of Constantine Porphyrogennetos are calculated to lead the reader astray : "The Blue faction stands at the right-hand porch of the Manaura, which is the door of the Augusteus" (p. 214). The Hall of the Augusteus lies to the east of the church of S. Stephen in the Daphne, as is evident from the extant writings of our historians, and this one in particular. From the flight of stairs leading up to the Manaura there was a way out to the gallery of the Lord, which led directly to the door of the Augusteus, which again gave entrance to the palace of the Daphne.

I come now to study the various chapels, lodges, and other structures in the Palace grounds erected by various Emperors, without much order, and with no harmony among them.

Detached Palaces.

THE MANAURA OR MAGNAURA.

The etymology of this name given by G. Kodinos, and repeated by other writers, is childish in the extreme.[1]   I have already referred to the site of this Palace and the remains still existing on the spot. The Turkish houses between them and the Pharos prevented me from measuring their distance from the latter.[2]

According to Kodinos[3] the Manaura was built by Constantine the Great, and after him Leo the Philosopher adorned it.[4] Next to the Chrysotriklinos, the Manaura was the most magnificent building in the whole Palace, as will be seen from the following citations from our historians.   Constantine Porphyrogennetos writes[5] : " He passes through the Sakelle and the Oval, and the narrow

---

[1] 'Ω μάνα ὑπὸ αὔρας ἀπόλλυμι, pp. 120, 278.   The derivation given by others from the Latin Magna Aula, seems to me nearer the truth.

[2] As to the site of the Manaura, Luitprand describes it (Ant., vi., 5,) as, Domus palatio contigua. Du Cange, Cpolis. Chris., lib. ii., cap. 5, places the Manaura beside the palace of Blachernai.   Ce qui pourroit me porter a croire que ce palais [Blachernai] n'est autre que celui de Magnaura—le palais des Blaquernes celui de Magnaura. Hist. de l'Empire, Part 1. Du Cange was misled by not knowing that both palaces, Blachernai and the Akropolis, had Magnaurai. J. Labarte, p. 193, " Of the palace of Blachernai nothing now remains except the tower erected by Theophilos on the land-walls, a pitiable wreck, falling in pieces day by day." Βυζαντιναι Μελέται, pp. 83, 192.

[3] P. 18. In the Anthology, Vol. II., p. 231, the following epigram by an unknown author is found : —

ΕΙΣ ΤΟΝ ΤΡΙΚΛΙΝΟΝ ΤΗΣ ΜΑΝΑΤΡΑΣ.

'Οτραλέως τολύπευσαν τόνδε δόμον βασιλῆες,
αἰχμὴν ὀλβοδότειραν ἀπὸ σταυροῖο λαχόντες,
αὐτὸς ἄναξ Ἡρακλῆς σὺν Κωνσταντίνῳ υἶι.

He certainly refers to the place of that name in Blachernai.

[4] Theophanes Con., p. 374.

[5] Vol. I., pp. 125, 545, 567 ; G. Kodinos, p. 120. The Manaura mentioned in the Chronicon Paschale, Vol. I., p. 623, is not the one in the Great Palace. Banduri, Vol. II., p. 601.

doorway leading to the terrace of the Manaura, and enters the great hall." He uses the same expression in connection with the great reception which took place in this hall of the Manaura : " Thence he passes through the Sakelle, the Oval, and the narrow entrance leading up to the terrace of the Manaura." [1] From this it is plain that the Manaura lay further north than the church of our Lord, and accordingly on a higher level.

From some words of Kedrenos I think that, in addition to the ground floor mentioned in the history of the Palace, the Manaura had also upper rooms, traces of which exist in the remains of the building still extant. Describing the last hours of Constantine Porphyrogennetos he writes : " Some days before his death, for several evenings, stones discharged from above kept falling into his apartments with a great din, and caused a prodigious noise. Believing that they came from the upper rooms of the Manaura, he set guards there for several nights in the hope of apprehending the perpetrators of the deed." [2]

In the Manaura the Emperor exhorted the people on the first Monday of Lent to keep the holy forty days faithfully, and in the fear of the Lord.[3] It is recorded that the Emperor Leo, when suffering from a disease of the bowels, and near his

---

[1] Ἔκτισεν ὁ βασιλεὺς τὸν στρογγύλον ἡλιακὸν τῆς Μαγναύρας. G. Kedrenos, Vol. I., pp. 698, 709.

[2] *Ibid.*, Vol. II., p. 338.

[3] Cons. P., Vol. I., p. 155. Διαλαλία was the term applied to the Emperors' addresses to the people.

end, " was scarcely able to address the people in Lent according to the Imperial custom."[1]   Theophilos also addressed them in the Manaura[2] : " And going out to the hall of the Lausiakon, he proceeded to the Manaura, and there spoke to the people, that they should accomplish the fast in chastity and the fear of the Lord."[3]

" He goes through the Manaura and the galleries above it."—" Sitting in the chamber of the Manaura."—" Proceeding, they sat on the newly-built throne, which stands in this hall of the Manaura."[4]   From other passages of this writer we learn that the courtiers and all the chief citizens often assembled here on great festivals.

In the eastern end of this hall there were three chambers and four great pillars.[5]   The courtiers invited stood on either side.   In the middle, steps led up to the chambers.   The one on the right was the wardrobe, or, as the Byzantines called it, the vestiary, of the Emperor, where he entered on great festivals and receptions to robe.   When he addressed the people he stood on the steps with a carpet spread beneath his feet.   After the address the people exclaimed, " May God grant you to reign many years."

From the Manaura, all went by the right-hand

---

[1] Theophanes Con., pp. 377, 870 ; G. Kedrenos, Vol. II., p. 273 ; Leo Gram., p. 285 ; Cons. P., Vol. I., pp. 432. 549.

[2] Genesios, p. 51 ; ὁ Θεόφιλος . . . ὑπὸ τῆς νόσου σφιγγόμενος ἄνεισι κλινήρης πρὸς τὴν Μαγναύραν. G. Kedrenos, Vol. II., p. 273.

[3] Cons. P., Vol. I., p. 155.

[4] *Ibid.*, pp. 137, 138.

[5] *Ibid.*, pp. 570, 571.

door to the hall of the Candidati, and through the Excubita, the Schools, and the Chytos of the Bronze Gate to the holy well in S. Sophia.

The election of the Patriarch was conducted in this hall. The Metropolitans met in the catechumeneia of S. Sophia and voted for whom they desired. Then they and those whom they had chosen by this preliminary vote went together to the Palace—that is the Chrysotriklinos—where the Emperor selected one from the three already chosen. The senate and clergy next proceeded to the Manaura, where the Emperor, standing on the steps, said to the Metropolitans and the senate:—"The grace of God and our empire which proceedeth therefrom, hath promoted this most holy man to be Patriarch of Constantinople."[1] Kodinos Kouropalates records this address as follows: "The Holy Trinity, through the empire which it hath granted us, promoteth thee to be Archbishop of Constantinople the new Rome, and Oecumenical Patriarch."[2] After this the Patriarch-elect, accompanied by the clergy and courtiers, proceeded to the Patriarcheion, while the Emperor returned to his own apartments.[3]

---

[1] Joannes Lydos writes as follows of the Candidati: κανδιδάτους δὲ τοὺς λευχείμονας Ῥωμαίοις ἔθος καλεῖν . . . κανδιδάτοι δὲ καὶ οἱ μέλλοντες εἰς ἀρχὰς τῶν ἐπαρχιῶν παριέναι ἐλέγοντο, ὅτι καὶ αὐτοὶ λευχειμονοῦντες προῄεσαν, p. 142. *Cf.* the *Chron. Pasch.*, Vol. I., pp. 501, 502.

[2] P. 103.

[3] Cons. P., Vol. I., p. 564. Ἱερᾶται τοίνυν οὗτος [ὁ Ἀρσένιος] καὶ Πατριάρχης χειροτονεῖται κοινῇ τῶν τε ἀχιερέων γνώμῃ, καὶ τοῦ βασιλέως τὰ μέγιστα συναινοῦντος καὶ ἐπικυροῦντος ὡς ἔθος τὴν ἀρχιερατικὴν ψῆφον ἐκείνων. N. Gregoras, Vol. I., p. 55 ; Kodinos Kouropalates, p. 101 ; G. Phrantzes, p. 305.

Constantine Porphyrogennetos describes the fabulous wealth and splendour of this Hall, which were displayed when a reception took place.[1] On the day appointed, the Senate made their way early to the Manaura, and all the officers of the Palace soon followed them. The Emperor—or Emperors —came from the Chrysotriklinos, passed through the gallery of the Forty Saints and the Sigma accompanied by all the courtiers, and entered the church of Our Lord. Then they went up by the narrow entrance to the Terrace of the Manaura, which, I think, was the name given to a narrow open piece of ground in front of the great entrance to the Manaura. All went into the great hall where the throne of Solomon was set. This throne, the magnificent ornaments of which all our historians have extolled, stood in the great hall or chief apartment of the Manaura. Other thrones in the Chrysotriklinos and the Hall of Justinian are mentioned. This throne was occasionally brought into the Consistory under a strong and unceasing guard of silentiaries and chosbaïtai.

At another reception the Emperor entered the Hall of the Manaura with his courtiers, "and having put on his octagonal mantle and great white diadem, ascended the throne of Solomon and sat there."[2]

The Emperor entered the right-hand eastern portion of the Hall of the Manaura, where the Imperial

---

[1] Theophanes Con., p. 378; Cons. P., Vol. I., p. 566.
[2] *Ibid.*, pp. 583, 593.

robes were kept, and robed there, while the courtiers summoned to attend arranged themselves in the places set apart for them. The people, standing outside at the public western entrance to the Manaura, wished the Emperor a long reign. Then his Majesty took his seat on the throne of Solomon, and received and greeted the invited courtiers, who were presented by the Master of Ceremonies, made obeisance to the ground, and then retired to their places. Such is the ceremony as described by Constantine Porphyrogennetos.

After the entrance of the logothetes, the organs sound. Then "the lions begin to roar, and the birds on the throne, and likewise those on the tree, sing harmoniously, and the animals at the throne rise up from the steps." A little later, "the organs play, the lions roar, the birds cease singing, and the animals sink back to their places." This is repeated two or three times while the Emperor sits on the throne of Solomon, and his train utter felicitations." [1]

There were great pillars in the Manaura supporting the ceiling or the upper chambers. Our writers give us no precise information about them. [2]

At the reception of the ambassadors from the Amerimne [3] or Emir, very valuable Persian hangings

---

[1] As to the organs, see Cons. P., Vol. II., p. 137.

[2] *Ibid.*, Vol. I., p. 571.

[3] Written also 'Αμερουμνῆ or 'Αμερμουρῆ, properly Emir-ul-muïmin, or Commander of the Faithful. The same correction applies to 'Αμεραυνουνῆς in the Continuation of Theophanes (pp. 82, 96, 97). See Cons. P., Vol. I., p. 624. A. Maliakas' *Turkish-Greek Lexicon*, *s.v.* 'Εμίρ.

were spread in this hall. The ambassadors entered from the west end, and ascended to the Manaura by stairs.[1]   Mention is also made of a metatorion in the Manaura, next to the vestiary, where the Emperor rested during the festivals.   This hall had its own papias or janitor.[2]

It was in the Manaura that Theophilos convened the assembly of those " who enjoyed the Imperial wealth and shared in the Imperial honours."[3] Theophilos also established the learned mathematician Leo in the Manaura, and gave him the most gifted youths as pupils.[4]   Probably this school was held in the private apartments of the Manaura, and not in the great Hall of the receptions.   Constantine Porphyrogennetos makes no mention of this.[5]   In all likelihood the school was dissolved after the death of Theophilos.

Shortly before this, Theophilos, who was dying of a disease of the bowels, gathered his officers and friends together in this Hall, and speaking with a great effort, commended to them his wife and his

---

[1] Cons. P., Vol. I., pp. 201, 576.

[2] *Ibid.*. pp. 583, 725.

[3] Theophanes Con., p. 85.   Συναθροίζει σοφοὺς κατὰ τὴν Μαγναύραν, ὡς τοὺς μὲν φιλοσοφίας γεωμετρίας, τοὺς δὲ ἑτέρους ἀστρονομίας.   Genesios, p. 98.   Le Beau ascribes this to Bardas Caesar.   *Hist. du Bas.-Emp.*, Vol. XV., p. 64.

[4] Theophanes Con., pp. 192, 694, 806 ; προσλαβόμενος αὐτὸν (ὁ Θεόφιλος) εἶχεν ἐν τῷ παλατίῳ τῆς Μαναύρας, παραδοὺς αὐτῷ διδάσκειν καὶ μαθητάς.   Leo Gram., p. 225.

[5] Ὁ Βάρδας δὲ διεῖπε τὰ πολιτικὰ καὶ τῆς βασιλείας . . . ἐπεμελήθη δὲ καὶ τῆς ἔξω σοφίας . . . διατριβὰς ἑκάστῃ τῶν ἐπιστημῶν ἀφορίσας, τῶν μὲν ἄλλων ὅπῃ περ ἔτυχε, τῆς δ' ἐπὶ πασῶν ἐπόχον φιλοσοφίας κατ' αὐτὰ τὰ βασίλεια ἐν τῷ Μαγναύρᾳ.   G. Kedrenos, Vol. II., p. 165.   On the Manaura, Bronze Gate, and Hippodrome, see *ibid.*, p. 204.

son Michael—"having made an assembly of them in the Manaura, and being with much difficulty raised and lowered on his couch by his attendants."[1]

Basil, the Macedonian, after his proclamation, being in lack of money for making the wonted largesse to the people, found much money in the private treasury to the east of the Triconchos. This had been derived from melting down the golden plane-tree, the two golden griffins, the two lions of hammered gold, the golden organs, various gold ornaments belonging to the table, and the Imperial robes of cloth of gold. His predecessor, Michael the Drunkard, son of Theophilos, had intended to spend it on his pleasures, but his death saved a part of the treasure, which Basil devoted to the maintenance of the army.[2]

The golden organs which we saw were mentioned by a later ruler, the Emperor Constantine VII., a descendant of Basil the Macedonian, were probably renewed by the art-loving Porphyrogennetos himself.

The magnificent receptions of the dignitaries took place in this Hall. "When a reception is held in this Hall, as is the wont of the Emperors of the Romans when they are about to receive any one of those who are great and famous in the government of any nation "—"when a reception took place in the Manaura as usual."[3]

The nuptials of the Emperor were sometimes

[1] Theophanes Con., p. 138.
[2] *Ibid.*, pp. 173, 257, 659.
[3] *Ibid.*, p. 317 ; G. Kedrenos, Vol. II., p. 237.

celebrated in the Manaura. "In the reign of the Emperor Leo, the Emperor took to wife the daughter of Martinakos and wedded her, celebrating the nuptials in the Manaura and the Nineteen Couches."[1]

We have a concise account of the Manaura in the *Antapodosis* of Luitprand, ambassador to Nikephoros Phokas. He says: "In Constantinople, near to the Palace, there is a very large and beautiful house called the Manaura. Constantine arrayed it as follows in honour of myself and the Spanish ambassadors who had lately arrived. Before the Emperor's throne stood a tree of gilded bronze, the branches of which were filled with birds of every sort made of the same material, and each singing according to its kind. The Emperor's throne was so constructed that it now rose, and now subsided without any visible means of motion. Whether this immense throne was wooden or bronze I do not know. It was guarded by gilded lions, which beat the ground with their tails, and roared with gaping mouths and lolling tongues. I entered the chamber leaning on the shoulders of two eunuchs. As soon as I entered, the lions began to roar, and the birds to sing according to their kind. But as I had been forewarned of it, I was in no wise alarmed, nor surprised."[2]

These words of Luitprand confirm what I said

---

[1] Theophanes Con., pp. 694, 846.

[2] *Ant.*, vi. 1. Luitprand has written many valuable observations on Constantinople and the Palace. We must, however, dissent from the vulgar abuse of Nikephoros Phokas, in which this fault-finding and acrimonious ambassador indulges. Βυζαντιναὶ Μελέται, by S. Zampelios, Athens, 1857, p. 517.

above about the re-erection of the golden organs by Porphyrogennetos or some other successor of Theophilos.

Of the numerous accounts of the splendour of the Manaura the best is given by Constantine Porphyrogennetos when describing the reception of the Saracen ambassadors[1] by himself and Romanus Porphyrogennetos. He describes with great minuteness not merely the general disposition, but the whole arrangement of the Palace. For this reason, and for the sake of the description of the Palace and the various ceremonies performed there, I transcribe the passage that the reader may test the accuracy of the foregoing. I omit some details of the numerous decorations employed on these occasions which the show-loving author describes at great length.

The heading runs :—" Concerning the reception held in the splendid and spacious hall of the Manaura under Constantine and Romanus Porphyrogennetoi, Emperors in Christ of the Romans, at the reception of the ambassadors from the Emir, from Tarsus, concerning the armistice and the peace of 31st May, in the fourth indiction."[2]

---

[1] The Byzantines called the ambassadors of the Mussulman rulers Saracens. The word is from the Arabic *sharq*, the East, *sharqir*, Oriental. Compare *garb*, West, *magrib*, Western, the term given by the dwellers in Syria and Egypt to their co-religionists who come from Barbary, Algeria, and Morocco for worship or trade. The Crusaders borrowed the word *Saracens* without representing the rough Arab *sh*. The tenth century Arab traveller Ibn Batûtâh records that the Constantinopolitans called the Mussulman inhabitants *Sharkiyyin*, *i.e.*, "East-men." See the *Saturday Review*, Nov. 8. 1884, p. 605.

[2] Vol. I., p. 570 (A.D. 915-948.)

Chains of copper, silvered over, from the monastery of SS. Sergius and Bacchus, were hung on either side of the great Hall of the Manaura, where the throne of Solomon stood. From them the great golden candelabra of the new church, founded by Basil the Macedonian, were suspended. On the right side of the hall, between the great pillars, the golden organ was placed, with that of the Blue faction higher up, more to the east, while the organ of the Green faction was on the left side. All the anadendrarion[1] was transformed into a covered passage[2] by means of silk awnings. On either side of the pillars, the hangings of the Palace[3] hung from these awnings to the ground.

At the reception of the Spanish ambassadors the same preparations were made, only the anadendrarion was not decorated with silken awnings, but with hangings, and enamels[4] from the treasury were hung up.

For the adornment of the Manaura and other halls, the officials in charge requisitioned not only the decorations of the churches, but also many

---

[1] A line of trees planted for a walk or shadow in the middle of the Manaura and the Schools, the Lights, and the Hall of the Candidati. Cons. P., Vol. I., p. 584; II., p. 256.

[2] Τροπική, the name given by the Byzantines to a vaulted passage or an awning constructed in the open air by means of cloths or boughs. A τροπική in the Lausiakon has been mentioned.

[3] *I.e.*, the Chrysotriklinos.

[4] Χειμευτικὰ ἔργα εἶναι τὰ καλούμενα ἐγκαυστικά. Γαλλ. email. Σμάγδος, ἔγκαυστον, ἐκ τοῦ Ἰταλ. smalto. Koraës' *Posthumous Works*, Vol. I., p. 127; Cons. P., Vol. II., p. 204. This latter writer often mentions enamels or encaustics. Χειμευτής, a worker in enamel. Τότε καὶ ἀνήρ τις χειμευτὴς ἐκ τῶν τῆς χείμης τεχνῶν εὐφυὴς ὢν ταῖς ἀπάταις ὀφθαλμοπλανῆσαι. G. Kedrenos, Vol. I., p. 629.

pieces of silver-work belonging to the guest houses, hospitals, monasteries, and churches outside the city. In addition to these, they also took many valuable articles from the silversmiths. Special mention is made of the numerous chains and candelabra belonging to Basil the Macedonian's New Church, which shows us the surpassing beauty and wealth of this church, so lauded by the Patriarch Photios.

Outside the Bronze Gate the prefect decorated either side of the passage from the Bar with curtains, hangings, and silken stuffs. A chain was hung in the centre of the Bar with the great silver candelabrum of the church at Blachernai. The sakellarios decorated the hall where the baldaquin stood and the magistri were appointed,[1] with the curtains of the Chrysotriklinos. The portico of the Augusteus, or Golden Hand, was also decorated with bright hangings from the same hall. The passage from the Augusteus to the Apse was hung with embroidered curtains. In the same way the prefect adorned the Palace hippodrome with blattia and various imperial hangings.

All the floors were strewn with ivy and laurel; the more private apartments with myrtle and rosemary. After the curtains were hung in the great Hall of the Manaura, it was all strewn with roses, and costly Persian carpets were spread at the entrance.

---

[1] Cons. P., Vol. II., pp. 302, 652. I do not know which hall the writer indicates. *Cf.* Vol. I., p. 578.

After describing the ornaments of the Manaura and the surrounding palaces, Constantine Porphyrogennetos gives an account of the dresses of the subordinates and magnates. Candidati, holding the Roman sceptres, stood right and left of the Emperor's throne in the Manaura. Above the steps, men of the great company were stationed with the Emperor's silken, gold-embroidered banner. Others near these held the Emperor's golden banners. Above these, on the same steps, stood the choristers of the churches of the Holy Apostles and S. Sophia, acclaiming, and singing imperial odes.

The rowers of the Imperial galleys stood in the Hall of the Candidati on the side next to the church of Our Lord, in the baldaquin and the Onopodion. Next to these, were the cadets, the fullers [1] of the wardrobe, and the sewers, the former in their proper skaramangia with swords, the others in dark mantles.

Inside the Bronze Gate—that is, at the Bar— Toulmatzoi or Dalmatians [2] were stationed holding flags, and armed with leathern bucklers, swords, and quivers filled with arrows. Outside the Bar, or in the Gallery of Achilles, partly in the neighbourhood of the Numera, partly at the Chamber of the Milion, stood a crowd composed of the remainder of the sailors, some Dalmatians, and the

---

[1] Σαπωνισταί, sunt qui vestes sapone mundant et lavant. Cons. P., Vol. II., p. 680. A large number were employed about the Palace owing to the great use of white robes by the Emperor and courtiers.

[2] See Cons. P., Vol. II., p. 682.

baptised Russians bearing flags, and armed with targets and swords.

The Halls of Justinian and Lausos were illuminated with candelabra. At the Tripeton, or porch of the Chrysotriklinos, the Emperor's two silver and two golden organs were placed.

Inside, the Chrysotriklinos was decorated as at Eastertide, with the Pentapyrgion, the Emperors' thrones, the couches, and golden table.[1] Crowns and ornaments from Our Lady of the Pharos and other churches in the Palace were hung in its eight bays. In addition to these, various enamels preserved in the Treasury, the Imperial mantles, and S. Peter's golden scapular,[2] set with pearls, were employed. From the silver doors were hung the golden sagum, and the crowns and enamels "one by one," that is, " a crown in the middle with an enamel on either side." The eastern bay, in which was the great picture of God, was all adorned with crowns. The other seven were hung with candelabra from the church of Our Lady of the Pharos. In the eastern bay the three lights were replaced by three crowns—in the centre the green one from the church of the Holy Apostles, on the right the blue crown from Our Most Holy Lady of the Pharos, on the left the blue one of the arch-martyr Demetrios.[3] These three were prepared by order

---

[1] At the reception of the Spanish Ambassadors, the Chrysotriklinos was not decorated because the ambassadors did not banquet there.

Greek πλαρδνιον or πλατώνιον. An embroidered garment; derivation unknown. See Cons. P., Vol. II., p. 682.

[2] Not the chapel of S. Demetrios beside Our Lady of the Pharos, but the church in the Akropolis beside the gate of S. Barbara, commonly known as S. Demetrios, the arch-martyr.

of the pious Emperor Constantine.   A variety of other pieces of embroidered work from the church of the arch-martyr Demetrios and the Treasury were carried here, and also to the Pentapyrgion.

These were the arrangements in the Palace. It is impossible for us now-a-days to understand many of Constantine Porphyrogennetos' descriptions of ecclesiastical vestments and embroideries which no other writer mentions.   From his detailed description, which the reader cannot pursue without some degree of weariness, we obtain an excellent idea of the wealth of the Palace, and the inexhaustible magnificence of gold and silver which belonged to its many churches.

Other ambassadors were not received with so great a display and such busy commotion throughout the Palace.   I have contented myself with setting forth only a part of the wealth of information derivable from the above account, that the reader may not be burdened with an enumeration of dresses and ornaments, of which we in the present can form but little idea.

I come now to the portion which is of most concern to us, for the actual reception of the Saracen ambassadors throws light on many parts of the Palace.

When the Emperor came out of the Chrysotriklinos, and entered the metatorion of the Great Hall of the Manaura, the ambassadors were directed to enter into his presence.   They set out from their lodgings beside the Saracen mosque,[1] and proceeded

---

[1] [See ch. i.. p. 33. Tr.]

to S. Sophia by the same road as that which Manuel Komnenos afterwards followed at his triumph. They went into the church, passed through the chamber called Anethas, and by the Holy Well into the Milion, and arrived in front of the Imperial Bronze Gate, which was gay with decorations. No doubt the ambassadors were brought through S. Sophia that they might admire the splendour of the church.[1] At the Gate they dismounted, and proceeded on foot through the Gatehouse, the Hall of the Schools, and the Tribune; then turning to the right, they took their seats to await the arrival of the Emperor.

When the Emperor entered the Manaura, the singers and the members of the factions began to sing the Imperial odes. He entered robed in his octagonal chlamys and great white diadem, and took his seat on the throne of Solomon. Then all around him wished that he might reign for many long and prosperous years. The choristers of S. Sophia and of the Church of the Holy Apostles began the customary Imperial odes, and the βῆλα, or sceptres,[2] were carried in with the usual ceremonies. Last came the Saracen envoys supported by the captain of the Palace and the master of horse. They wore σπέκια,[3] and other robes which the Emperor had ordered to be used on this occasion. After the usual ceremonies, the Saracens went out through the anadendrarion, the hall of the Candidati, and the

---

[1] Non-Christians were never allowed to enter the Byzantine churches.

[2] [See Cons. P., Vol. II., p. 667. Tr.]

[3] A robe with embroidery and tassels. *Ibid.*, p. 619.

one which contained the Kamelaukion. Thence they passed through the portico of the Augusteus or the Golden Hand, to the Hall of the Augusteus, where they sat waiting the Emperor's return to the Palace, *i.e.*, the Chrysotriklinos.

After some time, they were summoned thence, and accompanied his majesty on his way to the Chrysotriklinos. After this second reception, they crossed through the gallery of the Augusteus to the hippodrome, and thence to the Skyla at the end of the Hall of Justinian. They took their seats in the western or upper part of this Hall, on the benches near the Skyla. Embroidered robes and other apparel were sent to them by the Emperor at the hands of a chamberlain.

Candidati holding the golden Roman sceptres stood on either side of the Hall while the banquet lasted. The magistri wore the garments appropriate to Eastertide. The accubitor, the logothetes, and the other patricians wore σπέκια.

All the time that the Saracens were in the Chrysotriklinos banquetting with the Emperor, the choristers of the Holy Apostles stood in the bay leading to the Emperor's bed-chambers, and those of S. Sophia in the opposite bay of the Pantheon, and sang the usual hymns. While the courses were being brought to table, the singers were silent, and the organs sounded. When the Emperor rose from the table each of the Saracens received pieces of money on a golden tray according to his rank, before retiring. After the banquet, all the Saracens withdrew, and sat on the benches in the eastern or lower part of the Hall of Justinian, next to the Mesokepion. The Emperor sent a chamberlain to them with sweet scented flowers and rose water. Embossed handbasins[1] were then brought to them to wash in, with costly towels, and various perfumes.

They took their departure through the gallery of the Lausiakon, the Tripeton, and the Chrysotriklinos. From the last they went across the Terrace of the Pharos by the side of the New Church, to the Tzykanisterion, where thy mounted and rode to their lodgings, which were called χρυσιῶνα.[2]

Some days later, the Saracens requested another interview with the Emperor. This time they were received in the Chrysotriklinos, which was decorated with the crowns from the churches of Our Lady of the Pharos and S. Demetrios, and strewn with laurel, rosemary, and roses. The Saracens went in by the gate of the Skyla, through the Hall of Justinian and the gallery of the Lausiakon, and being conducted by the logothetes through the Tripeton to the presence of the Emperor, who was seated on his throne, they talked over their business with him. Those who accompanied the ambassadors stood without in the Tripeton awaiting their return. This was not through the Tzykanisterion, as on the former occasion, but through the same

---

[1] Χερνιβόξεστα—διὸ καὶ σκεύη πρὸς τούτοις δύο ἐκ χρυσοῦ τε καὶ λίθων πολυτελῶν τὴν σύστασιν ἔχοντα, ἃ ἡ κοινὴ γλῶττα καὶ μὴ καθαρὰ, καλεῖ χερνιβόξεστα, αὐτῷ ἐπεδέδωκεν. Theophanes Con., p 96.

[2] [Either like our Goldsmith's Lane, or else a sort of custom-house. See Cons. P., Vol. II., p. 692. Tr.]

galleries as those by which they entered, and the Augustaion.

All these full and particular accounts of Constantine Porphyrogennetos, which enter into such minute details about dress and decorations, throw light on our history, and give some idea of the wealth of the churches and Palace, and of the court-life of the Emperor. Without this writer we should know nothing about these Imperial ceremonies. Contemporary and later writers are all silent about them, and simply make passing mention of some buildings connected with the Palace, but give practically no information about their site.

Many ornaments, wall-paintings, and enamels were due to the artistic taste of Constantine Porphyrogennetos. This, no doubt, accounts for the minute detail with which he describes these ceremonies. Perusal of his writings is no doubt often troublesome and vexatious, nevertheless they are the most valuable of all Byzantine works relating to Constantinople, and to the Palace in particular.

CHAPTER XI.

THE TZYKANISTERION.

THE Tzykanisterion,[1] which is often mentioned by Constantine Porphyrogennetos and the other Byzantine writers, was in the early days of the Empire situated to the south of the Pharos and the other Palace buildings. In it the members of the Imperial family exercised on horseback. The Continuation of Theophanes speaks of the Emperor Romanus playing at ball in the Tzykanisterion with the nobles and many skilled players, and beating them all.[2] According to Kodinos, Theodosios the Younger built the Tzykanisterion, and Basil the Macedonian extended and levelled it.[3] After a time, but how long we cannot determine precisely, the Tzykanisterion is described as being in the most northerly part of the Palace precinct, where there was a gate of open work leading to the city. Constantine Porphyrogennetos twice speaks of the Saracen ambassadors going from the terrace of the Pharos, down through the terrace of the New Church and the Great Hall, into the Tzykanis-

---

[1] That is, tennis court. Τζυκανίζειν, Pila ludere, Meursius. Von Hammer derives the word from the Persian *Tschewkan*. *Opolis.*, Vol. I., p. 240. By the Greeks it is spelt τζυκανιστήριον, τζηκανιστήριον, τζουκανιστήριον, and τζικανιστήριον.

[2] Theophanes Con., pp. 472, 717.   [3] P. 81.

terion.[1] The exit from it to the city was termed the "Eastern Gates." "Having received perfumes they went back through the Chrysotriklinos and the Eastern Gates, as we have already described.[2]"

A study of the Palace explains the entrance and exit of the ambassadors by opposite doors. Those of the Pope and Catholic European sovereigns had their lodging near the church of SS. Sergius and Bacchus, which was situated south of the Hippodrome. It appears that the priests of Western embassies often made processions to this church singing Latin processional hymns. The nearest Palace gate to this church was the Karean, and by it accordingly Luitprand entered. In proximity to the other end of the Palace was the μιτάτον or Mohammedan mosque, which the Crusaders in Galata burnt in 1203. The Mussulman merchants of Constantinople lived in the neighbourhood of this mosque, and here, too, the Saracen ambassadors, who came to the city from time to time, had their lodgings.[3] From them they passed along the outside of the Palace walls, through the narthex of S. Sophia, and entered the Palace by the Bronze Gate. On their return they went down to the Tzykanisterion, and out through the Eastern Gates, which were near the mosque, in the neighbourhood of which they lodged during the whole of their stay in Constantinople.

---

[1] Cons. P., Vol. I., pp. 557, 586. εἰς τὸ καταβάσιον τοῦ τζυκανιστηρίου. Theophanes Con., p. 859; Leo Gram., p. 273. The Palace buildings, therefore, stood higher than the Tzykanisterion.

Cons. P., Vol I., pp. 557, 592; Theophanes Con., p. 438.

[3] Porphyrogennetos calls the residence of the Saracen ambassadors χρυσιῶνα, pp. 583, 588. I am of opinion that it was beside the mosque.

These facts seem to me to explain why Luitprand and the Saracen ambassadors entered at opposite ends of the Palace precinct.

" The one entered from the Tzykanisterion, the Mangana of the Akropolis, and the tower of Eugenius." [1]—" The people were divided into three parts, one attacking the hippodrome, the other the excubita, and the remainder the Tzykanisterion." [2]

At the present day the railway runs through its site, which is covered with gardens, fruit trees, and cypresses, while bake-houses are built beside the sea-wall.

THE EAGLE.

Two buildings, the Eagle and the Pyramidal Houses, are said to have stood near the Palace wall, where the Sultans built their treasuries after the capture. The Eagle was the name given to a lofty structure of Basil the Macedonian.[3] The historian writes : " The other imperial places of resort which have a more easterly and loftier situation than the Chrysotriklinos, and also stand further west than the New Church, and from their great elevation in the air, have received the designation of the Eagle, etc."

I think that the text here is corrupt. East of the Chrysotriklinos the ground slopes very steeply down to the sea ; the words, καὶ μᾶλλον ὑπερκειμένην ἔχει τὴν ἵδρυσιν cannot be applied to such a descent.

---

[1] G. Kodinos, p. 81.   [2] G. Kedrenos, Vol. II., p. 538.
[3] Theophanes Con., p. 335 ; Byzantios Κπολις., Vol. I.. p. 200.

Moreover, no one makes mention of any building west of the New Church and Chrysotriklinos. It is probable, therefore, that these oversights of our writers may stand in need of correction. In this building there was a chapel of Our Lady. It is probably the place mentioned by Kantakouzenos : "The Emperor dwelt in another of the splendid houses called the Eagle.[1]

THE PYRAMIDAL HOUSES.

In these, which were beside the Eagle, there was a chapel of Our Lady. They are very seldom mentioned in the history of the Palace, and no remains either of them or of the Eagle are to be seen in the neighbourhood. Constantine Porphyrogennetos never refers to them. I cannot determine their sites with any accuracy from the notices in the Continuation of Theophanes.[2] In all likelihood they were summer-houses built beside the walls by some of the Emperors.

THE MESOKEPION.

The Mesokepion was a garden which lay east of the Hall of Justinian and the Lausiakon, and south of the Chrysotriklinos, from which it extended to the Karean Gate. The buildings already enumerated within the Palace precincts were not built close to the walls, because the lofty sea walls hindered the view to the sea, and the buildings would also

---

[1] Vol. III., p. 304.   [2] P. 336.

have been exposed to foreign vessels sailing past the Akropolis. The Boukoleon alone was close to the sea wall. "The same friends (the Saracens) were accommodated in the Hall of Justinian in the eastern part next to the Mesokepion."[1] According to Porphyrogennetos, it extended from this Hall to the sea-wall.

In the Continuation of Theophanes, which gives a full account of the Palace buildings erected by the Emperor Theophilos, it is said that he erected a terrace facing the north, "from which one could see the old Tzykanisterion while it existed, in the place where the New Church is built, and the two fountains, and the Mesokepion made by order of the illustrious Emperor Basil."[2] This terrace was near the Hall of the Pearl, and from its height one could see the lower or eastern parts of the Palace where the old Tzykanisterion and the Palace garden lay. The ground east of the New Church, which Basil planted with trees, is termed the Mesokepion[3] by the writers of the Continuation.

THE PALACE OF THE BOUKOLEON.

In my former description of the remains which are still preserved in the Palace grounds, I mentioned those of the Palace of the Boukoleon, and

---

[1] Cons. P., Vol. I., p. 585; II., p. 695.

[2] Theophanes Con., p. 144.

[3] *Ibid.*, p. 329. ὃν ἀπὸ τῆς θέσεως Μεσοκήπιον ὀνομάζειν εἰώθαμεν. It was visible not only from this terrace, but also from all the palace of the Triconchon.

the neighbouring harbour of the same name.[1] Little is said about this Palace before the time of Nikephoros Phokas.[2] This Emperor surrounded the Palace with the walls, the strong remains of which were discovered beside the other walls during the operations at the railway. Kedrenos writes of them : "the building of the Palace wall vexed the men more than aught else." In this Palace Tzimiskes murdered Nikephoros Phokas with the help of Theophano, widow of Romanus.[3]

Mention of the Palace of the Boukoleon is made by Willelmus Tyrius, Archbishop of Tyre, who came to Constantinople in 1172, to ask Manuel Komnenos' assistance against Saladin.[4]

At the capture of the city by the Latins in 1204, Mourtzouphlos fled for his life to this Palace, and he and the women with him got out of the city from it through the harbour of the Boukoleon. According to the French historian, Ville-Hardouin, the most beautiful ladies in the world were found here, where they had taken refuge, Agnes of France, and Isaac Angelos' young widow, Margaret of Hungary.[5]

After the complete capture of the city the Latin rulers sometimes stayed here, sometimes in the

---

[1] There was a vaulted house beside this harbour where the Imperial barges were laid up. The modern ἀκάτια of the Turks like their σουλτανικά, are in imitation of those of the Byzantines.

[2] Βυζαντιναί Μελέται, p. 114.

[3] G. Kedrenos, Vol. II., pp. 369, 375.

[4] *Cpolis. Chri.tiana.* lib: iv., p. 59.

[5] Ville-Hardouin, *Conqueste de Cple.*, Paris, 1870, pp. 92, 98. I have written most fully on the palace and harbour of the Boukoleon in my Βυζαντιναί Μελέται, p. 106. For particulars of the wealth found in the palace, see the *Fontes Rerum Austriacarum*, Vienna, Vol. I., p. 356.

Palace of Blachernai,. which was situated beside the land wall of the seventh quarter.[1]

Mention is made of a chapel in this Palace dedicated to Our Lady.[2]

THE HARBOUR OF THE BOUKOLEON.

Here I shall transcribe some of the particulars which I have given elsewhere[3] about the harbour of the Boukoleon. Many other writers have spoken of its site, its size, and its connection with the palace of the same name. The discovery of the remains of the palace has helped to decide the first of these. A small depression to the south of the ruins now marks its position. After the capture, the Turks blocked up the entrance, and now every vestige of the stone wharves and Imperial jetties has perished. All the interior of this still harbour, which many vessels once entered, is now covered with gardens, trees and a small pond. Previous to the excavation at the Palace, topographers identified the harbour of the Boukoleon either with that of the Sophies,[4] or

---

[1] Debet vero Imperator habere universam quartam partem acquisiti Imperii et palacium Blacherne et Buccam leonis. *Urkunden zur Älteren Handels- und Staatgeschichte der Republik Venedig,* von Tafel und Thomas. Wien, 1856, Vol. I., p. 447.

[2] *Exuviae Sacrae,* Comte Riant, cap. 157. Pope Innocent III., in his 32nd epistle, lib. 15, speaks of the churches of the Boukoleon and Blachernai. Another writer, Rigord, mentions the Imperial chapel in the Boukoleon. *Hist. de l'Empire, sous les Empereurs François,* pt. i., p. 155. It is strange that none of our native historians should have mentioned this chapel whose magnificence is so extolled by the Crusaders. It was in it that the relics of the Passion were kept, which were removed to Paris in 1234.

[3] Βυζαντιναὶ Μελέται, pp. 112, 117.

[4] Now *Kátergha limané.*

with the harbour of Julian beside the Iron Gate.[1] They never placed it inside the Palace precincts. Labarte alone, with his wonted acuteness, endeavoured to follow the guidance of the Byzantine writers, and to point out its true site. He places the Harbour of the Boukoleon beside the Palace of the same name, but outside the sea-walls, being led astray by Buondelmonti's map, as given in Du Cange's *Constantinopolis Christiana* and Banduri, which pictures two jetties on the outer face of the sea-wall, stretching into the sea, and gradually contracting towards the mouth of the harbour so formed. This preposterous picture Labarte accepted as correct, without bearing in mind the strength of the current and the depth of the sea, which would render it impossible to build a jetty against the irresistible flow past this point. At the same time, our thanks are due to Buondelmonti for shewing us that the site of this harbour was beside the Palace of the same name.

Kedrenos writes, "Theophano conducts him (Tzimiskes) by night to the artificial harbour below the Palace."[2] The words of Anna Komnenê[3] are also worthy of attention. "Beside these walls, a harbour hewn out of the rock and built of marble had been constructed, where the stone lion captures the ox. He has hold of the ox's horn, and clutching him by the neck, is fastened on to his throat. For which cause, in sooth, the whole place is called

---

[1] Now *Djetladhé kapú.*
[2] Vol. II., p. 375.   [3] Lib. iii., p. 137.

Boukoleon, both the buildings on the land, and the harbour as well."

This harbour had a marble landing-place adorned with lions and columns, from which the Emperor and his courtiers embarked when they went by water to Blachernai or the Life-receiving Fountain. It was a large harbour, as I would infer from the following words: "As the Patriarch Nicholas did not consent to this, Romanus was warned by Theodore, his tutor, to come with all his fleet to the Bouko-leon."—"He came armed, with all his fleet, to the Boukoleon."[1] If the harbour of the Boukoleon be identical with that termed the harbour of the Sophies or the Kontoskalion, as most topographers maintain, what are we to say of the words which Phrantzes uses in describing the capture : "To the Consul of the Catalans, Peter Giuliano, it was appointed to keep guard in the neighbourhood of the Boukoleon and as far as the Kontoskalion."[2]

THE NEW CHURCH.

"The cross is placed for veneration in the same New Church" On the first of May, the dedication of the New Church was celebrated by the Emperor, Patriarch and courtiers, going in solemn procession from the chapel of Our Lady of the Pharos.[3] The procession was made to the New

---

[1] Theophanes Con., p. 886. ἐκ τοῦ κατὰ τὸν Βουκολέοντα λιμένος εἰς τὸν ἐν τῷ φάρῳ τοῦ μεγάλου παλατίου νεὼν τοῦτον ἀνήγαγε. N. Choniates, p. 289.

[2] P. 252.

[3] Cons. P., Vol. I., pp. 549, 775.

Church, and after the Liturgy, a reception was held in the Chrysotriklinos.

This church was built by Basil the Macedonian in the ninth year of his reign (876 A.D.), and was on that account sometimes termed the Basilikê or Imperial Church. It was dedicated to Jesus Christ.[1] "In the building of the church which was then being constructed at the Imperial Court, to the name of our Saviour Jesus Christ, the Leader of the heavenly hosts, and Elijah the Tishbite."[2] It had two chapels, dedicated to the Archangel Michael and Elijah the Tishbite, [and another to S. Clement]. The floor was laid with various precious marbles, fitted together like mosaics, and rivalling—we are told—the variegated and charming lustre of peacocks.[3] In the description of this famous church by the Patriarch Photios,[4] it is said that the ceiling bore a figure of Christ, surrounded by companies of attendant angels. A figure of the Virgin occupied the apse of the sanctuary. On the walls were depicted choirs of apostles, prophets, martyrs, and patriarchs. According to Photios,

---

[1] Fabricavit [Basilius] ecclesiam quam neam . . . in honore summi et celestis militiae principis archangeli Michaelis. Luitprand, *Antap.*, lib. i., cap. 20 ; lib. iii., cap. 34 ; G. Kodinos, p. 82 : Theophanes Con., p. 691.

[2] *Ibid.*, pp. 308, 319.

[3] *Ibid.*, p. 326. The wealthy Peloponnesian lady Danelis covered the floor with pile-carpets (ρακοπαπήτων). *Ibid.*, p. 319 ; G. Kedrenos, Vol. II., pp. 191, 814.

[4] G. Kodinos, p. 194. The dedication took place on the 1st of May, in the 14th year of Basil's reign. Theophanes Con., pp. 692, 845. πολλαχοῦ τῆς πόλεως τῷ ἀρχιστρατήγῳ Μιχαὴλ ναοὺς ἐδείματο ἐκ καινῆς, ὧν εἷς καὶ ἡ ἐν τῷ παλατίῳ λεγομένη νέα. M. Glykas, p. 549.

the church was dedicated to Our Lady. The five domes of the gilded ceiling were full of pictures. Gold, silver, precious stones and abundance of rich marbles were to be seen on every side. The floor was covered with silken stuffs.

The site of this magnificent church is made clear by the following words of Porphyrogennetos: "They descend the stair of the Boukoleon, and turning to the right, descend to the narthex of the great New Church."[1]

At the western end of the church, either in the narthex or the fore-court, were two fountains,[2] one at the north, the other at the south side, in which the water flowed up from a spring in the marble, and issued from the mouths of bronze cocks, goats and rams. On the south and east there was an open space, extending as far as the Imperial buildings about the Pharos, where the Emperors with their families and specially invited friends played at ball.

From the narthex the Emperors went up again to the Palace of the Chrysotriklinos through the private ascent and the highest terrace of the narthex.[3] This ascent was in all probability covered over, and reserved for the Emperor's exclusive use.[4]

Basil bought up the private houses which originally stood here, levelled them to the ground, cleared the site, and devoted it to a sacristy and

---

[1] Cons. P., Vol. I., p. 117. The ground falls rapidly from the Chrysotriklinos to the Boukoleon.

[2] Theophanes Con., p. 328.

[3] Cons. P., Vol. I., pp. 116, 121.   [4] *Ibid.*, p. 549.

storehouse for the church.[1]   Similar houses belonging to private persons are mentioned in the precincts of Blachernai.[2]   This is the place called by the later writers the Mesokepion. Basil planted all the space extending as far as the sea-walls with various plants, and introduced a copious supply of water.

For the building of this church he collected marbles, mosaics, and pillars from many ruined churches and houses.   To these he added the bronze pillar, with a figure of a bishop, which stood in the Senate-House.[3]   The bronze doors of the church he brought thither from the portico of the Forum.[4]   This church, the most magnificent in the whole Palace, is, I conjecture, the one referred to by Choniates[5] as the New Monastery, "the famous church in the Palace," which Isaac Angelos stripped "of all its wondrous furniture and sacred vessels."

At the celebration of the inauguration of this New Church, the Emperor and courtiers went "to the narthex next the sea."   Constantine Porphyrogennetos seems to call the space behind the bema

---

[1] Καὶ ἄλλους δὲ πολλοὺς θείους ναοὺς ἐντὸς τοῦ παλατίου ἐδομήσατο, εἰς ὄνομα Ἡλίου τοῦ προφήτου, καὶ τοῦ μαρτύρος Κλήμεντος καὶ τοῦ Σωτῆρος Χριστοῦ, καὶ τοῦ ἀρχιστρατήγου.   G. Kedrenos, Vol. II., p. 240.

[2] Βυζαντιναὶ Μελέται, p. 96.

[3] Theophanes Con., p. 691.

[4] G. Kodinos, p. 125.   This Forum is the place where the burnt pillar still stands.

[5] P. 582.

a narthex.[1] The text is probably faulty, for it does not seem possible that this church could have a narthex at the east end behind the bema.

We saw above that, contemporaneously with the erection of this church, Basil built three chapels to Elijah the Tishbite, the Archangel Michael, and S. Clement. A procession was made to this church on November 8, the festival of the Captain of the Heavenly Hosts."[2]

THE CHAPEL OF ELIJAH THE TISHBITE.

From the chapel of the Pharos they went up to the chapel of S. Elias. "When their majesties enter the sanctuary of the oratory of S. Elias."[3] "Immediately to the east of the Palace is built the church of the Tishbite, which is full of all kinds of wealth and splendour, not inside merely but also outside."[4] The ceiling of this church was covered with gold mosaic, wonderfully fitted together. "On the 20th of July a solemn procession is performed in the Palace in commemoration of Elias the prophet."[5] From the language which Constantine Porphyrogennetos employs in describing the festival, I am inclined to think that this chapel was outside the New Church.

---

[1] Vol. L., p. 121. Reiske rightly remarks (Vol. II., p. 216): Qualis hic θάλασσα significetur, aut quis horum verborum sensus sit, fateor me nescire.

[2] *Ibid.*, Vol. I., p. 121.

[3] *Ibid.*, pp. 116, 117 ; G. Kedrenos, Vol. II., p. 240.

[4] Theophanes Con., p. 329.   [5] Cons. P., Vol. I., p. 776.

THE CHAPEL OF THE ARCHANGEL MICHAEL.

This chapel also was in the New Church. Whether it, and the chapel of S. Elias, communicated with the church I do not know. I have already said that Basil planted the ground east of these chapels; this seems to show that they were not close to the sea-wall.[1]

THE CHAPEL OF S. CLEMENT.

Basil erected another chapel in the New Church dedicated to the holy martyr Clement. It contained various sacred relics of the martyr.[2]

From an expression of Porphyrogennetos, to which I have already referred—"They go down from the Palace of the Boukoleon, and, turning to the right, descend to the narthex of the great New Church "—I conjecture that the site of this church and its group of chapels is correctly represented by the place which I have assigned them on my plan.

East of the Pharos, at a short distance from the Thracian railway, there is still preserved a long building, many years deserted, built entirely of hewn white stone. Some small vaulted chambers stand behind it, which have been partially demolished by former occupants. The floor of the underground vaults is laid with stone, about $7\frac{1}{2}$ inches thick.[3] This building is quite different from the surrounding Ottoman houses. On its south

---

[1] Theophanes Con., p. 328; G. Kedrenos, Vol. II., p. 239.
[2] Theophanes Con., p. 330; G. Kedrenos, Vol. II., p. 240.
[3] Ten δάκτυλοι.

side there is an open space. A short time before I saw it, three large marble pillars and their capitals, which were plainly of Byzantine workmanship, had been unearthed in a shattered condition. The Greek proprietor of this house was anxious to make further excavations, but was prevented by his Turkish neighbours.

According to a common tradition amongst them, Sultan Achmet, who in 1610 erected the adjoining mosque which bears his name, gave this house to his chief eunuch for a residence. The Byzantine writers speak of no other buildings here, except the New Church and the adjacent buildings already referred to. I think that this is the spot where Basil the Macedonian erected the splendid church which he adorned with all manner of marbles and columns. Besides, this house is built, as I said, entirely of white stone, contrary to the practice of the Turks, who do not favour stone buildings. Probably Sultan Achmet's chief eunuch built this house out of the ruins of the New Church and its chapels. The three pillars, moreover, have formed part of a very great building.

These facts support the view which I have often expressed, that in the Palace precincts many remains of the Palace, and undoubted examples of our palatial architecture, are shut up in the houses and close-fenced gardens of the Turks. To add to our difficulties, the crowded dwellings and the network of narrow and tortuous streets make any attempt to fix the site of an ancient building difficult and often untrustworthy.

THE PORPHYRY CHAMBER.

Anna Komnenê describes the site of this chamber clearly.[1] "The Porphyry Chamber is a certain building whose form is comprehended in a square from the foundation to the spring of the roof, and thence it rises to a pyramid. It looks on one side to the sea and the harbour, where the stone oxen and lions are. The floor and walls are covered with marble, not such as might be at hand, nor such varieties as are more easily procurable, but such as the former Emperors used to bring from Rome. The stone is this sort : the body of it is purple, and white sand-like specks are scattered over it. Because of this stone, I think, they called the building the Porphyry Chamber." It was reserved for the accouchement of the Empresses. "They anciently named it the Porphyry Chamber, whence the name of the Porphyrogennetoi spread to the world."[2] "The Πορφύρα is so called because the Empress used to distribute purple to her ladies at the Brumalia."[3] Kantakouzenos, in his account of the entrance of Andronikos, the younger, writes : "He returned again to the Palace and lodged near it in the Emperor's houses of the Porphyrogennetos;" and again : "The Emperor,

---

[1] Vol. I. p. 334.

[2] *Ibid.*, p. 295. τῆς δὲ δεσποίνης πρὸς τὸ τεκεῖν ἐλθούσης ᾠκονομήθη μὲν ἡ πορφύρα καὶ εὐτρεπίσθη πρὸς τὴν ὑποδοχὴν τῆς γεννήσεως. *Cf.* N. Choniates, p. 219 ; G. Kedrenos, Vol. II. p. 27.

[3] Theophanes Con., p. 147. Porphyrogenitum autem non in purpura sed in domo quae Porphyra dicitur natum appello. Luitprand, *Ant.*, lib. ii., cap. 6.

going to the house of the Porphyrogennetos, first ordered that no one should approach the Emperor's apartments." [1]

In 1354, the enemy entered the Palace, and plundered the arsenal at the dockyard of the Boukoleon, while Andronikos the younger " was emboldened to advance on the Emperor's apartments, and to go to the house of Porphyrogennetos and lodge there." [2] We do not know why he took up his quarters in this palace instead of elsewhere. Probably the other palace-buildings mentioned in earlier days were by this time in ruins or quite unfit for habitation. Byzantios gives a vivid description of the villanies enacted in this palace. [3]

Along the right hand side of the railway, where it passes through the Palace precincts, vaults and strong Byzantine foundations, which probably belong to this palace, were laid bare. No other such building in this neighbourhood is mentioned in history. [4] The navvies engaged on the railway demolished most of these relics, and what remained the Turks used for building purposes. Some vaults are still preserved beside the line.

THE FIVE CHAMBERS.

This building, which was a hall of very great size situated beside the Gallery of Marcian, was the

---

[1] Vol. I., p. 305 ; II., p. 290 ; J. Kantakouzenos, Vol. II., p. 607 : Πορφύραν ὀνομάζουσιν ἐκεῖνον τὸν οἰκίσκον. Manasses, v. 4470.

[2] J. Kantakouzenos, Vol. III., p. 290.

[3] Κπολις, Vol. I., p. 206.

[4] According to Luitprand (*Ant.*, i., 7) Constantine the Great built this chamber.

work of Basil the Macedonian, who, we are told, conveyed to it the choicest examples of lovely and beautiful work.[1] " The work of the same hand and mind (Basil the Macedonian's) was the great hall beside the Gallery of Marcian, called the Five Chambers." The chapel of S. Paul was in this hall.

In the account of the reception of Elga, Porphyrogennetos says : "Another banquet was held in the Five Chambers of S. Paul."[2] In the Continuation of Theophanes, where the writer is describing the buildings of Basil, he says :[3] " Among them is the venerable chapel of the Holy Herald, S. Paul. Its pavement has silver bands encircling the marbles, and in richness and beauty it is evidently nothing behind the others." The chapel of S. Barbara, which communicated with it, was the work of Leo the Philosopher.

Alexios Komnenos, when overtaken by his last illness, was conveyed to the Five Chambers, where he died.[4] I do not know whether the following refers to this chapel of S. Paul: "The fourfold apse of S. Paul he adorned with various pictures, and ordered the old ornamentation to be cast away and new set up, and also placed many designs and pictures in gold in it."[5]

---

[1] Theophanes Con., p. 335.

[2] Vol. I., p. 598.   [3] Pp. 147, 331, 335.

[4] Byzantios, Κπολις., Vol. I., p. 205.

[5] Theophanes Con., p. 450.

THE CHAPEL OF S. BARBARA.

This chapel was in the Five Chambers beside that of S. Paul, and was built by Leo the Philosopher, son of Basil the Macedonian [1]—" The very beautiful chapel of the heaven-soaring Paul, with which is connected that of the martyr Barbara, built by the most sapient Leo, etc." [2]

The passages from Constantine Porphyrogennetos, above referred to, do not tell us whether these chapels were inside the Five Chambers or not. The Byzantine historians have recorded very little about the building.

THE GALLERY OR PASSAGE OF MARCIAN.

I have already mentioned [3] that some portions of the Palace fortifications, anciently known as the Gallery (διαβατικὰ) or Passage (περίδρομοι) of Marcian are still in existence. This name was given to the wall which extended from the Skyla to the Karean Gate and the shore, where it was connected with the sea-walls. From the Skyla and the Gallery of Marcian the Emperors went to the church of S. Peter. " Their majesties . . . . proceed through the Tripeton, the Lausiakon, the Justinian, the Skyla, and the Gallery of Marcian outside, (τῶν ἔξω διαβατικῶν) to the chapel of the Holy Apostle Peter which is there." [4] I think that instead of τῶν ἔξω διαβατικῶν we should read τῶν ἄνω.

---

[1] *Ibid.*, p. 335.   [2] *Ibid.*
[3] [In chapter i., p. 22. Tr.]
[4] Cons. P., Vol. I., p. 122 ; Labarte, p. 215.

The fragments which happily are still preserved, on the right-hand side of where the railway issues from the Palace precincts, shew us the nature of the gallery. In Porphyrogennetos, however, it is seldom alluded to. Mention is made of certain churches built beside these walls, probably opposite the Five Chambers. The tower called Βύκινον or Βούκινον lay at one extremity of the inner Palace wall. It had been destroyed long before the time of our writers, and it is impossible for us now to determine its site. The same is the case with the Kentenarion, from which Andronikos the tyrant shot at his enemies in 1185.

THE CHAPEL OF S. PETER.

I have not succeeded in discovering any remains of this chapel. It lay in the Palace precinct, beside the walls, as appears from the quotations above. Basil the Macedonian built a chapel to S. Peter the chief of the Apostles at the extremity of the Gallery of Marcian as an ἀκροπύργιον.[1] The sea-end of the Gallery of Marcian at the present day is an old Turkish tower, which has long been used as a beacon. No trace of these chapels now survives. On the right hand side of the Turkish tower there are some arches which formed part of the residence occupied by Justinian before he became Emperor. South of this house, beside the sea-wall, there may be seen

---

[1] Theophanes Con., p. 331. Gyllius, lib. ii., cap. 16, says that the churches of these saints did not exist in his day. Cons. P., *loc. cit.*

great columns and Byzantine capitals, the remains of ancient buildings, which have been cast into the sea. These unfortunately are now being destroyed.

THE CHAPEL OF THE ARCHANGEL MICHAEL.

This chapel was connected with that of S. Peter at the end of the Gallery of Marcian.[1]

From the passages already quoted, it is impossible to determine where these buildings lay. Any traces or remains of them I have never been able to discover, although I have frequently made careful search. The chapel of the Theometôr lay above these two.[2] I suppose that they were all inside the Palace.

THE MONASTERY OF KALYPAS.

This monastery, which was situated in the Palace, is only once mentioned. " Alexander confined him in the monastery of the Palace called Kalypas."[3]

Equally unknown is another mentioned in the same collection. " In the monastery of the Palace which is called Kampas."[4] Many statements in our historians are inaccurate. These monasteries are never mentioned by Constantine Porphyrogennetos. No doubt they were not in existence in his time.

---

[1] Theophanes Con., p. 331 ; G. Kedrenos, Vol. II., p. 240.

[2] Theophanes Con., *loc. cit.*

[3] Theophanes Con., p. 717 ; on p. 873 it is called Καλυππᾶς.

[4] *Ibid.*, p. 379. [Probably the apparent difference is due to a copyist's error. Tr.]

In the study of the Palace we have difficulty in fixing the position of buildings, which are mentioned only once, without any indication of better known adjacent buildings. Take, for example, "the spiral stair of S. Christina."[1] Mention is also made of a bridge which was, as I suppose, beside the descent to the Boukoleon in front of S. Christina. "And they form a consistory at the foot of the bridge."—"The patricians stand at the table of the bridge."[2] It was probably thrown over some chasm here for the convenience of those who crossed. ·No one else mentions the chapel of S. Christina. Perhaps it was a holy well.

Meletius, in his valuable work,[3] enumerates all the churches and monasteries founded in Constantinople and the suburbs from the earliest times to the final capture. These particulars were taken by him from Du Cange's *Constantinopolis Christiana.* Their number in both works is about 370. All of them, however, did not endure until the time of the capture by the Turks. Some of the churches and chapels which the historians, and Constantine Porphyrogennetos in particular, mention as being in the adjoining buildings, or in the Palace precinct, have not been described in the works of Du Cange and Meletius, since they, more especially Du Cange, could not avail themselves of the guidance of Constantine

---

[1] Cons. P., Vol. I., p. 214.

[2] *Ibid.*, p. 215.

[3] Μελετίου Γεωγραφία Παλαία καὶ Νέα, Venice, 1807, Vol. III., p. 71.

Porphyrogennetos.[1] In addition to this, the various writings of the Crusaders, and the account of the sacred relics brought to Europe from the churches, enlighten us greatly on the churches which then existed.[2] The Crusaders deprived the churches of the city and Palace, sometimes openly, sometimes secretly, of ivory, of the silver and gold bindings of church books, of sacred vestments of all sorts, and of richly adorned reliquaries. Most of these they conveyed to Venice, where many fell a prey to the flames in the burning of S. Mark's in 1231. Others which were preserved in the royal collections of France, were destroyed amid the political upheavals of last century.

I have recalled these facts because, in my opinion, the pillage of the Palace churches, and the denudation of the Imperial residence, probably moved the Emperors to leave the Palace on the Akropolis, and take up their abode in the lofty castle of Blachernai. Moreover, it is well known from the many writers of the times of the Crusades that during all their stay in Constantinople the Frankish Emperors did not live in the famous Chrysotriklinos and Manaura, but in the Boukoleon and Blachernai. While the palace of the Boukoleon, which was for the most part the work of Nikephoros Phokas, and his principal stronghold,

---

[1] In subsequent editions of Meletius, the editors might have made many additions from the Byzantine writers which were unknown to Du Cange, but afterwards available.

[2] *Les Dépouilles Religieuses enlevées à Constantinople au XIII., par les Latins.* Par le Comte Riant. Paris, 1875.

is but seldom mentioned by our historians, the foreign Crusader writers in their turn have left nothing of importance about the Great Palace, which Constantine Porphyrogennetos and our other writers have described so fully.

I have now to enumerate the churches and chapels which I have already mentioned, and endeavoured to place in their true positions in the Palace precincts or the neighbourhood. Of these, unfortunately, only one, the church of S. Sophia now remains.

CHURCHES AND CHAPELS IN BUILDINGS ADJOINING THE PALACE.

1. S. Stephen, beside the Stand of the Great Hippodrome.
2. The chapel of Our Lady, in the first porch of the Mangana of the Hippodrome.[1]
3. S. Sophia.
4. S. John the Baptist, or the Baptistery, beside the Horologion of S. Sophia.[2]
5. The church of Alexios.
6. The chapel of S. Constantine.
7. The chapel of S. Helena. Both these were on either side of the base of the statue of Justinian.

---

[1] Cons. P., Vol. I., p. 334. See also the chapter on the Hippodrome, p. 46.

[2] Ἰωάννου τοῦ Θεολόγου ἐκκλησία, εἰς τὸ ὡρολόγιον, πλησίον τῆς Μεγάλης ἐκκλησίας. Meletius, Vol. III., p. 83. S. Ioannis Baptistae aedem ad Horologium, haud procul ab aede Sophiana. Du Cange, p. 102.

8. The church of S. John, or the Diippion.[1]
9. The chapel of S. Theophylaktos in the Patri-archeion.
10. Our Lady in the Copper-market, with its two chapels on either side of the bema.[2]

CHURCHES AND CHAPELS IN THE PALACE PRECINCTS.

1. The chapel of S. Theodore in the north-east chamber of the Chryostriklinos.
2. Our Lady of the Pharos.[3]
3. The church of S. Demetrios.
4. The church of S. Basil, east of the Laùsiakon.
5. The chapel of S. Ann, beside the Vestiary of the Augusta.[4]
6. The church of S. Stephen in the Daphne.
7. Church of Our Most Holy Lady, south of the covered hippodrome.
8. Chapel of the Holy Trinity.
9. The Baptistery or the Crosses.

---

[1] Ἰωάννου τοῦ Θεολόγου ἐκκλησία εἰς τὸ Μίλιον ἢ Διΐππειον . . . τοῦ Θεολόγου εὐκτήριον, κτισθὲν ὑπὸ Βασιλείου τοῦ Μακεδ. εἰς αὐτὴν τὴν εἴσοδον τῆς λεγομένης Μονοθύρου. Meletius, *ibid.* I think Du Cange is mistaken when he writes : S. Phocae aedem in Milio, loco nuncupato Dihippio. Ἀρχιμανδρίτης τοῦ ἐν ὁσίοις Φωκᾶ, p. 133. The Diippion is never said to be the church of S. Phokas, Meletius has followed this error. Φωκᾶ μαρτ. ἐν τῷ Διΐππείῳ. Vol. III., p. 89. Under the 9th of March, the Synaxaristes mentions the monastery of S. Phokas, but its whereabouts is unknown.

[2] Ὅπου ἦτο ἡ συναγωγὴ τῶν Ἑβραίων. Meletius, *ibid.*, p. 75.

[3] Τῆς Θεοτόκου ἐν τῷ Φάρῳ, πλησίον τοῦ μεγάλου παλατίου. *Ibid.*, p. 78. Deiparae Phari, aedes sacra extitit in majori Palatio Constantinopolitano. Du Cange, p. 95.

[4] Ἄννης κατὰ τὸν Αὐγουστιακὸν κοιτῶνα. Meletius, *ibid.*, p. 91. S. Annae oratorium in Magno Palatio. Du Cange, p. 144.

10. A chapel unnamed in the stand of the open hippodrome, mentioned only by Constantine Porphyrogennetos.

11. Church of Christ the Saviour at the Bronze Gate.

12. Church of the Holy Apostles near the Bronze Gate and the Schools.[1]

13. The church of S. John, beside the gallery of the Forty Saints, and north of the Secret Fountain.

14. Church of Our Lord, beside the Consistory and the Oval.

15. Chapel of Our Lady in the Eagle.

16. Chapel of Our Lady in the Pyramidal Houses.

17. Chapel of Our Lady in the Palace of the Boukoleon, mentioned by the Crusader writers.[2]

18. The New Church, built by Basil the Macedonian.

19. Chapel of S. Elijah the Tishbite.

20. Chapel of the Archangel Michael.[3]

21. Chapel of S. Clement in the New Church.

22. Chapel of S. Paul, built by Basil.

23. Chapel of S. Barbara, built by Leo the

---

[1] Τῶν Ἁγίων Ἀποστόλων ἐν τῷ Τρικόγχῳ. Meletius, p. 82 ; Du Cange, p. 111.

[2] Ὁ πλησίον τῶν Βουκολίων. Meletios, p. 78. It was dedicated to Our Most Holy Lady. Riant, *Exuviae Sacrae*, cap. 157.

[3] Τοῦ ἀρχαγγέλου ἐν τῷ Τρικόγχῳ τοῦ παλατίου. Meletius, p. 80.

Philosopher; both these were in the Five Chambers.

24. Chapel of S. Peter, beside the Gallery of Marcian.[1]
25. Chapel of Michael the Heavenly Captain.
26. Kalypas, the monastery of the Palace.[2]
27. The Monastery of Kampas in the Palace [?].
28. The spiral stair or descent of S. Christina.

Our historians have told us but little about the clergy who served these many churches. The Emperor, with his family and court, used to go to the adjoining church of Our Lady of the Pharos. On great occasions (which the Byzantines called δεσποτικὰς ἑορτάς) he went to S. Sophia. We often read of the protopappas of the Palace, the superior of the clergy who officiated in the Palace churches.

THE BATHS.

"And the Augusta enters the Baths." These, "the most beautiful and great and splendid Imperial Baths," lay above the New Church, between it and the Pharos.[3] According to the writers in the Continuation of Theophanes, they were erected by Basil the Macedonian, but I think that he only enlarged or restored them, because there were similar baths in the Palace before his time. Beside them there were the two fountains

---

[1] Τοῦ ἀποστόλου Πέτρου ἐν τῷ παλατίῳ, ἢ ἐν τοῖς ἀνακτόροις. *Ibid.*, p. 84. S. Petri Apostoli templum intra Palatii septa. Du Cange, p. 115.

[2] Meletius, p. 92. Calypa, Monasterium in M. Palatio. Du Cange. p. 154.

[3] Theophanes Con., p. 336.

of the Green and Blue factions which Basil demolished, putting an end at the same time to the festivities which they were wont to celebrate there. " And purposing to wash in the great bath in the Palace, and having entered it, he was miserably drowned in the swimming-bath.". The situation of this bath in which Romanus Argyros was drowned, at the instigation of Zoe, is not clear.[1]

Another bath is mentioned in the life of Leo the Armenian.—" Suspecting that he is plotting a rebellion, he puts him in chains in the bath Pithekeion."[2] I do not know the reference of the words : " at the furnace of the Imperial Baths." [3]

THE BATH KATOPTRON.

Kodinos mentions this bath in passing, without any further explanation. It is doubtful whether it was in or outside of the Palace.

THE BATH OF THE HOUSEHOLD.

Kodinos notices this great bath of the household, which was beside the Tzykanisterion, and had seven chambers (ἐνθήκας), twelve porches, and a great swimming-bath adorned with figures. This bath was in existence until the reign of Nikephoros

---

[1] G. Kedrenos, Vol. II., p. 507 ; M. Glykas, p. 585 ; Byzantios, Κπολις., Vol. I., p. 210.

[2] Theophanes Con., p. 610 ; Genesios, p. 21.

[3] Theophanes Con., p. 35. ἐμβληθέντος ἐν τῇ καμίνῳ τοῦ ἐν· τῷ παλατίῳ λουτροῦ. G. Kedrenos, Vol. II., p. 62,

Phokas (963).. Tzimiskes demolished it, and used the material to build the Bronze Gate, where he was buried.[1]

THE BALNEARIA.

" The archbishop enters, as is his custom, through "the balnearia,"—" The candidati stand before the hippodrome, behind the door of the latrines ($\chi\rho\epsilon\iota\hat{\omega}\nu$),[2] of the balnearia."—"The Emperor goes out through the balnearia." C. Porphyrogennetos' words are not easy to understand now; but I cannot conceive that the Emperor and the Patriarch went through the latrines of the baths as Reiske would explain it.

THE STABLES.

It is difficult, not to say impossible, to determine the site of the stables, which are so often referred to. " He departs thus to the stables,"—" outside the stables of the mules "—" to the Augusta's stables "—" the overseers of the stables "—" five chains were hung outside the stables of the mules " —" the prefect decorated the outside of the stables of the mules, and the first school." [3]

Michael, the son of Theophilos, built a stable for

---

[1] G. Kodinos, p. 19.

[2] Cons. P., Vol. I., pp. 422, 699. Reiske translates, τὴν θύραν τῶν χροιῶν [sic] τῆς Βαλνιαρίας: portam necessariarum seu latrinarum balnei. On p. 822 (Vol. II.) he says : Χρειῶν, necessariae Latinis et χρεία Graecis novis sunt latrinae.

[3] Cons. P., Vol. I., pp. 271, 311, 572, 583, 715.

his horses, which he adorned with marbles, and furnished with abundance of water.[1]   I think that this stable was inside the Palace ; but where precisely, no writer tells us.   " Michael, the son of Theophilos, built the vaulted stable, and adorned it with valuable marbles."[2]

The Entrance to the Stables mentioned by C. Porphyrogennetos[3] was on the left side of the Manaura. Probably it was here, at a distance from the Palace, and apart from other buildings, that the Emperors erected their stables.

THE CISTERNS.

The Palace no doubt had an abundant supply of water from cisterns and underground conduits.   It came chiefly from the great cistern of Philoxenos, which was situated west of the Great Hippodrome.[4]   Mention is also made of cisterns in front of the Manaura, and of another between the Hall of Justinian and the hall of ceremonies, which contained abundance of drinking water, and fish for the sport of the Emperors.   Heraclius filled these up, and turned them into gardens, because Stephen the mathematician had warned him that he would

---

[1] Theophanes Con., pp. 666, 825 ; Leo. Gram., p. 239.   The stables of the Patriarch Theophylaktos, mentioned on p. 449 of the Continuation, were within the Palace walls.

[2] G. Kodinos, p. 82.   [3] Vol. I., p. 215.

[4] Now *Bin bir direk*.   The Continuation of Theophanes says about Theophilos : τὰ πρὸς τὴν θάλασσαν τοῦ παλατίου τείχη τῶν ἀρχαίων θεμελίων οὗτος παρεκβαλὼν, καὶ πρὸς τὰ ἡλιακὰ, ἔνθα πρότερον κινστέρνης οὔσης συνέβη βασιλικὸν ἀποπνιγῆναι υἱὸν, παραδείσους ἐργασάμενος.   P. 88.

die by water.[1] The water from the cistern called the Emperor's cistern did not flow into the Palace, for it lay at a higher level.

All the Palace cisterns have now disappeared. The cistern of Philoxenos is dry. Most of the water used within the Palace at the present day comes from the hydraulic pyramid in front of the Hippodrome, which is connected with the great aqueduct of Valens. Kedrenos writes of the cisterns of the Palace : Basil "built also the Palace in Pegai . . . having cleared out the cistern which the Emperor Heraclius had filled up with earth and turned into a garden for plants and vegetables. He had done the same with those which were in the Palace, before the Manaura, and between the Hall of Justinian and the Lausiakon."[2] These few words do not aid us in further settling the site of the cisterns which are not now in existence.

I have described the Palace of the Byzantine Emperors chiefly on the authority of Constantine Porphyrogennetos. Other writers, earlier or later, supplement what he has written. The remains which have been discovered, contribute greatly to

---

[1] *Ibid.*, p. 338; M. Glykas, p. 550. There was then, as now, an overseer of the waters. Βασίλειος ὁ Μαλέσης . . . τὸ τοῦ λογοθέτου τῶν ὑδάτων ὀφφίκιον περιεζωσμένος. M. Attaliates, p. 167. Andreossy, in his valuable work, *Cple. et le Bosphore de Thrace*, Paris, 1828, p. 385, says : "Le système des eaux qui abreuvent la capitale de l'Empire Ottoman est recommandable . . . on aura lieu de se convaincre que c'est un des plus grands travaux que les Empereurs grecs nous aient laissé."

[2] Vol. II., p. 241 ; Malalas, p. 477. All that is said about the cisterns is very vague.

the more exact arrangement of the whole Palace, with the many halls and galleries, which connected its manifold buildings.

Fortunately for the description of the Palace, I was able to attain exact measurements of the Palaces of the Boukoleon, and Blachernai. The Boukoleon, which was a long, narrow building, measured 98˙28 m. long and 17 m. broad [319 ft. by 55 ft.]; while that of Blachernai, which was founded on the prison of Anemas, was 65 m. long [211 ft.] and somewhat more in breadth. These measurements indicate that the palaces which the Byzantine Emperors erected in the Palace precincts were not of great size. The same conclusion is suggested by the number of the halls and chambers which were scattered over the whole extent of the Palace ground.

The palaces, especially the Manaura and the Chrysotriklinos, had domes, and like the churches lead-covered roofs. We very seldom read of fires breaking out in the Palace. The majority of the buildings were of one storey, and had vaults in the basement, supported on stone or marble pillars such as are still to be seen in the remains of the Numera, the Pharos, and the Manaura.

The sloping nature of the Palace site is rendered plain by the number of staircases and descents mentioned in the description of the buildings. We do not know which of the passages were covered or not ; neither do we know the size, height, breadth and length of the many buildings, and the passages by which they were connected. Nevertheless I must admit that we learn a great deal about the Palace of our Emperors from the study of the ceremonies celebrated there.

After Constantine Porphyrogennetos wrote his description of the ceremonies in the middle of the tenth century, the Emperors erected no more buildings of any importance, at least nothing of the sort is alluded to in the subsequent history of the Empire.

After that time, the Byzantines as they gazed on the dome of S. Sophia, or the immense structures in the Augustaion, conjured up the names of the great builders, Justinian, and his successors Theophilos and Basil the Macedonian, who erected so many buildings in the Palace and the city. Then the Italians began the ruin of the state by unjust monopolies, by hindering Byzantine navigation in the Euxine, and by claiming the sole right to convey the rich merchandise of Pontus, India, and China to Constantinople and their own country. The customs of the city were far exceeded by those of her independent rival Galata on the other side of the Golden Horn. From 'the eleventh century onwards, the Italians and Crusaders pillaged the Empire and took all sorts of valuable Greek and Byzantine work to Italy, where it is still preserved. In consequence of this the palaces remained as Constantine Porphyrogennetos described them.[1]

---

[1] Les princes croisés affoiblirent extrêmement l'Empire d'Orient par la façon dont ils le conquirent ; et le Grecs, en le reprenant, ne recouvrerent, pour ainsi dire, que le cadavre de l'ancien. M. Guys, *Voyage Littéraire de la Grèce*, Vol. I., p. 336.

From the historians we learn that our Emperors after the time of the Crusaders, and especially after they regained the government in 1261, resided in the palace of Blachernai. In it and the Boukoleon, the foreign emperors had already resided during the Latin domination. After Michael Palaiologos erected the new walls, this Palace—the Holy Palace—was neglected. Probably the gold and silver ornaments were removed, and the numerous chambers were used only for the public festivals and processions, and the banquets of the courtiers with the Emperor.[1]

In consequence of its neglect, and the poverty of the Emperors to which I have already adverted, no expensive repairs were made upon the Palace. I do not however agree with Labarte's statement that the ancient walls were demolished and the materials taken to build the new ones. The emperors could not betray so many splendid buildings and adornments of marble and precious mosaics to the wretched and impoverished inhabitants of Constantinople. My own opinion is that these walls —those beside the Augustaion and the Gallery of Marcian—were demolished by the Turks, who when they gained the mastery of Constantinople, collected materials from every quarter towards the

---

[1] Benjamin of Tudela, though he never alludes to the Palace in the Akropolis, extols the Palace of Blachernai, or Bilbernae, as he calls it. He says, "The throne in this palace is of gold, and ornamented with precious stones ; a golden crown hangs over it, suspended on a chain of the same material, etc. Bergeron, p. 12; *Early Travels in Palestine;* Wright, p. 75.

building of their numerous mosques, a work begun even during the lifetime of the conqueror Mahomet.[1]

From the historians after the Latin domination, we learn a few particulars about the Palace. These gleanings throw some light on the very obscure history of the Palace after the restoration in 1261. "Vekkos had the dignity of chartophylax, attached to which office is the privilege that his consent must be obtained before any priest can bestow the blessing. But a priest who officiated in the church situated beside the Pharos of the Great Palace, was in the habit of giving the nuptial blessing without having obtained his consent. When this became known he was suspended from the exercise of his functions as a punishment."[2]

When Michael Palaiologos lived in the palace of Blachernai, it appears as if the patriarch resided in a monastery in the vicinity, to be nearer to the Emperor, though not in the Church of Our Lady at Blachernai, where the Emperor and those in the Palace worshipped. "The monastery of the district was assigned as a resting-place to the train of the Patriarch." Shortly before this the same writer says: "It was the height of summer, and the Emperor was taking the air in the middle of the Oval, and the Patriarch was residing beside him in the neighbourhood."[3]

---

[1] Βυζαντιναὶ Μελέται, p. 297.

[2] G. Pachymeres, Vol. I., p. 225.

[3] G. Pachymeres, Vol. I., pp. 405, 409. Our historians mention no chapel within the palace of Blachernai.

Contemporary records, however, show us that there were still some ceremonies performed in the Great Palace. Pachymeres says : " It was the day of an assembly in the Sacred Palace, and the assembly was sacred, and entirely composed of holy monks and other men in holy orders, and monks, and the Patriarch and all his synod were present." [1]

Nikephoros Gregoras, in his account of the reign of the younger Andronikos, says, " He could not endure to be taken up with courtly occupations and employments, nor did he perform the duty of an Emperor in the greater festivals." [2]

At the coronation of Michael, son of Andronikos Palaiologos, in 1290, in the church of S. Sophia, all the distinguished citizens, courtiers, and military men were invited, together with the Italian traders and those whom " the requirements of embassies brought to Constantinople." All the extent of the Augustaion was filled, and innumerable foreign tongues—says the chronicler—were heard in this crowded space. After the ceremony, those who were invited went to the Great Palace, where the festivities were celebrated in the great hall of Manuel.[3] From this the Emperor went to Blachernai where he usually resided.

The Chryostriklinos is mentioned in some ceremony, to which the Emperor invited the notable

---

[1] *Ibid.*, p. 392.   [2] Vol. L, p. 565.
[3] Κατὰ τὸν Μανουηλίτην βασιλικὸν τρίκλινον. I do not know what hall is meant by this.

citizens and the monks, and since the building could not contain all the guests, they went out to the lower ground, where the Emperor Andronikos Palaiologos addressed them.[1]

When Michael Palaiologos entered the city in 1261, he at first lodged "in the palace which is next to the Great Hippodrome." The palace of Blachernai, where the Crusaders lived, had for long been neglected, and "filled for the most part with dust and smoke."[2] The Latins had before this been convinced that it was impossible for them to continue in Constantinople, since the Europeans were indifferent, and their Greek subjects hostile. On this account, they removed the precious treasures of our churches, and the gold and silver vessels of the Palace to Europe.

Owing to the residence of our Emperors at Blachernai after the restoration, little is thereafter said of the Great Palace. But some of the many ceremonies detailed by Constantine Porphyrogennetos, continued to be performed. Sentinels still guarded the Palace, and the usual sentries kept nightly watch on its towers and battlements.

Nikephoros Gregoras says of the younger Andronikos when he went round the wall of Constantinople : " The Emperor observed that the sentries,

---

[1] G. Pachymeres, Vol. II., p. 336; Kantakouzenos, Vol. II., p. 542, calls the fortress where Apoksuchos was put to death, "The Palace of Constantine the Great." It is what is now known as *Tekfur serai*, north of the quarter called Kalligarea.

[2] N. Gregoras, Vol. I. p. 87.

who watch by turns all the night long, do not cease to keep one another on the alert by continual shouts." [1]

As to the condition of the Palace and the splendid houses beside S. Sophia, the same writer says that the greatest confusion prevailed both in the language and the dress. Some of the citizens wore Latin, others Mysian, Triballian, or Phœnician head-gear, or else they entered the Palace in the garb of country-folk. [2]

Gyllius says of the Chrysotriklinos, that while writers very often spoke of it, and everyone in Constantinople knew its name and its whereabouts before the capture, yet in his time, no one knew of it, or cared to know. [3]

Gregoras says, " And now it was suggested to me to collect for the future information of those who may encounter this, something about the Imperial Palaces, and those splendid houses which are being destroyed almost entirely, or turned into a dung-hill ; and so likewise with the use and wont of the patriarchs, and the very great and splendid houses which once formed the chief ornament and support of the Great Church of the Wisdom of God . . . for destruction and dissolution are triumphant over all alike."

Pachymeres records the fall of the great Hall of Justinian in the reign of Andronikos Palaiologos

---

[1] Vol. I., p, 408.   [2] *Ibid.*, p. 567.

[3] Lib ii., cap. 24.   [4] Vol. II., p. 145.

(1283-1320). It was never re-erected. "As for the Hall of Justinian, which the younger Justinian built . . . through age it leant to one side, and latterly fell when a strong wind was blowing, so that those who saw its place could not tell whether a house had once stood there or not." Our historians relate many other things about the palace, but these all refer to the then favourite palace of Blachernai.

FINIS.

INDEX.

GREEK WORDS EXPLAINED.

Printed in the United States
129157LV00003B/42/A

9 780766 196179